EXCHAN
TRADED
FUNDS

Jim Wiandt
Will McClatchy

John Wiley & Sons, Inc.

Contents

Foreword

On December 31, 2000, there were 65.6 billion dollars invested in what we now call exchange-traded funds, or ETFs. On April 30, 2001, even after a falling market, the amount of funds under management for ETFs had reached 73.3 billion dollars. On the American Stock Exchange, trading in ETFs now dwarfs that of all other equity, even though there is now also trading on other U.S. exchanges and trading systems. The New York Stock Exchange has one ETF currently trading and is planning to introduce more.

A number of stock exchanges around the world, including the exchanges in Hong Kong, Singapore, London, Frankfurt, Sydney, and Toronto, are already trading ETFs. Many others are planning to introduce them soon, including the Tokyo and Osaka Stock Exchanges in Japan and stock exchanges in other European countries. When I reflect on what started as a simple goal and how it all evolved into ETFs, and the number of critical requirements that had to be met and overcome to make the ETF possible, I can only wonder how we were able to accomplish it.

At the time of the writing of this foreword, I had already spent a total of over 35 years in commodity trading and commodity and stock exchange management, where much of my work involved the design of new financial instruments. Prior to that, I had embarked on a career as a physicist and engineer specializing in acoustics. After World War II, my work devolved mainly into international trade and management, including trading and managing international commodities. The development of the ETF design would have been difficult without this experience and background. Further, I know of no other financial instrument for which its genesis evolved principally from a stock exchange's need to find something to trade. Generally, it is the other way around.

The American Stock Exchange, commonly known as the AMEX, originated at the curb on Broad Street in New York. Traders stood at their selected lampposts on the street curb and brokers leaned out of the upstairs windows and yelled or hand signaled orders to the traders below. When I joined the AMEX staff in December 1976, it was still referred to as the Curb Exchange. Originally, it served as the market for smaller stocks that didn't qualify for listing on the New York Stock Exchange. When the Nasdaq dealer market opened to non-dealer investors, many of the smaller new company stocks began to trade there instead of on the AMEX. The AMEX soon began to experience difficulties in obtaining new listings.

Responding to this, the AMEX began all types of new programs to attract listings. Most of these programs, unfortunately, were not as successful as AMEX management had hoped. The trading volume remained at approximately 20 million shares per day, a very small number compared with the growing trading volume on the NYSE and Nasdaq.

My position at the Exchange was head of new product development on the derivatives side of the Exchange's business, where we were doing relatively well. In my work, I have always thought in terms of looking "outside the box" in new product design. Accordingly, in viewing the Exchange's efforts to increase its trading volume, I thought that it ought to be looking for trading in different classes of securities not already trading on an Exchange, rather than continuing to fight what was obviously a losing battle.

The most obvious securities of this type were mutual funds, then increasing rapidly in popularity. I was encouraged by Professor Burt Malkiel of Princeton University, who was then chairman of the Exchange's New Product Committee and a member of the Exchange's Board of Directors. Professor Malkiel had written the book *A Random Walk Down Wall Street* that made the case for investing in broad market indexes.

My first approach was to determine whether mutual funds in their present form could be traded. A visit with Jack Bogle, then head of the Vanguard Group, discouraged this. Jack made the point that mutual funds could not deal with rapid movements in and out of his funds without substantially increasing operating costs. Jack was the innovator of low-cost mutual fund operations.

To solve this problem, I returned to my commodity experiences and thought that we might separate the functions of fund management and exchange trading by using what would essentially be a warehouse-type operation. Portfolios of stocks conforming to an established index would be deposited with a trust bank, which would then issue a depositary receipt to the depositor. The receipt would be divisible into a large number of pieces—50,000 has become typical. The divided pieces could then trade on the Exchange as equity securities. These pieces would not be redeemable by the fund, but could be reassembled into the full depositary receipt and submitted to the trust bank in exchange for the underlying share portfolio.

This was the key concept of the ETF from which all of the other features evolved. As the design developed, another feature appeared—the potential for arbitrage. This was seen as the mechanism that would cause the pieces or shares to track the value of the underlying portfolio during the trading day. Since new ETFs could be created at any time during the trading day by purchasing the portfolio of stocks to be delivered to the fund at its NAV at the close of trading, if the share price rose above the value of the underlying portfolio, those shares could be purchased and deposited with the trust bank in return for a new divisible warehouse receipt. New pieces from the receipt could be sold to take advantage of the price gap and earn an arbitrage profit. If the shares traded below their intrinsic value, the reverse transaction could be executed. The arbitrage transactions would quickly close any price gap.

Many other features developed as the design of ETFs evolved. The SEC's approval of selling traded shares on a downtick permitted the ETF shares to serve as a substitute for a future contract in hedging operations. Few, other than very large investors, can deal with the daily variation margin in futures trading, and this downtick approval feature provided both large and small investors with the ability to hedge their positions by short sales of ETFs. The importance of this feature was demonstrated by short sale hedging on the Nasdaq 100 during the Exchange's recent precipitous price drop. The assets under management of this ETF doubled during the drop through the creation of more shares needed to lend to short positions to make delivery. Another feature is that purchase and redemption from the underlying fund in shares, not cash, results in investors going in and out of the fund without creating a tax event for the fund. This helps minimize year-end capital gains distributions by the fund. Still another feature is the distribution of created shares to investors in book entry form only at the Depository Trust Company. This eliminated the need for the fund to keep track of individual shareholders, a very substantial reduction in the cost of operating these ETFs.

The sum of these and additional features of ETFs have made them attractive to investors and have resulted in their rapid penetration of the investment market. Listing these features doesn't mean that they were easy to achieve. The first response of the AMEX attorneys to the concept of ETFs was that the SEC would never approve such securities. When we finally obtained the Legal Division's approval to proceed, they proposed using a unit investment trust structure because it required neither a board of directors nor corporate management, among other reasons. The outlook was difficult.

What changed the climate for the security at the SEC was, interestingly, the crash of '87. The failure of the "portfolio insurance" concept simply to sell stock index futures short when the market started down was a major factor. In the '87 crash, the drop was so precipitous that there were no futures buyers to sell to. I believe that this caused SEC management to begin thinking of hedging instruments under SEC jurisdiction, which could better serve for hedging. To me, this was a very important factor in getting SEC approval of the many exceptions to the 1940 Act, which the ETFs required. Even with this, it took three years and the expertise of attorney Kathleen Moriarty to finally obtain that approval.

Beyond obtaining regulatory approval, another major matter to deal with was the National Securities Clearing Corporation's system for clearing trades between the stock exchanges. The ETF design required that the underlying stocks purchased to create the ETFs had to be transferred to the fund depository without cash payment, since the issued ETFs were the payment. The NSCC system consisted only of transferring purchased shares in one direction, and cash payment in the other. Fortunately, Mr. David Kelly, then president and CEO of NSCC, thought well enough of the prospect for the proposed ETFs that he persuaded his board to authorize him to modify the NSCC system to accommodate the required transfers. This was not a trivial task and would have seriously hindered the utility of the security design had it not been done.

We had chosen the S&P-500 index as the basis for our initial ETF because it was and is the most widely followed index by institutional investors. We negotiated the license with James Branscome, then in charge of Standard & Poor's Index Division. Jim, too, believed that the design would be successful.

Upon receiving SEC approval, we promptly launched our Standard & Poor's Depositary Receipt, or SPDR, on the AMEX and were almost immediately branded as the "spider people." As could be expected, acceptance of ETFs was slow in developing and it was two years before the rapid increase in trading volume and assets under management began.

A recent major development in ETFs has been the expansion of Barclays Global Investor's involvement. BGI's first active role was as fund manager for the Morgan Stanley Capital International ETFs, initially called World Equity Benchmark Shares, or WEBS. These ETFs are based on MSCI international country indexes and are closely followed by U.S. institutional investors. These were the first ETFs to use an investment company structure rather than the UIT used for the SPDR.

Ms. Patricia Dunn, CEO of Barclays Global Investors, the world's largest manager of institutional investment funds, saw the potential for ETFs to become a major rival to traditional mutual funds. She proceeded to set up a major program for introducing ETFs based on almost every sector of the U.S. securities market and of many international markets. Management of this program for BGI is under the direction of Garrett Bouton and Lee Kranefuss. BGI's expansion in these securities resulted in the first major marketing program applied to ETFs. After only one year of operation, the program has achieved over 11 billion dollars of assets under management with assets continuing to increase even during the recent major market decline.

What is now clear is that the ETF design does not have to be restricted to indexes—though the SEC, it should be noted, has expressed some doubts as to the feasibility of actively-managed ETFs. As long as the basic design features of the ETF are followed, any portfolio of securities can be traded using this design. Requirements are: disclosure of the next day's creation/redemption basket closely tracking the composition of the underlying securities portfolio; purchase and redemption of the ETF securities with stocks; no trading in the underlying portfolios during the trading day; and, for low cost operations, issuance of the securities to a clearing and depository system such as that of the Depository Trust Company. Not all securities that are sometimes known as ETFs meet these requirements.

In view of this remarkable and almost unprecedented development of the ETF market, what can we expect next? It has now been almost 13 years since I first started down the road of trying to find something for the AMEX to trade. Since retiring from the AMEX in January of 1996, I have served as chairman of the board of the two iShares Fund Groups and have consulted for BGI in its ETF program. ETFs have more than achieved my original goal of providing the AMEX with securities to trade. By far the majority of trading on the AMEX and a major part of its current development efforts are on these securities.

What was not anticipated was the rapid expansion of ETF trading on stock exchanges around the world. It is clear to me that the ETF design is only beginning its trading and investment penetration. Its design has made it a multipurpose instrument for many of an investor's needs. Its basic concept meets the requirements that I have always believed essential for any instrument to succeed: it is simple in concept and its usage is understandable by non-professional investors.

Nathan Most
Chairman of the Board, the iShares Trust

Preface

In early 2000, we, the senior editors of IndexFunds.com, were hard at work searching out and publishing news and data on index mutual funds. Long accustomed to numbingly consistent portfolio performance but decidedly dull investment vehicles, we were ready for some pizzazz. On cue, something exciting…dare we say sexy, entered the rather drab, albeit highly successful world of index, or broad market, investing. New products that we could not easily categorize, exchange-traded funds (ETFs), were suddenly a major topic on our discussion boards as they became popular among indexers.

Why the excitement? ETFs make investing money in equity indexes easy, direct and cheap. They greatly add to the flexibility of mutual fund investors and drive down some of the costs that eat away at returns. Prior to the availability of ETFs, investors had to choose between the control and versatility of direct stock ownership and the simplicity and safety of diversification through mutual funds. Buying Brazilian stocks in the morning and Swiss stocks in the afternoon, whether for speculative or long-term investment purposes, was once the special province of highly-paid traders and money managers. No longer.

We were not entirely certain how to treat ETFs at first. Clearly, they were a new tool for our audience since they did in fact help investors make low cost index allocations. But they also attracted highly speculative hedge funds and day-traders who were gobbling up odd-sounding financial products like Spiders (SPDRs or Standard & Poor's Depositary Receipts) and Cubes (Nasdaq-100 QQQs). Many long-time index investors were suspicious of transaction costs and the use of ETFs by short-term traders.

Should we embrace or reject this strange hybrid? The ETF peg didn't necessarily fit into the indexing hole where we normally put mutual funds. Regardless, IndexFunds.com started covering the indexing aspects of ETFs heavily. Soon, we were singing praises for their low fees and tax efficiency for buy-and-hold strategies, and we even came to admire the usefulness of their more speculative aspects to certain investors as well.

While perhaps not the best reason to invest in them, we confess that ETFs make indexing fun! They have all the flair of stocks and are commented on heavily by pundits and market predictors. We generally caution the reader not to pay much attention to the steady stream of "noise" emanating from the financial media industry. But it is nice to see a little flash and dazzle enter the indexing world. Used properly, ETFs *can* be good tools for the index investor. The fundamentals long espoused by index investors need not change. Wise investors should first get a fundamental grasp of their goals and concerns. Proper asset allocation is the most important step in portfolio management. Maximizing equity returns by owning a well-diversified, low-fee, tax-efficient portfolio is also essential.

ETFs are also a fascinating microcosm of financial markets. A bewildering number of investor types and financial institutions use them in different ways and for different reasons. Even the debate over whether they are better than mutual funds or other instruments involves nuanced arguments over the actual costs of doing business in the financial markets and the effects of decreased tax exposure. Although brokerage firms, magazines and sites like ours had written excellent studies and articles on various aspects of ETFs, virtually nothing comprehensive has been written on the subject. At the same time, the general financial media was at times circulating misinformation. We felt compelled to fill the gap with this book in order to educate and, on occasion, dispel myths.

We wanted to make it accessible to the less knowledgeable investor but also provide a solid reference for the professional trying to come up to speed on exchange-traded funds, or looking for a single source of ETF data and information.

ETFs are not a flash in the pan or a bubble. Spanning nearly every class of indexed equity available, and fast moving into fixed income and actively managed funds as well, they are now available to investors around the world. Smart financial professionals from the very largest firms are betting large amounts of money on them, and hundreds of products have been introduced or are waiting for regulatory approval. More importantly, investors love them. We hope you enjoy reading about them.

Jim Wiandt, Publisher
Will McClatchy, Contributing Editor and Co-Founder
IndexFunds.com
—San Francisco, California, July 2001

Acknowledgments

A book like this one, written properly, is not a solitary endeavor. Without the remarkably generous contributions of many industry professionals, this book would not have had the scope and accuracy that it now enjoys. Critical to the effort were some of the people who were there at the beginning to see the early ETFs develop and finally prosper at the American Stock Exchange. They're as fine and interesting a group of people as you'll ever meet. Nate Most at iShares, Gary Gastineau at Nuveen, and Kathleen Moriarty of Carter Ledyard all reviewed the manuscript exhaustively and provided us with endless subtle details and humorous stories.

Also commenting thoroughly on the manuscript and favoring us with long and enjoyable discussions were Jay Baker of Spear Leads, Herb Blank of QED International, Lee Kranefuss and Steven Schoenfeld of Barclays Global Investors, Diane Garnick at State Street Global Advisors, Debbie Fuhr of Morgan Stanley, Jan Altmann and Stephan Kraus of the Deutsche Börse, and Wayne Wagner of the Plexus Group.

Special thanks also go out to John Prestbo of Dow Jones, Brian Mattes at Vanguard, Mike Traynor of Susquehanna, Jim Polisson, Brad Zigler and Tom Taggart of BGI, Joe Keenan and Thomas Centrone at the Bank of New York, Julie Stav, Mike Cavalier and Larry Larken at the AMEX, Rob Gibson from the Chicago Stock Exchange, Jeffrey Villwock of Harpeth Capital, William Miller at Morgan Stanley, John Rekenthaler from Morningstar, Gus Fleites of State Street Global Advisors, Jim Duffy and Jyoti

Bhagavan at the NYSE, Jason Toussaint of MSCI, Jean-Michel Savre of Euronext, James Kelley of Addison Capital Management, Kenneth D. Pasternak of Knight Trading Group, Jim Novakoff, Rick Ferri, Bill Bernstein, Jason Zweig, Jonathan Clements, C. Michael Carty, Freude Bartlett, Gail Bateson, Jim Pacetti, Kevin Eagle, Deborah Mittelman, Mercer Bullard, Gavin Quill, and Eric Tyson.

Finally we stand and applaud for the support and attentiveness of Debby Englander, Greg Friedman and Alexia Meyers at John Wiley & Sons, the remarkable patience and diligence shown by Susan London-Payne at Argosy, the unending support of my wife Noemi Ezkurdia, and the hard work of John Spence, Adrienne Pauly, Maureen Burke, and Michael Collins in seeing that the book was brought to fruition.

CHAPTER ONE

THE BEST OF BOTH WORLDS

Mutual funds, long the investment of choice for individuals as well as pension funds, have a major new competitor.

> "Financial products come and go, but I think exchange-traded funds will probably end up being considered the leading financial innovation of the last decade."
>
> **Deborah Fuhr, vice president and global head of marketing for ETFs and OPALS at Morgan Stanley Dean Witter**

Exchange-traded funds (ETFs) are investment funds that trade like stocks. Cheap, flexible, and tax-friendly, they allow investment of any size in a myriad of different portfolios of equities, bonds and even real estate in the United States and across the globe. They are approaching $100 billion in assets and have the support of some of the largest, most respected firms on Wall Street.

Furthermore, they have found enthusiasts among a wide variety of investors, from individuals with a long-term buy-and-hold strategy to institutional hedge funds placing million-dollar bets on markets across the globe.

1

You may find that you can put these fascinating new financial instruments to work for you.

Comparatively low management fees for most ETFs are often what first catches the eye of investors. The fees for the cheapest ETF, for example, are about half the cost of the cheapest equivalent mutual fund and ten to twenty times cheaper than the typical mutual fund that attempts to outperform the S&P-500 index. Barclays Global Investors' iShares S&P-500 index fund (IVV) gives investors a stake in 500 of the largest U.S. companies for only .0945 percent in annual management expenses. The lowest-cost mutual fund in that category, the Vanguard 500 Fund (VFINX), has a total expense ratio of 0.18 percent, while the industry average for actively managed funds exceeds 1 percent, with a large number charging more than 2 percent. For an investment of $10,000 over 10 years, the difference is notable.

ETFs are more than just cheap funds. They are an entirely different animal from traditional mutual funds. ETFs can be bought and sold instantaneously on major stock exchanges, as opposed to mutual funds, which almost always trade at end-of-day prices.

Why is being able to buy or sell immediately so exciting to investors? Because with an ETF, the investor has the peace of mind of knowing exactly the price they are paying. When the market is low, the investor can buy in immediately. Waiting until the close of the day could mean letting the market rise considerably. Perhaps more importantly, in a market drop the investor can get out before panic selling takes hold.

Finally, ETFs delay capital gains taxes. Whether you pay the IRS now or later can make a big difference to your overall returns. In Chapter 2 we examine these and other benefits of ETFs, as well as possible flaws, in greater detail. Not everyone admires ETFs. In particular, critics have asserted that hidden transaction costs make them relatively expensive. Vanguard Chairman John Bogle, who popularized cheap index mutual funds, derides ETFs openly while his firm is busy launching them to satisfy demand from its own customers. Investors can decide for themselves what assumptions are reasonable and come to their own conclusions about ETF strengths and weaknesses.

Exactly what is an ETF if it is not a mutual fund? ETFs are indeed investment funds, but they have a few twists. As with mutual funds, ETFs come about when multiple investors pool their money with a financial serv-ices company such as State Street Global Advisors, Barclays Global Investors, or Merrill Lynch. These firms state in a written prospectus how the money will be invested, typically in a portfolio of stocks. Every investor takes proportional ownership of the fund and the underlying portfolio.

The key twist of most ETFs is that creating shares and unwinding them occurs outside the normal stock exchange transaction process, thereby avoiding trading expenses. When demand for an ETF is anticipated, a large intermediary firm (*authorized participant* or AP) transfers securities to the fund manager who places them in a trust. In exchange, the AP is given ETF shares. After the new securities are issued, they can be sold on the market as ETFs. The shares then trade freely between investors on stock exchanges. When overall demand drops and institutional investors decide to exit an ETF, the securities are retired and the underlying stock portfo-lio is transferred to the firms that are redeeming their ETF shares. While it is true that underlying stocks are often bought or sold alongside the cre-ation or redemption, this process allows the fund to avoid the cumbersome stock sale process, thereby saving money and lowering taxes. At least that is the theory. There are several variants to this process, some of which con-tain important implications. Details of ETF operations and the major ways to structure them are covered in Chapter 5.

Recognize these? They're all ETFs:

- SPDRs: depositary receipts mimic S&P-500 index, trade on AMEX, introduced in 1993

- iShares (formerly WEBS): numerous funds tracking numerous U.S. and foreign indexes

- DIAMONDS: track the Dow Jones Industrial Average

- QQQ: tracks the Nasdaq composite index, a large index consist-ing mostly of leading technology companies

- HOLDRs: Merrill Lynch's grantor trusts, with excellent tax benefits and sector coverage but expensive set-up fees

The most popular ETF in the world is the SPDR (Standard & Poor's Depositary Receipt, trading symbol SPY), developed by the American

Stock Exchange (AMEX) and managed by State Street Global Advisors (SSgA). The buyer of this ETF is investing in the S&P 500 portfolio of 500 of the largest U.S. stocks.

Hundreds of ETFs have been created around every conceivable type of equity index, including many that track stock markets of individual countries, industrial sectors and smaller-sized companies. Appendix C and D contain a comprehensive list of ETFs with their historical returns, a description of their structure, instructions to order the prospectus, and comments by us on their strengths, weaknesses, and appropriateness.

How to buy an ETF

Actually buying an ETF is easy. The investor simply calls their broker (or goes online if they have an Internet broker), obtains the latest quote for a price for the ETF desired and places a bid on a major exchange. If a seller accepts that bid, the investor becomes the proud owner of shares of an ETF. The process is no different than with an individual stock.

Retail and institutional traders have shifted billions of dollars into ETFs, often for very different reasons. Chapter 3 explores why an individual investing for retirement may find them attractive and provides various model portfolios containing different ETFs for typical investors. Chapter 4 discusses large funds' use of ETFs, while Chapter 8 discusses how day-traders and hedge fund managers use them.

In practice, ETFs are almost exclusively index funds. As such they are NOT an attempt to outperform a particular market of stocks. On the contrary, they almost always guarantee close tracking of the market, or index, they target. This is how they keep management fees so low.

Actively managed ETFs are just over the horizon. The world's first active ETFs were launched in Germany in 2000, and numerous proposals for U.S. versions are said to be under review by the SEC. "Most people are not willing to believe that a highly skilled, trained person cannot beat the index," said Nate Most, a pioneer in the creation of ETFs. "As long as that is true, [actively managed ETFs] will be a product that people will want and it will come to pass."

> "Active management is a beauty contest in which the average contestant is kind of ugly."
>
> **John Rekenthaler, Morningstar**

The sheer number of markets represented by ETFs, however, means that investors are still making important bets. Investors who feel they are avoiding all responsibility by placing their entire portfolio in an ETF of the Standard & Poor's (S&P)-500 index are doing nothing of the sort. They are choosing one portion of the market that happens to be dominated by large-capitalization, growth-oriented U.S. companies.

As James Kelley, a professional financial advisor to individual investors at Addison Capital Management, said, "These are stocks and they need to be managed. We want to beat the markets with the markets and ETFs give us the chance to do that."

Chapter 6 is a study of the history of index funds, providing insight into their evolution and helping explain which types of firms like them and which feel threatened. It also reveals the work of pioneers, tinkerers, and showmen who created and popularized this product.

For investment professionals or readers familiar with this new investment tool, Chapter 9 (Advanced Topics) will prove enlightening. Subtle economic issues that may have real implications on returns are explained here. Such investors can also browse the appendices for volumes of useful data and information about all 169 ETFs that were listed globally as of June 30, 2001.

Regardless of where investors place their money, they still have to perform two critical tasks: basic financial planning and asset allocation. The variety of ETF offerings allows investors to assemble from smaller parts a complete portfolio ideally suited to them. This will make ETFs even better tools for asset allocation. The simplicity of ETFs lets them execute the plan easily in ways that have never before been possible. (For now all

ETFs are based on stocks, with bonds ETFs based on bonds available only in Canada, but soon likely to come to many other countries.)

Financial planning is the process of laying out financial goals such as retirement, addressing a person's tolerance for risk and reducing liabilities to reasonable levels. *Asset allocation* is the selection of the type of investment appropriate for the financial plan. There are many types of equities and bonds, such as large capitalization stocks and short-term bonds. It is important to find a mix that matches the goals, risk tolerances and time horizons identified during planning.

Once the crucial task of asset allocation is addressed, the selection of funds can begin. Just as there are major differences in price and performance between mutual funds, so too are there differences between exchange-traded funds. You should pay careful attention to the individual product actually bought. Examining product listings in the Appendix is advised before final purchases are made. Of course, every investor should read the latest prospectus for a product before investing in it. A prospectus may be ordered by calling a fund's toll-free number or visiting its Web site, which can be found in Appendix C.

We encourage readers not to get too lost in detail or to allow this fairly straightforward investment vehicle to become more complicated than it really is. Stocks go up more often than not, but they also go down. Market experts do a notoriously poor job of timing these ups and downs.

The charm of ETFs, in our opinion, is in how they free the investor from the onslaught of financial noise at a relatively modest cost. Investors can devote time to the meat of the matter: how to choose among the markets wisely to hit financial targets with appropriate amounts of risk.

CHAPTER TWO

COMPARING ETFs TO TRADITIONAL MUTUAL FUNDS

The relevance of ETFs for most individual investors turns on this critical question: mutual funds or ETFs? Mutual funds are a fine choice, especially the inexpensive index variety. But there is increasing evidence that ETFs are superior to mutual funds in many of the major features. Most experts who have thoroughly examined ETFs recommend that investors consider ETFs carefully. In this chapter we will present data and opinions on both sides to help you decide for yourself.

Claimed benefits of ETFs fall into the main categories of low fees and expenses, trading flexibility, and delayed taxes.

POSITIVES CLAIMED BY ETF FANS	NEGATIVES CLAIMED BY ETF CRITICS
1. Inherently less expensive	1. High trading costs (loss to ask/bid spread and opportunity costs, which large fund can help protect investor from)
2. Highly liquid and tradeable in real time	
3. Greater tax efficiency than traditional mutual funds, shielding investors from the actions of other fund investors	2. Investor must pay commission to buy.
	3. Funds often trade at a discount or premium to the real underlying net asset value.
4. Allows investor to sell an index short and buy w/ leverage (on margin). There are also listed options on some ETFs.	4. Short track record. Can funds guarantee liquidity in a crisis?
5. Offers index exposure to new markets not always available to fund investors	5. Offer greater temptation to irrationally sell (greater exposure to buy high, sell low phenomenon)

Claimed disadvantages of ETFs include transaction costs, both visible and hidden, paid by the investor while buying and selling the actual ETF. Hidden costs are the most subtle to analyze and have produced the strongest debate.

What is our view? After reviewing the evidence, we feel ETFs have several advantages over mutual funds and at least one area of weakness:

- Annual fees are generally lower as claimed

- Tax benefits are superior but sometimes overstated

- Flexibility is far greater but not of value to every investor
- Transaction fees can be unacceptably high for the unwary investor

But before we tackle the data and the arguments pro and con, consider a recent study of *perceived* benefits by individual investors done by Financial Research Corp (FRC). "Given what you hear in the media you would guess the most attractive features would be continuous pricing and trading and tax flexibility," said Gavin Quill, senior vice president at the market research firm which polled nearly 892 retail investors. Very few had invested, and only 41 percent were moderately or very informed about them, but all were decision makers controlling assets.

ETFs were briefly described and respondents were presented with the following list of ETF benefits:

1. Continuous pricing during the day
2. Lower expense ratios relative to actively managed mutual funds and most index funds
3. Greater tax efficiency than most mutual funds
4. Greater trading and tax flexibility than mutual funds
5. Comparable trading and tax benefits to individual stocks but with the built-in diversification traditionally associated with mutual funds
6. Ability to invest in an entire market sector with one trade
7. Access to market sectors and indexes that mutual funds do not currently offer

It turns out that the main attractions are "very boring things":

1. Tax efficiency
2. Trading and tax flexibility
3. Lower expense ratios

Dead last was continuous pricing. "This doesn't seem to match with trigger happy or weak-willed individuals that critics feel will gravitate to ETFs," said Quill. "Just because they can trade all day doesn't mean they will trade all day." Many studies have shown that heavy trading in any security leads to high expenses that are extremely difficult to overcome through superior stock picking. Clearly FRC's study turned up lots of buy-and-hold investors interested in ETFs who are quite aware that their final returns after tax are the only measure of success.

Now for evidence of whether ETFs are better products than traditional mutual funds.

ANNUAL MANAGEMENT FEES AND EXPENSES

Exceptionally low annual fees may be reason enough for many investors to flock to ETFs. This is the easiest comparison to make, because expense ratios paid to managers, custodians and others attached to a fund are clearly stated in every prospectus. Sometimes fees are waived, but legally they cannot be raised above what is found in the prospectus.

Index mutual fund investors typically watch their fees very carefully. The whole theory of indexing rests on the notion that trying to pick stocks is pointless, and therefore fees paid to fund managers should be kept to a minimum. The compounding effect of savings in fees over time can be impressive, as Figure 2.1 shows.

Index funds are largely commodities. One S&P-500 fund is pretty much the same as another, although some funds eke out slightly better returns with clever techniques to protect against costly index changes and with better tax accounting practices.

Amazingly, a plain vanilla S&P-500 ETF can cost as little as half as much to own as even incredibly cheap S&P-500 mutual funds. Table 2.1 offers management fees for some of the lowest-cost offerings in each camp as of June 30, 2001.

John Bogle, retired Chairman of the Vanguard Group, and other index mutual fund proponents have long charged that low fees are one of the biggest reasons for leaving actively managed mutual funds for index funds.

FIGURE 2.1   LOW FEE EFFECTS

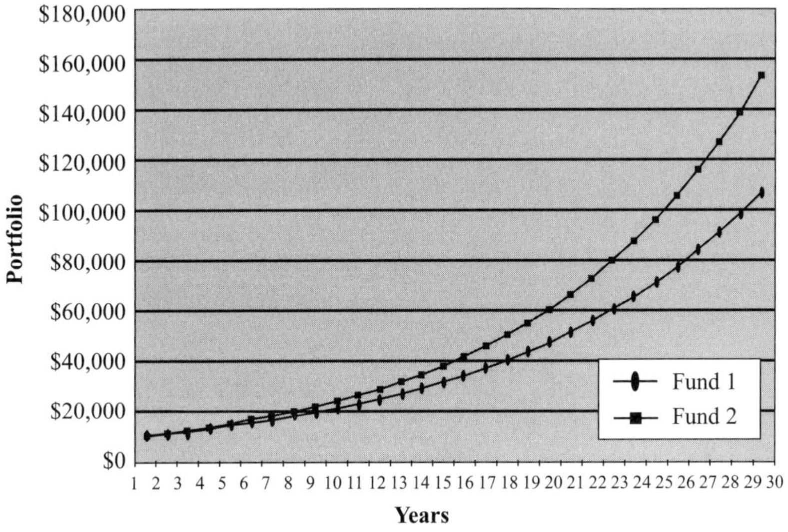

Now it appears this argument puts Bogle's cherished Vanguard S&P-500 fund at a disadvantage. No wonder his firm has come out with VIPERs, its own brand of ETF. Bogle himself, however, was not very pleased with the announcement.

TABLE 2.1   COMPARISONS OF TOTAL ANNUAL FEES
                 FROM LOWEST COST PROVIDERS

ASSET CLASS	ETF TOTAL EXP.	MUTUAL FUND TOTAL EXP.	ETF ADVANTAGE
S&P 500	.0945%	.18%	.0855%
Broad Market Index (US)	.15%	.20%	.05%
Sector Funds (Utilities)	.28%	.38%	.10%
Single Country (Japan)	.84%	.98%	.14%
International (Europe)	.60%	.29%	(–.31%)

Source: Morningstar, June 30, 2001

> "An ETF is like handing an arsonist a match."
>
> **John Bogle, Founder of the Vanguard Group**

> "Now that they are giving out the can of gasoline, the question is who at Vanguard is going to light it."
>
> **Augustin Fleites, principal responsible for ETFs at State Street Global Advisors**

Actively managed mutual funds may claim that they deserve to earn higher management fees, but there is overwhelming evidence to the contrary. So many studies of this question by academic researchers not affiliated with Wall Street firms have been made that it is not practical to review them here. Suffice it to say that not one Nobel Laureate economist (including, most vocally, William Sharpe at Stanford University) believes an active fund manager is likely to give the individual investor a long-term edge anywhere near the cost of that manager. A must-read for anyone curious about this question is the classic book *A Random Walk Down Wall Street*, which reviews the numerous relevant studies. This classic tome to index investing is by Burton Malkiel, who later worked with John Bogle in developing the groundbreaking Vanguard-500 index fund.

The critical point in the comparison of actively managed funds vs. ETF index funds is that the bigger the difference in fees, the more unlikely the actively managed fund can outperform its target index without taking on extra risk. By lowering fees, ETFs have raised the bar for stock-pickers, and history has shown that active managers are unlikely to pass over it.

Now for *transaction fees*. They come in a variety of flavors, and overall, ETFs are at somewhat of a disadvantage, depending on the product. Transaction fees include:

- Visible fees paid by the individual investor
- Hidden fees paid by the individual investor

- Visible fees paid by the investor's fund

- Hidden fees paid by the investor's fund

In summary, an ETF investor cannot escape paying some visible and some hidden fees during the purchase of ETF shares, while mutual fund investors can get around both by going directly to a mutual fund group. In practice, it is out of convenience that many mutual fund managers pay their broker to make the purchase. Neither type of investor can get around either visible or hidden fees incurred by the funds they select, such as management fees, and in the case of traditional mutual funds, transaction costs paid by the fund itself.

Jim Pacetti, president of ETF.com Inc., says, "All the costs that are inherent in the ETF are also present in a mutual fund. With ETFs they are all broken out."

Overall, we feel that for the individual investor using a discount or low-cost broker, the two fund types probably offer similar total transaction costs. Here are the details.

VISIBLE TRANSACTION FEES PAID BY THE INVESTOR

Both visible and hidden transaction fees exist for the ETF investor, while mutual fund investors can, with slight inconvenience, avoid them. ETFs cannot be purchased for free from their issuers the way mutual funds can, although most investors prefer to buy funds through a broker and incur fees anyway. Investors who buy ETFs through their broker pay trading fees just as they would any other stock. Investors using an online discount stockbroker generally pay a flat fee per trade, often as little as $10. Such a cost or "load" for an investment of $10,000 comes to an insignificant $1/10$ of one percent. For an investor who only invests $1,000 in a fund, the cost jumps to 1 percent of the original investment, a sizable penalty. In our view, for the investor with less than $1,000, ETF transaction fees are too expensive. Anyone with more than $10,000 to invest should not be concerned. In between is a matter for legitimate debate. Investors using full-service brokerage houses should adjust these amounts to reflect higher costs.

Paying that low $10 transaction fee, however, becomes exorbitant when it occurs frequently such as with the dollar cost averaging investment strategy. This common and sensible strategy involves adding small amounts to an account at regular intervals to help impose discipline, avoid sitting on too much idle cash, and lessen the risk of buying at a peak. The price of entry is thus an "average" over time. Here the $10 fees can really add up, and ETFs may not be appropriate.

An obvious solution would be to spread out the periods in which investments are made, perhaps from monthly to quarterly. Cash should be put away in an interest-bearing money market account, and yes, that takes a little discipline. But nearly everyone needs a little ballast in their boat. Studies have shown that at least some small amount of bonds or other fixed-income instrument both improves return and lowers risk for a portfolio as a whole. A small amount of cash kept in a money market account for a few months is perfectly reasonable.

Mutual fund investors who buy through their broker shouldn't gloat, however, as many pay for the privilege. The fact is that a "supermarket" stockbroker with every type of stock, bond and fund is a convenience, but few conveniences in life are free. Such stockbrokers nearly always charge for selling a mutual fund.

HIDDEN TRANSACTION FEES PAID BY THE INVESTOR

Every stock transaction has hidden costs. As a buyer of a stock, the ETF investor must be concerned, while the investor who invests directly with a mutual fund company can rest easy.

As with any stock, an ETF also has a *bid-ask spread*, which is the amount of profit taken out by market middlemen who help an investor to purchase or sell a stock (or in this case an ETF). At any given time just about every major stock has a buyer offering to buy (at the bid price) and a seller offering to sell (at the ask price). The difference, or bid-ask spread, is the price of doing business on the open markets. Without this profit incentive, middlemen such as stock market specialists and private electronic trading networks would not bother to bring buyer and seller together. Inevitably, the spread comes out of investors' pockets.

Many investors are surprised to find out that their own brokers may share in part of the bid-ask spread in a practice known as *payment for order flow*. Financial firms that specialize in bringing buyers and sellers together to profit from the bid-ask spread often return part of the spread to brokers for routing customers to them. There is no law that says the broker must obtain the very best price for a customer, although price is expected to be a major consideration. The U.S. Securities and Exchange Commission says that price is not the only measure of a well-executed trade. Speed is another, as is the ability to cross large amounts of stock or less commonly traded stocks. These are all elements of trading "quality," and reasonable leeway is allowed in the routing of orders to seek all of these features. In practice, payment for order flow is relatively modest, far smaller than the bid-ask spread. Clearly, though, investors should be aware of this hidden fee.

The bid-ask spread itself can be 1 percent or more of the value of a stock. At this rate it can have a significant effect on long-term wealth creation, especially if there is recurring buying and selling. In this regard, not all ETFs are created equal. Some have negligible bid-ask spreads while others have fairly large spreads. Clearly, ETFs based around major U.S. indexes with heavy interest fare well, while sector, small capitalization and country-specific indexes suffer from having to invest in harder-to-obtain stocks and less investor interest. Low liquidity is a catchall phrase for this situation, and it is a sure predictor of a wide bid-ask spread.

It is important to recognize that ETFs eventually will have to be sold, so a "round-trip" cost of the spreads both in buying and selling reflect the true transaction cost. As a minor note, the long-term investor has the consolation of pushing the selling half of this cost out into the future when spreads are likely to come down.

Overall, our view of hidden transaction costs is that paying more than 0.5 percent in round-trip spreads for an ETF is the point at which the ETF begins to be at a clear disadvantage to a mutual fund. Lower annual fees, trading flexibility, lower taxes or other features may well justify this extra cost, but it should be weighed. For an in-depth analysis of ask-bid spreads and other ETF pricing issues, please refer to Chapter 9.

Buying mutual funds can have minor hidden transaction costs. Often, investors buy stocks when they appear cheap and start to climb. When investors send in their money to purchase stocks, their cash sits idle at least until the end of the day when their investment is recorded. In practice, it sits idle for longer than that since many invest by sending their check through the U.S. mail. Still, this is not a huge factor for the truly long-term investor.

Visible Fund Transaction Costs

Transaction costs occur whenever any fund seeks to build a portfolio from individual company stocks. In this comparison, mutual funds and exchange-traded funds work in somewhat different markets, but we doubt there is much difference. We would argue that exchange-traded funds probably have a slight edge.

Why? Because the creation/redemption system of the ETF allows the fund manager to bypass the official transaction market and its overhead. Mutual funds almost always buy and sell stock (or index futures as a temporary surrogate) every time investors bring in or take out cash. ETF fund managers do not actually buy stocks to create or redeem ETFs. Instead, they place stocks in trust and take them out as needed. Many of them have policies allowing for the use of options and futures contracts for additional flexibility. Chapter 5 discusses the operational details, which are by no means without cost but offer potential cost savings.

Hidden Fund Costs

The main transactional costs that traditional mutual funds face are hidden. A well-known phenomenon is "market impact," where large buy and sell orders tend to push up prices with large buy orders. It does not go unnoticed when a mutual fund goes into the market with millions of dollars of buy orders. Nimble stock traders are constantly on the lookout for trading patterns, and they make matters worse by getting in on the act themselves. One common tactic is to "front run" large institutional buyers by putting in their own small bids at slightly higher prices. Now the institutional buyer is in an even worse situation. This effect occurs as a result of the buying and selling that takes place when stocks enter or exit an index. It is almost universally accepted that large players impact market prices more than small players. The effect, particularly with indexes like the S&P 500, with one trillion dollars indexed to it, can often force fund managers to buy high and sell low.

This effect is particularly strong for the largest traditional mutual funds that have concentrated holdings, and those that are forced to buy and sell less liquid stocks. This effect is about the same for ETFs as it is for traditional mutual funds. One minor area of weakness for mutual funds is the way they bunch up massive amounts of orders at the end of the day, and common sense suggests that this could impact the price they pay.

Another cost to consider that comes in several forms is *cash drag*, where a portfolio supposedly designed to invest in equities remains partly in cash. Of course cash kept in interest bearing accounts is relatively safe, but since cash over time delivers less return than stocks, keeping even a small portion of a portfolio in cash will inevitably dampen performance over time.

Actively-managed mutual fund managers have learned, on occasion, to keep 5 percent or more of a fund in cash to mitigate the comings and goings of investors in order to take advantage of trading opportunities. Sudden market declines, of which there have been many in recent decades, frequently trigger a rush for the exit doors and force a manager to sell stock so they can give cash to investors who want out. The timing of these panics couldn't be worse for fund managers, who pride themselves on buying low and selling high but are forced to dump concentrated holdings of stocks in a down market. Tax consequences are dire for the remaining stockholders, as they pick up capital gains that may well belong in part to exiting investors. So fund managers are acting rationally by keeping extra cash on hand, but it can give an edge to ETFs which, because of their structure, do not suffer from distributions caused by net redemptions of other investors. ETFs have a small but not overwhelming edge here.

Index mutual fund managers, furthermore, do not face this problem to such an extent since they are charged with tracking an index and have a broad number of stocks in their portfolio. There simply isn't much cash drag in most index mutual funds, although they, like active funds, can suffer the tax consequences of net investor redemptions.

DIVIDEND DRAG

Similar to cash drag, dividend drag occurs when assets sit idle but safe. In this case, the assets are cash dividends received by a fund but not put to work immediately. The most advanced mutual funds allow investors to plow dividends back into the fund immediately as stock. ETFs, however, do not always do this for regulatory reasons. Some are able to immediately reinvest dividends and avoid the dividend returns lag.

The effect is noticeable but not huge. Investors are giving a little more performance for a little less risk. It is somewhat akin to holding a few bonds among the portion of a portfolio that was supposedly dedicated to stocks. Most investors who plan to own short-term bonds can simply ratchet up the stock portion of their portfolios by a percentage or two to adjust for it.

PHANTOM NAV DISCOUNTS

Initially critics decried ETFs trading at a significant premium/discount to the *net asset value* (NAV) or combined value of the underlying stocks they represent. This is a problem that regularly plagues closed-end mutual funds, where prices of the funds are generally lower (sometimes by 30 percent or more) than the NAV of their portfolios due to a lack of liquidity.

So far most critics appear misinformed. The biggest flaw in their arguments is their selection of end-of-day NAV figures as the measure of the true worth of a portfolio that is trading continuously. End-of-day NAV will always be an imprecise measure of a stock portfolio, especially one with small capitalization and international equities.

Consider an ETF trading in the U.S. that represents an index of stocks based in a country on the other side of the world. The U.S. exchange trading the ETF is open while the exchange trading the underlying stocks is closed (and no after-hours market is trading them heavily). The official end-of-day NAV is many hours old and will reflect yesterday's news, while the ETF trades actively and reflects today's news and currency fluctuations. At that time of day, which is going to be a more accurate reflection of the value of the underlying stocks? We put our money on the ETF, not the underlying stocks. We discuss this in greater detail along with several studies with convincing evidence in Chapter 9.

Certainly, domestic ETFs track major underlying indexes in proportion to the liquidity and importance of that index. The Nasdaq QQQs, for instance, has been noted by many observers for its particularly close tracking of the Nasdaq-100 index. "I get a report on my desk if we move more than a tenth of a basis point," noted Thomas Centrone of the Bank of New York, the custodian for the QQQ.

CONTINUOUS PRICING

The ability of ETFs to trade instantly at a known price at any time is one feature simply not available to mutual funds. Mutual funds, you will recall, have no intraday price and trade only at the end of the day. Investors, however, must give their orders to buy or sell by mid-day without knowing what price they will get.

Clearly, continuously priced and traded ETFs provide more freedom than mutual funds, and with freedom comes the opportunity to do foolish things. In our view, constantly churning an account in hopes of timing markets and panic selling during a market drop are among the foolish things that ETFs more easily allow.

What is continuous pricing worth to most investors? How much of a penalty does the mutual fund investor pay for being forced to take end-of-day pricing?

The answer depends partly on the type of investor involved. In general, investors who occasionally move significant portions of their portfolio in or out of ETFs are likely to find modest benefit while others are less likely to do so. It is also a matter of gut feelings. Does the investor feel comfortable placing an order at an unknown price or does the investor find that disquieting? Peace of mind is an underappreciated aspect of investing.

As C. Michael Carty, principal at New Millenium Advisors, Inc. says, "Would you buy a Ferrari at end-of-day pricing? With ETFs, you know what you are buying and what you are selling."

Long-term investors who either (a) add or shift relatively large portions of their portfolios or (b) maintain an asset allocation target with regular rebalancing, are likely to appreciate instantaneous trading. Most retail investors fall into this category.

Adding or shifting large portions of assets exposes mutual fund investors to risk. Just imagine deciding to liquidate an expensive, actively managed mutual fund to invest in a similarly targeted, but cheaper, mutual fund and not being able to reinvest immediately during a rising market. Even if your funds from the mutual fund were available at the close of the day, you would not be able to reinvest in another mutual fund until the close of the next day unless you had access to an ETF, or switched within a family of funds. Markets can easily go up 1 percent or more in a single day.

Rebalancing a portfolio can expose the investor to such a lag of the market (though, of course, they could also benefit in a falling market). *Rebalancing* is the process of selling a portion of the assets in a portfolio that have gone up to buy more assets that have stayed flat or gone down. This keeps the allocation of assets (60 percent stocks, 40 percent bonds, etc.) on target, and it forces the purchase of assets when they are inexpensive, and their sale when they are expensive, i.e., "buy low, sell high." During the Internet boom, investors who rebalanced tended to sell these pricey stocks at their peak, while investors who did not suffered the full degree of their crash. It should be noted that investors in a family of funds can switch instantly between funds at end-of-day prices. ETF investors can buy and sell *any* ETF share instantaneously to rebalance.

Consider the investor whose technology mutual fund climbs steadily for a year and spikes up sharply in the twelfth month. This investor decides midday to sell part of the technology mutual fund. By market close, that fund has dropped 2 percent, a perfectly ordinary event for that type of asset. Had he been an ETF owner, this would not have happened.

Long-term investors who add to their accounts in small amounts at regular intervals (such as automatic deposits from their salary) AND who never rebalance their portfolios to maintain set asset allocation, should see little benefit from trading flexibility. These extreme "hands-off" investors are in the minority. They never move enough assets around to benefit from instantaneous investing and aren't watching prices anyway. Because they invest such small amounts in an automatic fashion, choosing the end of the day as the regular interval to buy in (even if the order is sent ahead of time with no knowledge of the coming closing price) is reasonable.

If this type of investor never rebalances the portfolio to stick with an asset allocation plan, then instantaneous rebalancing is of dubious value. Since they never reallocate large amounts of assets from one asset type (large cap stocks, small cap, bonds, etc.), they never have much at risk by missing a single day in the markets.

Speculative traders of all stripes, including individual day-traders and institutional hedge funds have found ETFs indispensable. Previously, expensive options on indexes were all that many such traders had to work with in their quest to outguess the markets each day. With ETFs, they have an economical tool with which to take major market positions in real time.

TAX CONSEQUENCES

ETFs have a particularly attractive tax profile because the investor generally sees few capital gains until the actual shares are sold. Taxes are an important and frequently overlooked aspect of wealth creation. Studies have shown that over 2 percent of average investor returns are given up to taxes. That amount can grow to an enormous sum over time.

ETF investors do not suffer capital gains distributions when their fellow investors sell shares, because the underlying stocks are traded, not sold. These and other tax benefits related to ETF structure are discussed in detail in Chapter 9.

"Generally it is difficult for a comparable mutual fund to beat ETFs on taxation," said Rob Gibson, director of ETFs/New Products, Chicago Stock Exchange, Inc.

Mutual funds, especially active ones, can dump enormous amounts of capital gains on a long-term investor, even in a down market. Redemptions of shares by exiting shareholders force the sale of assets, resulting in capital gains for investors who are still in the fund. These gains are distributed proportionately to whoever is left in the fund at the end of the year. This tax bite is particularly strong after a significant contraction of assets in a fund (such as in a market drop) and is especially galling to calm investors who sit tight but are stuck with a tax bill left by panic sellers. Year 2000 saw many funds perform especially poorly and still hand out large capital gains distributions.

Because of their particular structure, ETFs can generate little or no capital gains until the investor exits. At that point, the difference between the original purchase price and the sale price is recorded as capital gain. Large company U.S. ETFs do an especially good job of this, while small company, smaller sector, and especially single-country ETFs have had problems with tax management. The listing of ETFs in Appendix C provides capital gains distributions for each product. Also, a reading of Chapter 9 provides the foundation for understanding how the fund managers exploit this structural benefit.

Mutual funds have tried to keep up with better accounting procedures that allow them to track which stock shares were bought at what time and in what quantity. In this way, they can keep the oldest shares locked away and sell the more recently purchased shares. The newer ones have a higher cost basis, or original purchase price, than the old ones and trigger lower capital gains when sold. The IRS defines capital gains as the difference between the cost basis and the final sale price. Capital gains on the stocks that have not been sold by the fund continue to grow, but taxes on these gains are put off until a later date. In taxation, delay is the key to success. Once again, Vanguard also has led the way in tax management for the mutual fund industry with several funds focused on careful tax management. But aside from these few mutual funds, ETFs should, in theory, proceed from year to year accumulating fewer unrealized capital gains than traditional mutual funds.

There is a misconception that ETFs do away with capital gains. This is not so. Every investor ultimately has to pay on the gains he or she has made. It's just a question of when. The distribution of capital gains by funds forces investors to pay taxes *now*. Tax efficient funds can delay capital gains while apportioning them more fairly among investors. These achievements are worthy and increasingly valuable over the long run.

The Chicago Stock Exchange's Rob Gibson cautions that there is no guarantee that ETFs will remain so tax efficient as their assets grow and they accumulate unrealized capital gains. Also, brand-new funds can show unwanted gains in the first year or two in a volatile market where investors are entering and exiting in large numbers.

"It's not so much the frequency of creations and redemptions as the timing of them," he said. Not every ETF has a desirable tax profile. "With country funds in general you are going to get a larger capital gains distribution," noted Gibson.

ETFs VS. INDEX FUTURES AND CLOSED-END FUNDS

Sophisticated individual and institutional investors have long played markets with index futures. Futures are essentially contracts that reward the investor if a particular index goes up. They can be bought and sold instantly and can deliver exactly the same investment effect as ETFs. Experts tend to agree that ETFs are easier to manage and generally cheaper for longer time periods.

Futures are more complicated to manage and analyze. They are not a straightforward purchase of assets but rather a speculation on the assets' behavior. The investor must understand the implications of possible market moves and account for them continuously. They cannot be purchased and forgotten. None of this work is overwhelmingly difficult, but professional assistance in the form of a knowledgeable broker or money manager and a CPA is recommended.

Is all this work worth it for the individual investor? Probably not. For longer-term positions, ETFs appear to be cheaper. According to one estimate by Lehman Brothers, the total cost of handling a large account with S&P-500 futures over one year was about .3 percent of assets, while the cost of owning S&P-500 ETFs with an equivalent investment exposure was only 0.22 percent. Salomon Smith Barney conducted a study in 2000 that revealed that while ETF commissions may be greater, overall costs may be less. Mispricing risk and market impact, especially, are far less with ETFs. In this study, short-term futures generated 0.297 percent (29.7 basis points) of mispricing risk cost and .222 percent (22.2 basis points) of market impact costs. *Mispricing risk* is, as its name suggests, the likelihood of prices straying from actual index values.

Lastly, ETFs are now available for a large and increasing number of equity markets, including industry sectors, portfolios based on company sizes, and country exchanges. Futures, we believe, will have a hard time keeping up with the diversity of offerings by ETFs.

Closed-end funds are even more clearly on their way out. *Closed-end funds* are mutual funds that trade like a stock and are particularly popular for country and sector markets. They will no doubt linger for years, but industry veterans privately acknowledge that, over time, they are likely to take a back seat to ETFs. Choosing them is a bit of a black art, as they often trade at a significant discount to their underlying NAV and that discount can change quickly. Fees are often substantial.

CONCLUSION

For the long-term investor, ETFs cost about as much to own as the least expensive index funds and perhaps even a bit less. They appear to have the edge in annual fees, are often tax-advantaged but suffer from some additional transaction costs. Compared to the average actively managed fund, they are truly a bargain. The one feature that no mutual fund can match is the simplicity, freedom and flexibility of owning an instrument that is bought and sold like a stock. Every investor must consider for himself or herself the value of this feature.

With over 100 U.S.-trading products (and 169 worldwide) covering most major and many minor market segments in the U.S. and across the globe, ETFs can be used to construct a portfolio suited to virtually anyone's financial plan. In the next few chapters, we investigate various strategies, plans, and portfolios.

CHAPTER THREE

ETFs FOR THE BUY-AND-HOLD INVESTOR

The buy-and-hold investor has as much to gain from ETFs as anyone. While media hoopla has focused on day traders using ETF, in reality, ETFs' greatest strengths lie in their long-term features. Especially when purchasing an index-oriented product, the keys to success over time are:

- Low fees

- Tax efficiency

- Broad diversification

As we saw in Chapter 2, the average investor who has little experience with ETFs can quickly grasp their relevance and is a lot savvier than the so-called experts of Wall Street would have the world believe. In this chapter, we will examine typical scenarios for individual, long-term investors. Compounding interest over time magnifies the advantages of low fees and tax efficiency. A dollar saved early on in the life of a portfolio grows exponentially and, especially towards the end of the investment period, can produce substantial results.

ETFs are somewhat hampered by transaction and opportunity costs. Assessing the pros and cons of various arguments for all such costs, we have selected the following assumptions we feel are realistic for an ETF and a mutual fund that tracks the S&P 500.

BEYOND THE NUMBERS

Today's financial advisers say that their investment clients seem to be comfortable with ETFs. Comfort with an investment vehicle is not a luxury but rather a necessity. Without confidence in the chosen strategy, an investor is not likely to stay the course. Advisors generally say ETFs help simplify the entire educational process because they involve:

- Fewer trades

- Less time explaining a plan to buy 5 securities rather than 100

- Simpler reports for clients to read

Investors can get hung up discussing the merits of each individual stock when a portfolio of stocks is presented to them. ETFs remove that granularity from sight since the portfolio can only be traded as a block. The investor can focus more on the big picture, say the advisors, and can ignore recommendations of individual stocks by brokerage house analysts and others. These analysts are notoriously shy about downgrading firms they feel are poor prospects if their firm stands to gain fees from the firm or if a portfolio manager in the brokerage house has invested in them. "Why does anyone believe that an analyst will give an honest opinion?" asks Jeffrey Villwock, a former brokerage research analyst and now managing partner at Harpeth Capital Atlanta. "There is nothing in the system that rewards them."

SCENARIO 1: A BASIC RETIREMENT PORTFOLIO

To see how typical buy-and-hold investors might approach ETFs, we can examine the case of the fictional Smyth family. Donna and Rich Smyth, both aged 35, are seeking to invest money for their two infants' college educations and for their own retirement later on. They currently have about $100,000 on hand and think they can save about $20,000 each year to put into the fund.

After speaking with a financial planner, examining historical returns, estimating inflation and considering their needs carefully, they determined that they wanted to place 70 percent of their assets in equities and could tolerate a drop of 30 percent at any given time. They understood that with equities no absolute guarantees exist, only that some indexes have tended to be more stable than others. They admitted to feeling uncomfortable about international and small company stocks and were happy to limit their investments to a few funds. They had no interest in following individual stocks.

The Smyths were just about ready to copy the strategy used by many of their friends and split their initial assets between Vanguard mutual funds when they heard about exchange-traded funds that track the same indexes.

To help evaluate their options, the Smyths built a table of pros and cons in the following areas to help weigh the alternatives (see Table 3.1).

Examining the table of pros and cons, the Smyths were persuaded by the consistently high scores of ETFs in key areas. Picking individual stocks involved too much risk and work. Owning a mutual fund, particularly the ones from Vanguard, was appealing but the flexibility of being able to time

TABLE 3.1   PROS AND CONS OF VARIOUS OPTIONS OPEN TO A SMALL INVESTOR

STRATEGY	FRONT LOADS OR BROKER FEE	MANAGEMENT FEES OVER 18 YEARS	BROKER FEES AND SPREADS	TAX EFFECTS	FLEXIBILITY
Buy 50 stocks and bonds	High	None	High	Excellent	Very High
Low cost mutual funds	None	Low	Very Low	Good	Low
Low cost ETFs	Low	Very Low	Low	Very Good	High

entry and exit had value to them. The Smyths valued a certain amount of control over their investment, including the ability to rebalance their portfolio. At the same time, they didn't want to worry about stock picking and preferred to spend their free time with their children rather than poring over investment journals.

As to the choice of indexes, the Smyths were also aware that their choices of indexes kept them away from small and international stocks (and indeed most real estate, value, and a host of other asset classes). They understood that they would not be as diversified as they could be. The simplicity of owning just a few funds and the lack of comfort with more volatile sectors was enough to convince them. They felt comfortable with a low-cost, no-load bond mutual fund for the fixed income portion of their portfolio, but which ETFs to pick for equities?

We asked several leading financial advisors and money managers who handle ETFs regularly to construct a typical portfolio as a starting point for this hypothetical couple. It was understood that more in-depth discussions with an investor would be necessary to customize a portfolio and make it suitable to their particular situation.

Rick Ferri, CFA, president of Portfolio Solutions, LLC, an investment management firm in Troy, Michigan, offered a radically simple portfolio. All assets can be placed in Russell-1000 iShares, an ETF comprised of large and mid-sized companies.

"This is the simplest, easiest portfolio you can do," he said. "If you can find one ETF that does it all, then don't complicate matters by buying more than one fund."

Jim Novakoff, president of Levitt Novakoff & Company, investment counselors in Boca Raton, Florida, suggested the following three equity ETFs (see Table 3.2).

TABLE 3.2   A PORTFOLIO SUGGESTION FOR A BEGINNING INVESTOR

Nasdaq-100 QQQ	20%
Dow Jones DIAMONDS	30%
S&P-500 SPDR	50%

"This is just a basic buy and hold portfolio," he said. "Set it and for-get it. I don't think you need to rebalance this thing, except maybe every 5 years." He noted that the major indexes tend to self-correct somewhat, so yearly rebalancing is not absolutely necessary.

Diversifying with International and Small Company ETFs

A certain degree of complexity benefits the investor. Financial theorists have concluded, after examining decades of global market returns, that large com-pany investors can improve returns without significant additional risk by adding international and small company stocks to their portfolio. Why? These latter stocks tend to perform better over time with greater volatility and risk, which is the natural trade-off of assets with greater promise and less stabil-ity. More importantly, since they do not move much in tandem with large U.S. company stocks, their volatility goes away partly when they are added to the portfolio. This basic trick of portfolio construction is particularly per-tinent to the ETF investor. Conveniently enough, just about every asset class is available in one ETF or another to allow this optimization to occur.

Is the average investor ready for this complexity? No, according to one top U.S. financial advisor specializing in ETFs. "If you are creating a port-folio that tracks to [U.S.] expectations you will want to underweight inter-national," he said. "Why is that? CNBC doesn't spend a lot of time on international stocks." CNBC is what investors watch for their financial news, and it spends an inordinate amount of time on U.S. markets.

At the same time, it should be noted that international and small com-pany stocks carry higher management fees, hidden transaction costs, and earlier declarations of capital gains taxes. Diversification is best suited for the prepared and well-read investor. For such an investor, ETFs are an ideal way to inexpensively add international, small company and other forms of diversification.

Scenario 2: Diversification

Shortly after the Smyths began their investment program, they mentioned it to their friends the Joneses, who were also reviewing their finances out of dissatisfaction with high-fee mutual funds.

The Joneses, both age 45, have accumulated $250,000 in stocks and bonds for their retirement. Their children are out of school, so their only concern is to have enough money to retire in about 15 years. The Joneses conferred with their planner and came to the same conclusion that ETFs were right for them, but they wanted greater diversification than the Smyths. In particular, international and small company stocks seemed like a good place to start.

Once again, we asked our practicing professionals familiar with ETFs on how to go about constructing a typical portfolio that might be suitable for this fictitious couple, at least as a starting point.

Ferri offered the following equity ETF picks with accompanying weightings (see Table 3.3).

"I like the Global Titans as a starting point," Ferri said. "You have international and U.S. exposure right there."

Broad international ETF funds are somewhat limited, he noted. "The problem is getting proper exposure in ETFs at this time," he said. "There are only a few regional funds." That is surely going to change as the flood of new ETFs reach the market in coming years.

Ferri feels that value stocks, or stocks with low earnings-to-price, or high book value-to-price or other standard measurements, perform better over time than growth stocks, so his next pick is a large company value component, the Russell-1000 Value iShares. Then he rounds out the portfolio with several ETFs based on Standard & Poor's indexes, which he likes because they are screened for financial solidity and other qualities.

TABLE 3.3   A PORTFOLIO SUGGESTION WITH INTERNATIONAL AND SMALL COMPANY DIVERSIFICATION FOR AN INDIVIDUAL INVESTOR

Dow Jones Global Titans streetTRACKS	50%
Russell-1000 Value iShares	20%
S&P MidCap-400 iShares	20%
S&P SmallCap iShares	10%

"This gives you about 25 percent exposure in international stocks, it gives you about 20 percent exposure to large and mid-cap value, which have historically shown to produce a slightly higher return for the overall market," he said. "Finally, you have a position in the S&P MidCap and S&P SmallCap."

Novakoff offers this portfolio as a starting point for this somewhat more sophisticated couple (see Table 3.4).

"It's pretty market neutral," he notes. "It may overweight small-cap just a tad."

AVOIDING DUPLICATION AND BETTING ON SECTORS

In the rush to create the perfect portfolio, investors and their advisors sometimes ignore assets right under their noses. During the day, most investors hold a job in a particular company in a particular industry. They hope to keep a steady revenue stream from this job, but what if the industry enters a recession and they are laid off?

This would be unfortunate, but the injury would be compounded if they were also heavily invested in their industry of employment. Of course,

TABLE 3.4   PORTFOLIO SUGGESTION WITH INTERNATIONAL AND SMALL COMPANIES FROM JAMES NOVAKOFF

Nasdaq-100 QQQ	20%
Dow Jones DIAMONDS	20%
S&P SPDRs	30%
StreetTRACKS SmallCap Value	5%
Russell-2000 iShares	10%
S&P SmallCap/BARRA Growth iShares	5%
Dow Jones Global Titans streetTRACKS	10%

many companies offer stock options as incentives, so heavy personal investment in a particular industry is the norm, quite aside from any formal investment.

When selecting portfolio components, investors should be aware of duplication. If they work for a firm that depends heavily on exports to Asia, it may not be wise to load up on Asian-country ETFs. A worker in a biotechnology company probably should not commit extra funds to a biotechnology ETF unless their insight into the industry exceeds the added risk of concentrating so tightly in one asset class. Because there are so many ETFs covering so many asset classes, both broad and narrow, the astute investor can avoid obvious duplication.

At the same time, some investors have particular insight and experience in an industry or country. They can use the granularity of ETFs to pursue their hunches without the risk of stock picking.

Scenario 3: Avoiding Duplication

The Joneses realize belatedly that they are overexposed to large growth company stocks. Mrs. Jones is an executive in a large growth company and holds substantial options to buy company stock in several years. Her financial planner noted that when her company options are counted in her total portfolio, she is very heavily weighted towards large growth stocks.

At the same time, she gets to know a fair amount about the pharmaceutical industry because of her work. She feels she has particular insight into this industry, likes it for the long-haul, and feels she knows when the sector has dipped and is a bargain.

In this scenario, our advisors cautioned that any solution to such a duplication problem should involve very careful analysis of a particular investor's situation. As with all the portfolios in this chapter, suggestions were offered as conceptual frameworks for action.

Ferri came up with a compact portfolio that decreased large growth company exposure for the investor (see Table 3.5).

"The best way to hedge against that risk is to buy large cap value," Ferri said. "I am going to assume that she is in a high tech industry, so I want to avoid that industry. The way to do that is to stay away from growth

TABLE 3.5   PORTFOLIO SUGGESTION FOR AN ADVANCED INVESTOR WITH HEDGING

Dow Jones Global Titans streetTRACKS	40%
S&P-500/BARRA Value iShares	25%
S&P MidCap/BARRA Value iShares	20%
S&P SmallCap/BARRA Value iShares	10%
Pharmaceutical HOLDRs	5%

and just go with value." He noted that some growth still remains in the Global Titans. As for overweighting pharmaceutical, Ferri wasn't enthusiastic. "My first impression is: 'Don't make those speculations,'" he said. "I don't think you should be making sector bets in a portfolio. The only reason I would put a pharmaceutical ETF in there is if the client absolutely insisted on it."

He feels that it will probably neither hurt nor help much if kept to a modest portion, say less than 10 percent.

Finally, he emphasized that "I would sit down with the client and say this is the initial information I have and this is a first broad brush stroke for where to begin."

Novakoff offered a somewhat more aggressive approach designed especially to address truly hefty options held by Mrs. Jones. An additional assumption was made that the company stock in question correlated with the Nasdaq-100 QQQs more than any other index. In such a case, then shorting the QQQ makes sense, while at the same time putting any company stock held outright on margin to purchase appropriate amounts of other broad market indexes. "If the investment advisor has determined that this portfolio is suitable in this specific instance, then this might be an appropriate strategy. You don't want to do anything resembling this without professional assistance."

His hypothetical portfolio based on these assumptions would look somewhat like this, with exact numbers dependent on the specifics of the situation (see Table 3.6).

TABLE 3.6   A PORTFOLIO SUGGESTION FOR AN
ADVANCED INVESTOR WITH HEDGING
STRATEGY

Short QQQ	In appropriate amounts
Borrow on margin from company stock	In appropriate amounts
Dow Jones US LargeCap Value streetTRACKS	Same amount as S&P-500 SPDRs
S&P-500 SPDRs	Same as Dow Jones U.S. LargeCap Value streetTRACKS
Russell-2000 iShares	About 10%
Dow Jones U.S. SmallCap Value streetTRACKS	About 5%
S&P SmallCap/ BARRA Growth	About 5%
Dow Jones Global Titans streetTRACKS	About 10%
Pharmaceutical HOLDRs	About 5%

ADVANCED FEATURES FOR THE AVERAGE INVESTOR

Have you ever held a group of stocks you wanted to own long-term, but you had a feeling that they were fully priced and not likely to appreciate? *Shorting* and *options* are advanced features available to ETFs that give them remarkable flexibility for all types of investors. Neither feature is available with mutual funds. Although both features are possible with individual stocks, it can become quite cumbersome and expensive to manage.

Shorting involves selling a stock that is not currently owned. An investor who shorts a stock is betting that it will go down and faces unlimited potential loss if the stock goes up. Shorting is to be used only when the speculator feels absolutely certain that a market is significantly overvalued and will come down. It is very easy to understand and implement but rarely appropriate for the buy-and-hold investor. Unlike traditional mutual funds, ETFs may be shorted and bought on margin.

Options, on the other hand, can be appropriate for a wide variety of investors, from the most conservative to the most speculative investor. *Options* center around the *call*, or opportunity to buy an ETF at a certain "strike" price before a particular expiration date, and the *put*, or opportunity to sell at a certain strike price before the expiration date. Options are traded openly and react to movements of the underlying ETF. Options for which underlying ETFs do not reach the strike price expire worthless. Options have been available for a small number of major ETFs but are expected to expand to more products. For example, if a January 2003 call with a strike price of 50 for the QQQ representing the Nasdaq-100 index sells at $5, the owner of the call has paid $5 for the opportunity to purchase the QQQ at $50 by January 2003.

It is important to keep separate and understand the implications of each flavor in its context. These include:

- Buying protective puts: conservative protection for an ETF owner against its fall

- Selling "covered" calls: conservative locking in of profits for an ETF owner with downside protection

- Buying simple puts: speculation that the underlying ETF will fall

- Selling puts: very risky speculation that an ETF will not fall

- Buying calls: speculation that an ETF will rise

- Selling calls: very risky speculation that an ETF will not rise

For the option seller or writer, there is always a modest cash premium taken in and a relatively large risk if the strike price is surpassed. For the option buyer, the opposite is true—there is a modest cash premium paid and a relatively large potential profit to be made if the strike price is surpassed. The various intricacies of the more speculative options strategies are beyond the scope of this book, but it should be noted that substantial knowledge, experience, and soul-searching are a prerequisite. Two conservative strategies for the buy-and-hold investor, the protective put and the covered call, however, can be addressed here.

An ETF *call*, once again, offers its owner the opportunity but not the obligation to buy a stock (or ETF) for an agreed-upon strike price before a specified expiration date. The call buyer pays the call writer for this privilege with an up-front premium. Writing a call without owning the underlying securities is speculative and ill-advised for most investors, but writing a *covered call*, or a call for an asset which one owns, can actually lower risk of loss. Selling a call gives the buyer the opportunity to purchase the stock from the call-writer if the price moves above the strike price. Thus, selling a call guarantees the writer will earn the call premium, but sacrifices potential upside beyond the strike price. The appropriate investor should resemble the farmer with a healthy crop still in the field that is already coveted by buyers. Obtaining the very highest price for the crop is not as important as securing some degree of insurance against disaster. The retired investor seeking a stable amount of income is the ideal candidate for this strategy.

Ever held a group of stocks you wanted to own long-term, but you had the feeling that they were fully priced and not likely to appreciate? You would be a candidate to sell a covered call. For an ETF investor, this means selling calls for an ETF which is currently in their portfolio. In exchange for a cash premium, the investor gives up all profit of appreciation above the strike price prior to the expiration date. Choosing the strike price determines how much potential profit is given away and how much is locked in.

Long-term options (LEAPS in the U.S.) lasting more than one year are a particularly clever way for the cautious investor to exploit covered calls. Premiums for these options, under the right circumstances, can be treated as long-term capital gains (although the IRS has debated whether to lobby Congress for different treatment), so taxes on this profit can be low. Generally this means owning the underlying ETFs for over a year before writing the call. LEAPS exist for several indexes mirrored by ETFs, such as the S&P 100, the S&P 500, and the Nasdaq 100. If LEAPS are exercised, the portfolio may be surrendered directly without additional penalty. Several top financial advisors specializing in ETFs are pursuing this strategy for certain clients.

Consider the following example that could allow an investor to step into technology stocks gingerly with downside protection. On March 12, 2001, the Nasdaq 100 was 64 percent off its 52-week high, and some investors were eyeing QQQs as a possible bargain. Volatility, however, remained, and few were willing to predict whether it had hit bottom. Options offered an interesting twist for the generally bullish investor. QQQ calls with a strike price of $48 and expiring on January 18, 2002 could be sold for $6. If the investor had purchased the QQQ at the closing price of $42.30 and immediately sold January 2002 calls, the net cash investment would have been as follows:

Investment made	$42.30
Premium sold	−$6.00
Net cash outlay	$36.30

Downside protection obtained by the premium as a percentage of the initial investment made in this case would be:

$$\$6.00/\$42.30 = 14 \text{ percent}$$

In other words, the underlying QQQ stock could fall $6 to $36.30 within the 312 days remaining in the option before the investor would suffer loss.

If the QQQ remained entirely unchanged, the profit realized would have in essence paid $36.30 for a stock that ended up being worth $42.30. On an annualized basis this would turn a tidy 19.3 percent return. In this case, the investor would still be positioned in an important index, ready for the long-term. Finally, if the stock had shot up to $48 or higher, no doubt the option would have been exercised just prior to expiration, so there is a maximum cash profit of:

$$\$48 \text{ final proceeds} - \$36.30 \text{ initial net outlay} = \$11.70 \text{ profit}$$

This turns out to be a whopping 32 percent and 38 percent return on an annualized basis.

This package of trades has a little of everything: some downside protection, a tidy profit if the market stagnates, and a handsome reward if it climbs solidly. The main thing given away is upside beyond $48 if the market skyrockets. This strategy is not appropriate if the investor believes an index is truly cheap and likely to climb quickly.

The profitability of this twin trade depends in part on bullish sentiment on the part of other investors. If many investors believe an ETF will go up, they will likely pay a significant premium for a call. The investor selling the covered call is neither highly bearish nor very bullish in the short-term but quite happy to lock in profits.

Buying a put, once again, means paying a cash premium for the right to sell an ETF at the strike price before the expiration date. For the owner of ETF shares, doing this protects them from loss beyond that strike price. It does involve cost up front but limits losses. The option may well expire worthless, so in some sense it is a speculative bet. But in the context of an investor with a highly appreciated portfolio, who can spend a small amount of cash buying insurance, we regard this strategy as conservative. This protective put strategy is dependant on overall market sentiment and works best when there are many bullish speculators willing to write the puts at low cost to the buyer.

Buying a *protective put* is for the buy-and-hold investor who has become bearish. This can occur because of a crumbling economy or a large run-up in an ETFs' price. For instance, by early 2000, QQQ, the Nasdaq-100 ETF, had appreciated greatly over several years due to meteoric rise of telecommunications, Internet and pharmaceutical high-flyers. The investor wanting to protect against a severe downfall might reasonably have purchased puts for the ETFs they owned.

CHAPTER FOUR

INSTITUTIONAL INVESTORS FAVOR ETFS

I n the early '90s, when exchange-traded funds (ETFs) first appeared on the financial landscape, institutions were among the first to buy them in order to capitalize on their low-cost, ease of use and other advantages. Plan sponsors soon discovered a bonus: they could now make hedging transactions that regulations in the futures market had previously prohibited.

Money poured into the new financial vehicles. Institutional investing in ETFs began to soar during the years 1993–1998 when large cap stocks (and therefore the S&P 500) were outperforming all others, and it continues at a strong pace today. From $1.1 billion at the end of 1995, ETF assets ballooned to over $70 billion by the end of 2000. Including Merrill Lynch HOLDRs ($5 billion) German DWS active funds ($4 billion) and a spate of new ETFs, total assets under management globally had reached over $95 billion in 169 funds trading in 10 countries. For a bit of perspective, however, at year-end, institutions had over one trillion dollars directly indexed to the S&P 500, and over $300 billion indexed to the Russell 3000. Thus, even with the exponential growth of ETFs, their assets still represented a tiny percentage of the institutional market's benchmarked money.

Still, in the 12 months leading to December 31, 2000, the number of U.S.-based ETFs available to investors tripled from 32 to 96, while assets under management nearly doubled over the same time period. As of June 30, 2001, there were 103 ETF products on the market in the U.S. (169 worldwide) with over $95 billion in assets under management globally, and there was no end in sight. Much of the trading in these products, particularly in the United States, is done by institutional players.

Diane Garnick of State Street Global Advisors explains, "When ETFs came around, small and medium-sized institutional investors finally had the opportunity to replicate the index at a reasonable price."

Even large institutions that can trade baskets of stock very cheaply may benefit from ETFs. William Miller, vice president at Morgan Stanley Dean Witter, notes that for the institutional player it is "cheaper to buy and sell ETFs than underlying equities in many cases."

Not everyone is in agreement on this contention, however. Gary Gastineau, managing director of Nuveen Investments and former director of product development at AMEX, said, "Why would a major institution use them? They could go to BGI and get virtually any index in the world replicated for an institutional portfolio, as long as it puts $10–20 million in it, for two basis points. Why would they buy an iShare?"

Steven Schoenfeld, the head of international equity management of the Global Index and Markets Group at Barclays Global Investors, weighs in: "I see institutions that argue with us over half a basis point difference in fees readily using the international iShares with a much higher cost structure because it serves other purposes. It's a very efficient way for them to directly modify their cash equitization levels. It's a great way to park assets."

EQUITIZATION ENSURES LIQUIDITY

Although ETFs are billed as passive investment vehicles, fund managers have found a number of ways to actively employ them. They use ETFs for equitization: rather than hold cash at low interest rates, capital inflows are now quickly equitized by investing in ETFs, assuring that funds are fully invested to take advantage of market upturns. And liquidity is less of a concern for ETFs than for traditional mutual funds because large investors have the ability to create or redeem shares. Only the liquidity of the underlying stocks in an index-linked ETF can limit its liquidity.

Despite the fact that ETFs are becoming a significant market, their share of the overall market for the underlying stocks is still limited. Morgan Stanley Dean Witter reports that a $100 million basket of stocks in an index underlying an ETF usually represents less than 10 percent of the average daily volume of each stock. So individual stock prices are not severely affected by the process of buying and selling underlying shares to create and redeem ETF shares. Furthermore, trading volume is not necessarily indicative of significant creation and redemption activity (see Figure 4.1). Even the granddaddy of all ETFs, the SPDRs (ticker SPY), only had creation/redemption activity on 15 percent of trading days in its history.

Once they were comfortable with using ETFs for equitization, plan sponsors next moved to use ETFs for enhanced indexing strategies. "That's

FIGURE 4.1   SPDRs CREATION AND DELETION
             FREQUENCY 1993–1999

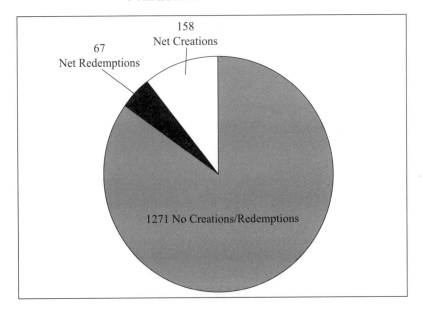

67
Net Redemptions

158
Net Creations

1271 No Creations/Redemptions

when they overweight certain sectors or underweight certain sectors, which gives them the ability to beat the benchmark," Garnick says. "If the S&P returns 10 percent, these managers try to return 12 to 15 percent by over-weighting sectors that they believe will perform well."

TWO ALLOCATIONS FOR ETFS

Garnick maintains that today ETFs can be used in two allocations: one allocation is to mirror the market, and the other allocation is for "active management." In actively-managed accounts, ETFs are used to control risk, to manage exposure, and to help mitigate the effects of fund management transitions. If a portfolio manager decides to move from small-cap to large-cap stocks, he can use a small-cap ETF to hedge while selling off the small-cap stocks. Owing to liquidity issues with the smaller stocks, it would probably take days to sell off all the small-caps from a fund. The ETF acts as a fund stabilizer during the transition period.

MANAGING STYLE DRIFT

Strange as it seems, too much success can put a fund manager's career in jeopardy. If a plan sponsor has allocated a certain amount of money to a value-oriented fund, and the high technology companies held by that fund spurt ahead and vastly out-perform the value-oriented index, the plan sponsor may actually be unhappy.

We'll take a hypothetical case to make this point. At a certain time in history, the value-oriented index is up 2 percent. The growth index during this time is up 22 percent and the S&P is up 18 percent. Even though the manager has not made any changes to his value-oriented fund, the high tech stocks within it have pushed his fund's returns to 6 percent. The sponsor may not be happy about this because he wanted his designated money in value, not growth. To rebalance his fund back to the value-oriented norm, the fund manager can purchase additional value-oriented ETFs and use them as ballast to bring his own fund back into character (value-oriented). In this way he can dilute the impact of his high-flying tech investments, please his investors, and keep his job.

WHY INSTITUTIONS USE ETFS

Not all institutional investors share the same goals when investing in ETFs. Among the reasons cited by institutional investors are:

- Core holding: For institutional and individual investors alike, ETFs provide broad market exposures from which custom portfolios of sector funds and/or individual stocks can be built. They can be tax-efficient, long-term holdings that reduce portfolio risk versus overall market risk.

- Building block: Index-linked ETFs offer an efficient way to add specific sectors or international diversification in order to weight a portfolio toward those specific sectors, styles, countries, or regions.

- Trading vehicle: Index-linked ETFs provide a low-cost, highly liquid vehicle for market-timers throughout the trading day (although brokerage fees can make this practice expensive). They are also useful for targeted asset allocation or sector rotation strategies, and because they are not subject to an uptick rule, they can easily be shorted throughout the trading day.

- Hedging instrument: Index-linked ETFs can be sold short to hedge a portfolio of stocks, closed-end funds, or open-end mutual funds. This allows investors to keep a portfolio intact while protecting it from overall market losses. In a market decline, profits on an index-linked fund short position could offset some of the losses incurred by the portfolio. Listed options are available on certain ETFs and can be used for income-producing, risk-reducing, and speculative strategies.

- Cash management: Investors can purchase index-linked ETFs to equitize cash inflows that eventually could be invested in stocks. They offer an alternative to futures and, in some situations, advantages over futures. ETFs can be bought in smaller sizes than futures, they do not require any special documentation or accounts, and investors do not have to deal with roll costs and margin requirements. In addition, ETFs track many indexes that do not have futures.

- Tax strategies: Index-linked ETFs can be highly tax efficient. They tend to pay out fewer taxable capital gains distributions than actively-managed funds. Because each separate ETF series is a different stock from a tax standpoint, they are not subject to *wash-sale* rules, which disallow a loss on a stock if the same stock is repurchased within 30 days. An investor under these rules could take a loss on one sector fund and immediately reestablish a position in another ETF fund in the same sector. Finally, ETFs may be used to hedge and defer income.

TRADING METHODS VARY

Although simplicity is emphasized when speaking of ETFs, it is important to understand that trading methods vary according to the portfolio involved and, in some cases, can become complex transactions. The costs involved for institutions in trading baskets of stocks help determine where and when it makes sense to use ETFs in portfolio management. There are several methods by which plan sponsors execute trades to manage their portfolios.

Agency trading: The broker executes trades for the investor on a best-effort basis in this method. The investor can give trading instructions on selected stocks and set time limits for execution. Also, the investor can set trading benchmarks, such as a day's closing price.

At the portfolio level, instructions can be given that the portfolio retains a desired characteristic during execution, such as sector weighting. For baskets with a mixture of buy and sell instructions, trading can be performed with controlled market exposure and cash levels. There are also some variants of agency trading that include incentives based on trading performance.

With agency trading, the investor has more control over the execution of trades, there is no capital commitment, and commission rates are lower than those of other basket trading methods. Also, with this method, the broker provides pre- and post-trade analytics.

The downsides of agency trading includes the fact that cost is not known before trading begins, and that there is also the potential for opportunity costs that tend to rise with the number of limit orders.

Principal: Here the broker commits capital to either buy or sell the designated portfolio immediately. The investor provides information (liquidity, tracking error, and industry composition) on the *basket* before the market closes. The dealer quotes a fee rate that will be charged (normally in cents per share for U.S. portfolios, and in basis points for non-U.S. portfolios). If the investor accepts the quote, he or she then discloses the holdings of the portfolio and the transaction takes place at closing prices.

Four important facts on principal bid should be kept in mind:

- Principal bid is usually done on a blind basis.

- Basket pricing is likely to be more efficient if it closely tracks an index with liquid futures.

- Liquid baskets usually result in a lower spread off of the trade that determines the price.

- The principal trade requires the broker to commit capital, so his risk premium will be embedded into pricing.

With the principal bid method, opportunity costs are eliminated and there is up-front certainty as to the trading cost.

The main drawback to principal bid is the higher commission rate to compensate the broker's willingness to commit capital.

Exchange for physical (EFP): This method involving futures is more complicated, and an EFP can be categorized as "pure" and "risk." In a pure EFP, the underlying portfolio equals the futures index composition; in a risk EFP, the portfolio deviates from the index.

The broker sets the bid-ask spread (based on the fair value futures basis). With risk EFPs, the spread widens as the portfolio deviates from the futures index.

EFPs take advantage of futures liquidity, and because the investor hedges with futures, potential opportunity costs are reduced. Compared to agency trading, there is a higher up-front certainty as to overall trading costs, and the investor can benefit from futures mispricing from fair value (but he or she can also lose because of mispricing).

Some limitations apply to EFPs: they are feasible only for portfolios that track an index with listed futures, and outside of the S&P 500, futures

TABLE 4.1   PRIMARY CHARACTERISTICS OF EACH
                 TRADING METHOD

Agent trading	Investor sets parameters for trade and commits no capital
Principal bid	Broker guarantees price, eliminating opportunity costs and charging per share commission
Exchange for physical	Portfolio based on futures index composition with futures to lessen opportunity cost
Basis trade	Like exchange for physical, except broker holds futures and spread is incorporated into price

liquidity is limited. The investor takes the futures market impact, and mispricing can work against him. In addition, as with principal bid, the broker is compensated with a higher commission for putting up capital.

Basis trade: Basis trades are similar to EFPs except that the futures are executed in the broker's account. However, unlike EFPs, with a basis trade the spread is incorporated into the stock price through an adjustment factor. The benefits of basis trade include taking advantage of the liquidity in the futures markets and the reduced potential for opportunity cost. Also, the fact that futures transactions take place in the broker's account is valuable for investors who cannot hold derivatives in their portfolios.

The drawbacks for basis trades are the same as those for EFPs.

Table 4.1 summarizes each trading method's primary characteristics.

INSTITUTIONAL INVOLVEMENT IN THE ETF CREATION AND REDEMPTION PROCESS

A unique creation and redemption process allows index-linked exchange-traded funds to closely approximate the holdings of the various indexes and keep their market price tightly in line with a particular index's underlying net asset value. The creation process is straightforward, and is described in detail in Chapter 5.

Authorized participants (APs) are the large financial institutions that initiate the creation of ETFs. They may do this because there is client demand for the ETF shares or because there is a pricing discrepancy that has opened an opportunity to profit. The AP purchases the underlying stocks in the index in the relevant market, delivers them to a custodian bank, and receives ETF shares in return, which can then be traded on the open market. The reverse occurs when the AP wishes to redeem the ETF shares. The ETF shares are delivered to the custodian, and the AP receives the underlying equities in exchange.

Only the really large players redeem whole baskets of stocks in-kind, but occasionally they have reason to effect these trades. A large investment firm holding shares of an ETF may decide it wants to give itself space to outperform an index and would prefer to own some of the underlying stocks in the index at a greater weight, or own stocks outside of the index. In this case, the firm will sell baskets of indexed stocks and cherry-pick the individual issues it wants to retain, selling off the rest.

Conversely, an investment firm may want to sell a particular stock that it holds in an ETF. The firm will opt to sell the ETF in order to back out of that particular stock, making up the cash as appropriate by buying back the other stocks (or simply retain them if it redeemed ETF shares).

Yet another reason large investors sell ETF shares is to own the actual underlying stocks in order to have a say in shareholding voting. To vote on company issues that management presents to shareholders—management changes, dividend changes, stock splits—shareholders have to own stock outright, not in an ETF. The fund manager controls the vote. In this case, the investment firm may sell an ETF and buy a block of stock in the company of interest. It is important to remember that while ETF shares are receipts that were traded for shares in the underlying stock, (a) trading prices are not directly determined by the price of the underlying stock, and (b) as with traditional mutual funds, the fund management acts as proxy to the shareholder vote for underlying shares. Most ETF fund managers do not use their shares to vote on shareholder resolutions, nor do they vote their shares in the same proportion as the rest of the vote.

ETFs Present an
Ever-changing Landscape

As institutional enthusiasm for ETFs grows, more and more firms are creating increasingly specialized ETFs sculpted to achieve or beat specific benchmarks. From their initial appeal as long-term passive investments, many of the newer ETFs are designed as tools to achieve specific short-term goals or comprehensive equity allocation by sector, style or region. The very definition of ETFs is becoming more complex—should investors still view them as core holdings in a long-term investment strategy, or should one flit from ETF to ETF with market fluctuations?

By the end of June, 2001, 169 ETFs were listed on the world's exchanges. They ranged from pure index-linked funds to finely-tuned, customized baskets of stock designed to exploit the outperformance (or, as we saw in 2000 with Internet funds, suffer from the underperformance) of particular segments of the market. Yet there were still gaps—not enough variety in international funds, only a small number of fixed income funds (based in Canada), and as yet only a handful of active funds in Germany. Investment managers wanted more, even as a plethora was being made available. Some industry participants predict there will be 1,000 ETFs by 2004. Others cite a slowing in the momentum for ETFs. Exchange-traded funds still represent a tiny percentage of mutual fund assets. Total ETF assets of the 169 funds trading globally at the end of June 2001 still amounted to less than those in the single largest traditional mutual fund. The Vanguard-500 fund contained over $100 billion, with ETF assets at about $95 billion. While some see the new vehicles fizzling, others see them chipping away at the share of assets in traditional index funds, which today control about 10 percent of total mutual fund assets in the U.S. Others boldly predict that ETFs will enter all realms of fund management, including active strategies, and supplant traditional mutual funds altogether. With the glut of new ETFs on the market, it is easy to imagine a drift toward using sector funds as short-term bets on sectors of the market. Gus Fleites, principal responsible for ETFs at State Street Global Advisors, commented at a recent conference, for example, that he'd heard that the average holding period for the technology-heavy QQQ was "about 3 hours." Time will tell if the trend toward sector bets intensifies and ETFs that are actively managed are ultimately introduced and gain headway, or if indexed, broadly-based funds continue to maintain their hold on assets. The advantages of the latter cannot be disputed, although it is possible that the tradability, lower costs, and tax-efficient nature of ETFs may translate well for actively-managed funds.

ONE CAVEAT

"The most important thing about investing in ETFs is having a valid investment philosophy," says State Street Global Advisors' Garnick. "The biggest hazard that investors have is not investing in the right underlying investments. An ETF gives you fantastic market exposure, which is the right way to think about it. But if you don't have a strategy behind which ETFs you're going to invest in, you can make mistakes." Garnick cites an example of going long on small caps and short on large caps just as large caps surge upwards and small caps sink. "It's exactly the same as owning stocks," she says, "if your underlying strategy, your thoughts about why you're buying an ETF are not valid, all that means is that ETFs are a faster, less expensive way to lose money."

STRATEGIC USE OF ETFS BY FINANCIAL ADVISORS

After ten years as a broker with major investment houses, Richard A. Ferri founded Portfolio Solutions LLC in July of 1999. Headquartered in Troy, Michigan, his three-member firm manages $100 million primarily for individual clients. They use ETFs—but sparingly.

"I use iShares for very special circumstances. I use them when there is nothing else to use," Ferri says.

Ferri's research revealed that every time investment firms made an asset allocation change and publicized this change, they would track not whether or not they were right, but the amount of commissions they would gain from that strategy. They'd look at the revenue stream gained every time they made an allocation change. Every quarter they'd make sure they did *something* to make sure they'd get a little boost in their revenue stream.

Ferri decided to go back and track whether these allocation calls were any good. Overwhelmingly, they were not. If you just left your money in a fund that was 60 percent stocks and 40 percent bonds, generally you did much better.

"I came to a very strong conclusion, which was supported by other sources, that the reason brokerage firms suggest asset reallocation is to generate commissions," explains Ferri. "It's very clear: the more market calls you make, the more commissions you get, and the wealthier you become as a broker."

Based on this research, Ferri concluded that what was best for his clients was a strategy that utilized indexing, passive investing, and static allocation.

THE FORAY INTO ETFS

Initially, the only way Ferri could buy index funds that were anywhere near affordable for his clients was to use Spiders ticker (SPY). He did not have access to Vanguard or Dimensional Fund Advisors (DFAs) because he was employed by a broker. He also bought some Middies (S&P MidCap funds—MDY).

Today Ferri uses ETFs as long-term, buy-and-hold investments. He does not trade them due to his aversion to churning accounts, but he does find ETFs an effective tool for select situations. He cites as an example a small, $4-million pension fund for a ten-person firm where most of the money belongs to the top officers who have been there a long time. He consults with them about what allocation between stocks and bonds is appropriate. After Ferri decides how much is going into stocks, he then decides how much of that will go into domestic stocks and how much into international stocks. He does not use international ETFs yet, because most of them are limited to individual countries and it's too complicated to buy the funds of 25 different countries.

Check List for Deciding on ETFs vs. Mutual Funds:

- ✓ What sort of funds, style, size and sector representation does investor want?
- ✓ Where are appropriate products available? Sometimes there are ETFs in categories where there are no mutual funds and vice-versa.
- ✓ What are the fees, costs, holdings, and tax efficiencies of the various holdings?

✓ Is uniform settlement possible upon rebalancing?

For his pension fund he uses all regular mutual funds for the international side, but on the stock side he looks for a large stock fund with a value tilt and another large stock fund with a growth tilt. He found what he was looking for in ETFs. He also found the same value and growth orientation in mid-cap ETF funds and small-cap ETFs. In all, he found six different categories of ETFs to choose from.

"My philosophy is buy a little of this and a little of that," Ferri says. He has difficulty implementing that approach with Vanguard funds because it does not offer a mid-cap value or a mid-cap growth fund—it has only a mid-cap fund. Ferri decided that ETFs were the better domestic fit in that case for his clients.

"On the domestic side I went ETFs, and for the international side I went regular mutual funds," says Ferri. "ETFs allowed me to be more flexible."

REALLOCATION PRESENTS CHALLENGES

However, when it comes time to make his quarterly reallocations to rebalance funds that have drifted from their original orientation, the mix of ETFs and regular mutual funds presents a problem.

When Ferri corrects for style drift in a portfolio of U.S. stock ETFs, he wants to do it instantaneously. When he sells the ETF that went up and buys the one that went down, he needs to do it at the same time. But ETFs have a three-day settlement period, whereas mutual funds have an overnight settlement. If he sells an ETF and wants to buy a mutual fund, he must wait three days to do it because the money's not going to be there.

"If I'm going to sell one, and I'm not going to get the money for three days, how can I buy the other one if it needs the money the next day?" asks Ferri.

That limitation illustrates how ETFs do not solve all investment needs. As Ferri makes clear, by late 2000, the product for some asset classes was only available in mutual funds, not ETFs. Bonds are a good example. There really weren't any ETF bond funds in late 2000 (a handful of Canadian-based funds were the only ones available), although Ferri expects them to arrive along with a host of other new ETF products as the industry matures. See Figure 4.2 for a list of ETFs as of June 30, 2001.

FIGURE 4.2   169 ETFs WORLDWIDE

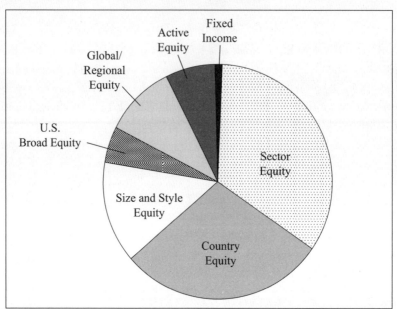

"I think there will be 1,000 ETFs in the next three years," he predicts. "Everything that has an index fund attached to it, someone—Barclays or Vanguard or somebody—is going to create an ETF so that you're able to buy and sell it during the day as opposed to having to wait until the end of the day. But to me, that's not that much of an advantage because I'm a long-term investor."

When enough ETFs are available, Ferri predicts money managers will use all ETFs or no ETFs because of the complications in correcting style drift. Plan sponsors will want everything they reallocate to have the same settlement date, otherwise they could end up cash short.

MARKET TIMING IRRESISTIBLE SOMETIMES

Despite his avowed aversion to short-term investing, Ferri admits he's found ETFs the ideal vehicle for quick strikes in the market. During the recent volatile period when the result of the U.S. presidential election was in doubt, he succumbed to temptation and made a purchase. "I wanted to go into the market [which had dropped] before Judge Sauls made his announcement about banning hand counts during the recent election," says Ferri.

Sauls was going to make the announcement about whether to proceed with hand counts during the day, so Ferri did not want to wait until the market closed to make a mutual fund purchase. In that particular case, it was a good thing he did move—the announcement came out, stocks took off, and his client made an extra 5 or 6 percent.

"But that was a rare case," admits Ferri. "I was buying into the market for this client every month anyway, but I had the discretion as to when."

This ETF flexibility is important during moving markets, but not so important when the market is flat, Ferri says.

And Ferri sees tax advantages in ETFs for some accounts. For a personal account, his firm may advise a client to buy 100 shares of an ETF in the S&P 500. Later they may advise buying another 100 shares and, still later, another 100 shares. Each of these buys has a different tax basis that must be tracked. If during the year the market goes down and one of the client's buys is showing a loss, the client can sell that particular tax loss and turn around and buy another ETF that is very similar. If the loss sell had been an individual stock, regulations would have prohibited the client from repurchasing that stock for 30 days. "So the ETF allows you to take a tax loss without ever being out of the market," says Ferri. It should be noted that some tax experts dispute the exact nature of the "substantially identical" language in Internal Revenue Service (IRS) code. It is unclear, for example, whether or not the tax wash rule applies when you sell, say the Spider S&P-500 (SPY) fund at a loss and then buy the iShares S&P-500 fund (IVV) within 30 days.

THE POTENTIAL FOR ABUSE

Ferri believes that ETFs were created to answer the clarion call of John Bogle and The Vanguard Group for lower investment management fees. Clients heard the message, were persuaded, and flocked to Vanguard index funds in droves. Competitors were caught flat-footed. With the success of index funds and particularly the S&P-500 fund, came a flood of copycat funds and ultimately low-cost ETFs with other advantages. It should be noted that, at least initially, no traditional retail fund managers launched ETFs for fear of cannibalizing their other funds. Vanguard, the manager of the world's largest mutual fund and the granddaddy of retail index funds, changed all that by announcing the launch of its own ETFs, VIPERs.

"Now all the investment houses can use ETFs to keep money from flowing (directly) to Vanguard," Ferri says. And because Vanguard now offers ETFs as well, Ferri thinks "the brokers can have even more fun—now they can churn Vanguard funds too."

Because the brokerage commission on ETFs is minimal, Ferri sees plans afoot by investment firms to offer a plethora of ETFs with many variations—at increased cost to investors. The simple truth of the matter is that with passive index-based funds it is hard to justify high expense ratios. And low expense ratios translate to low profit margins. Because of the squeeze, only the very large fund managers are able to compete. Ironically, ETFs may ultimately reinvigorate active management as fund managers seek ways to boost profits with a management style that can be justified as adding value.

"Realize that brokers get paid hardly anything for using these ETFs. It's not something they even want to think about," says this former broker. Still, they are better for profits than Vanguard, which gives brokers nothing. "When everybody was getting into Vanguard, and you were a broker at Merrill Lynch and all your clients were talking about was Vanguard, Vanguard, Vanguard—the brokers didn't have any answer to that. They could recommend Spiders, and that was okay, but now they have a portfolio of ETFs where they can say, 'I can show you something that is even better than Vanguard,' although whether it is or not is a question. Now, their argument goes, you don't have to transfer to Vanguard."

But Ferri maintains that's not where brokers want their clients' money to be.

"They'll put it in an ETF for a while and then recommend those clients rapidly trade those ETFs based on market timing or sector rotation," says Ferri. "They're going to create turnover in the portfolio [and fees for the broker]. That what the brokers want; that's not what the client should do."

According to Ferri, brokers claim their fees are low—even lower than Vanguard's S&P-500 fund with an internal fee of .18 percent. He paints a scenario: "Here comes a Barclays' iShare. The broker can say, 'Hah! I have iShare S&P-500 ETF at .0945 percent—only half the cost of Vanguard. So now, Mr. Client, you have no excuse to leave me.' The iShares product is a perfect weapon for brokers to use to retain their clients' assets that would otherwise go to Vanguard."

"The problem," according to Ferri, "is this: it's true. The iShares S&P-500 ETF is a loss leader for Barclays. It is the only one of its funds that has that low a fee. The other iShare funds—mid-cap, small-cap, growth, international—the expense ratios of these funds are higher, all the way up to around a 1 percent management fee."

Says Ferri: "Now the broker tells the client, 'I'm going to tell you about all these other iShares Barclays offers.' You're going to start diversifying away from the S&P 500. That's how Barclays makes money. That's how the broker makes money."

Ferri's bait and switch theory may hold true for some of the international funds (though even this is arguable since many of the iShares country funds do not have Vanguard equivalents); but overall ETF expense ratios are equal to or cheaper than those of traditional mutual funds—even Vanguard funds. This is all the more remarkable, because not all iShares funds are loss-leaders, but many of them are still cheaper that equivalent Vanguard funds—and Vanguard, which is owned by its shareholders, is running at cost. It only serves to underscore the point that ETFs are inherently cheaper to run than traditional funds. Barclays Global Investors and State Street Global Advisors can make a profit and still equal or undersell Vanguard on all 9 of the domestic ETFs that directly correlate to Vanguard funds. Comparisons are difficult with international funds, but clearly retail investors could find less expensive emerging markets and greater global and regional exposure with traditional Vanguard funds than ETFs at the end of 2000.

ETFs Serve a Purpose

Although Ferri is well aware of ETF limitations, he generally favors their addition to the investment manager's arsenal of trading options. Despite the disadvantages of ETFs in some areas (their three-day settlement restriction, and the inevitable bid-ask spread that adds to cost), Ferri says, "The bottom line is ETFs are much better than what was out there five years ago. The more arrows I have in my quiver, the better I can manage my client's money. My job is to know what best fits my client's situation for what they want to accomplish. For the right person in the right portfolio, ETFs make a lot of sense. In the long run, it is an advantage to have them out there because it does help drive fees across the board down, and that's a good thing. Anything that gets people to focus on fees, to focus on indexing, is good."

CHAPTER FIVE

INTERNAL WORKINGS OF ETFs

Investors can benefit from ETFs without knowing exactly how they work. But understanding the internal operations of ETFs will help clarify why they offer unique cost, flexibility, and tax advantages over traditional mutual funds. Plus, the alchemy of this unique financial instrument offers a fascinating insight into the modern world of money.

The key advantage of the ETF is that it sidesteps some of the costly buying and selling of underlying stocks that make up the target index. This allows investors to avoid some transaction costs and delay most U.S. long-term capital gains. Sidestepping normal cash-for-stock markets is done in-kind—where ETF shares are traded for the underlying stocks they represent. Although it might sound crude at first, it involves a myriad of specialized players performing intricate tasks to make ETFs an efficient instrument for buying and selling an entire market.

It should be noted that not all ETFs are created equal beyond the different indexes they target. Some are management investment companies structurally similar to mutual funds (BGI's iShares, State Street Select Sector SPDRs), others are relatively similar and are called unit investment trusts (Standard & Poor's Depositary Receipts [SPDRs] and

Nasdaq-100 Trust QQQs), and still others are traded as baskets of stocks or grantor trusts called HOlding Company Depositary Receipts (HOL-DRs), which stand somewhat apart from the first two. All types of ETFs are traded on the open market, highly liquid, and backed by major financial institutions, but different structures can lead to different holding costs and tax effects.

This chapter explores the inner workings of ETFs from the simplest overview to a more complex examination. First are the explanations that are easiest to grasp and explain to others. Next a comparison with mutual fund operations is made, because mutual funds are simpler in operation and are the principal alternative for most investors. Towards the end of the chapter, all the explicit details of ETF creation and redemption, and the intricate organization and structural details for various flavors of ETFs, are discussed to satisfy the truly curious.

Birth of an ETF

An ETF share is a blip on the screen of the investor's computer that ensures partial ownership of a portfolio of stocks, usually an index such as the Standard & Poor's-500 Index of the largest U.S. companies. It is a financial agreement sanctioned and monitored heavily by the Securities and Exchange Commission (SEC).

How does a share of an ETF come into existence? It occurs when an entire portfolio of stocks (usually an *index*) are placed in trust. The portfolio is not sold but literally bartered "in-kind" for the newly-minted ETF so that the latter serves as a kind of proxy. This private market of paper trading sidesteps some of the costly open-market costs of buying and selling securities. Figure 5.1 shows the steps to investing in ETFs.

Once created, the ETF share can now circulate freely. An investor, literally anywhere in the world, can buy it one minute and sell it the next or hold onto it for decades. The ETF lives and breathes freely in the open markets.

FIGURE 5.1   TRANSACTIONS FOR ETF INVESTMENT

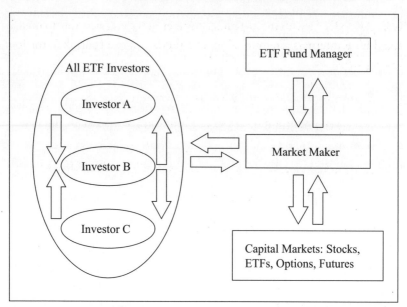

SOMEONE IS MINDING THE STORE

The reason an ETF, which is after all just a piece of paper, is seen as reliable is that the portfolio underlying it is locked away securely by the Depository Trust Clearing Corporation (DTCC), an entity registered and regulated by the SEC and owned collectively by the financial services industry. The DTCC was created by the merger of the Depository Clearing Company (DTC) and the National Securities Clearing Corporation (NSCC) under one umbrella in 1999. The DTCC is not set up to make money, but to run the most efficient markets possible. The primary job of the DTCC is to clear U.S. security trades, so if you have confidence that you will be paid for an individual stock that you sell, you should have confidence that the ETF you own has value. For most participants, this is a sufficiently solid base to believe that with an ETF they own a clearly-defined block of equities.

MUTUAL FUND OPERATIONS

Comparing ETFs with mutual funds is sometimes the easiest way to understand ETF internals. Traditional mutual funds grow and shrink in the following steps:

1. Investors transfer in cash to the mutual fund.

2. The mutual fund manager buys individual stock with the new cash.

3. Eventually exiting investors request redemption of shares.

4. The fund sells stock and delivers cash to the investor.

The relationship is a relatively direct one between the fund manager and the investor, aside from fund distributors or custodians who act as middlemen and safeguards. These latter participants ensure that funds are properly invested and that shares are properly credited. The investor's ownership proportion is determined by the *net asset value* (NAV) of the fund's holdings at the close of the day's trading (usually 4:00 P.M. EST for U.S. markets).

Figure 5.2 shows how mutual funds take in cash (or return it) from investors and create (or destroy) ownership portions. New cash is used to buy stocks, and stocks are sold to raise cash for exiting investors.

The only caveat, and an important one, is that if there are no *net* outflows from the fund, when one investor redeems, the cash of a new investor is relayed to him and his or her stock is held by the fund. Additional shares are bought by the fund as needed. With net outflows, of course, the opposite is true, and stocks must be sold to raise cash for the redeeming investors.

Note the following two critical features:

- Individual company stocks are almost always bought and sold (rather than traded) by mutual funds, both for new investment/redemption and changes to the underlying index.

- Capital gains are recorded in any sale for all mutual fund investors.

FIGURE 5.2   THE FLOW OF CASH FOR MUTUAL FUNDS

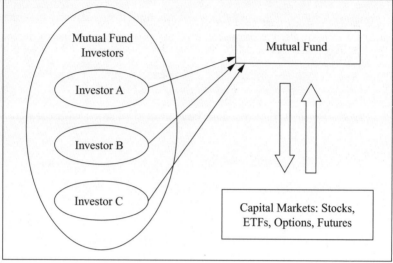

As we saw in Chapter 2, when individual company stocks are bought or sold, a whole range of transactional costs occur. Some of these are quite subtle and difficult to quantify, and, clearly, ETFs have their own transaction costs. In addition, capital gains are recorded. The effect of this is clearly known but depends on the income level and marginal tax rate of the investor.

ETFS TURN THE WORLD UPSIDE DOWN

ETFs invert traditional mutual fund operations because the fund is created before investors purchase ETF shares. ETFs grow and contract in the following steps:

1. Demand for ETF is anticipated by the fund manager.

2. Major institutions place entire portfolios of stocks in a funds portfolio.

3. ETF shares are created and exchanged for the stocks transferred to the fund.

4. ETF shares are sold on the open market and circulate freely.

5. Eventually demand for an ETF falls.

6. ETFs are repurchased on the open market.

7. ETFs are "redeemed" for underlying stocks held by the fund.

CREATION AND REDEMPTION

This life cycle contains a unique step, the creation/redemption process, in which ETF shares and underlying stock shares are traded "in-kind" without resorting to traditional cash sales of the underlying equities. The creation/redemption process depends on some form of market maker who operates in the middle of the ETF world such as it is depicted in Figure 5.3.

How Creation and Redemption Works

Authorized participants (APs), which are large financial players such as brokers or specialists, create ETF shares in block-size "creation units," usually in 50,000-share baskets. The creator then deposits this portfolio of stocks into the applicable fund in exchange for an institutional block (usually 50,000) of ETF shares. The ETFs can only be redeemed in creation units—"in kind"—for the portfolio of stocks held by the fund. This in-kind creation/redemption does not create a tax event for the fund, whereas a cash sale would. This avoidance of capital gains or losses in ETF trades provides a major advantage over traditional mutual funds that incur such tax events with each gain or loss. Because these gains or losses must be distributed to fund holders by traditional mutual funds, investor returns are reduced while non-taxed gains in an ETF continue working for investors.

Step-by-step, the creation process at the authorized participant level works like this:

The AP initiates the creation of ETFs either because he or she has orders to fill or simply needs to generate inventory. The AP purchases an

FIGURE 5.3   MAIN PLAYERS AND MONEY FLOWS

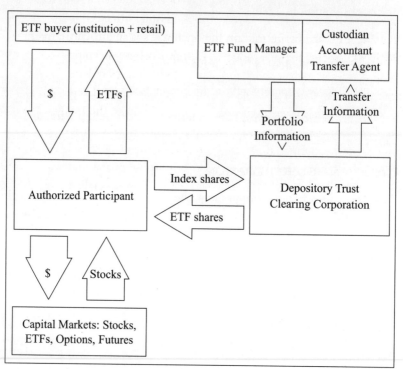

ETF basket of shares making up the relevant index—say the S&P 500—
and the value of the portfolio is calculated at the close of that trading day.
This basket of stocks is then delivered to a custodian bank. A cash component may accompany this basket to cover the creation fee (which cov-
ers custody and transfer charges) as well as accrued dividends, interest on
dividends, and any capital gains less losses on that portfolio basket that
have not been reinvested since the last distribution. At the time of settlement, the custodian delivers the ETF shares to the authorized participant,
usually in an institutional block of 50,000 shares.

The redemption process reverses the creation process. The ETF is calculated at the close of a trading day, and the ETF shares are delivered to
the custodian. At settlement, securities comprising the index (plus a cash
component that can be positive or negative) are delivered to the AP after
nominal transaction fees have been deducted. All creations and redemptions are effected after the market closes.

In-kind redemption sounds simple enough, but it can lead to real management headaches. Says Diane Garnick of State Street Global Advisors, "It's a dirt cheap way to redeem a fund but it's very difficult to manage. With 500 stocks, the possibility of mistakes arises—keeping track of all those dividends, splits, gains and losses. Nobody uses redemption except the specialists." Those specialists, companies like Spear, Leeds & Kellogg and Susquehanna Investment Group, not only make the trading market on ETFs but can also use their capital presence to take advantage of differences between the trading value and underlying net asset value in ETFs, while at the same time serving the lofty purpose of maintaining a high degree of liquidity in the ETF issues. Exactly how specialists make markets is discussed in greater detail in Chapter 9.

THREE TYPES OF ETFS

There are actually three different types of ETFs, (see Table 5.1) the management investment company, the unit investment trust and the grantor or "basket" trust.

TABLE 5.1   A COMPARISON OF THE THREE TYPES OF ETFS

	MANAGEMENT INVESTMENT CO.	UNIT INVESTMENT TRUST	GRANTOR TRUST
Leading products	iShares, Sector SPDRs	SPDRs, QQQs	HOLDRs
Tracks index	Yes, sampling OK	Yes, no sampling	No
Use of derivatives	Yes	No	No
In-kind redemption	Yes	Yes	Same as owning stock
Easily traded intraday	Yes	Yes	Yes

MANAGEMENT INVESTMENT COMPANY

Of the major types of ETFs, management investment companies most resemble a mutual fund. As the name implies, they are managed by a fund manager charged with coordinating fund activities, including setting policies on the index to be followed, dividend payments, and selection of specialists, distributors, administrators and other players.

The manager may charge a slightly higher fee in this type of ETF but has the flexibility to reduce costs and maximize performance by loaning securities and reducing cash drag. At this point in time, virtually all ETFs, except for HOLDRs and a handful of unit investment trusts, fall under this structure. With the management investment company (or open-ended) structure, the fund need not hold absolutely every stock of a target index—it can buy a representative sample that approximates the index. For indexes containing a very large number of small companies, this can be critical. Buying each and every stock can be laborious and costly. Likewise, futures and options are often employed instead of the actual purchase of stock. The fund can also lend its holdings for extra profit, to the benefit of the fund's investors.

Market makers, known as authorized participants (APs) in ETF lexicon, are the firms that deliver portfolios of securities, which are then exchanged for ETFs. Generally these are large Wall Street firms. Broker-dealers can serve as APs and can effect creations and redemptions, as can specialists who are selected by ETF fund managers to make markets by posting ETF bid and offer prices. In addition, custodial and fund-accounting services are required. For standard iShares these services are provided by Investors Bank & Trust. While for iShares country funds, PFPC serves as administrator and Chase Manhattan Bank serves as custodian. In addition, a transfer agent (also Investors Bank for iShares) passes on this information to the appropriate firms, and a distributor works with the authorized participant to ensure orders to create and redeem ETFs. For the iShares, this firm is SEI Investments Distribution Co. A complete list of all of the various participants in the process for each ETF can be found in Appendix C and D.

As mentioned, the Depository Trust and Clearing Corporation clears and finally settles stocks in its role as a kind of official referee and securities warehouse.

Unit Investment Trusts

Unit investment trusts operate much like management investment companies, but with less flexibility. The only ETFs that have the unit investment trust (UIT) structure are the SPDR Trust (SPY), Diamond Trust (DIA), Nasdaq-100 Trust (QQQ), and S&P MidCap-400 Trust (MDY). The unit investment trust structure was originally selected for ETFs because it was cheap and easy to manage. These funds, however, do not have some of the advantages of the management investment company, like the ability to immediately reinvest dividends, lend securities and use derivatives in managing the portfolio.

The main difference between unit investment trusts and management investment companies is that there is little managerial discretion with UITs. The target index must be followed rigidly and dividends are paid out and not reinvested. As a practical matter as well, derivatives are not used to create the ETF.

In general, unit investment trusts are excellent vehicles for highly-liquid large company indexes.

Grantor Trusts

Referred to as exchange-traded baskets, grantor trusts are the distant cousins of the ETF family, but they do have the essential trait of being able to be traded instantly. Merrill Lynch's HOLDRs, which target industrial sectors, are the primary grantor trusts in the U.S. They are most valuable to investors with strong convictions about a particular industry and less valuable to the investor painting a portfolio with a broad brush.

Grantor trusts give investors a relatively direct link to the underlying stocks. Investors essentially own the underlying stocks and generally trade the trust shares in lots of one hundred. Likewise, for a small fee, the underlying securities may be created or redeemed by investors themselves in 100-share units.

In fact, HOLDRs do not even try to track an index. They simply hold a static basket of underlying shares. Thus there are no authorized participants working away diligently in the background to keep ETF prices in check with the underlying NAV of a moving index. The HOLDRs trust mirrors the target stock basket on the day a specific HOLDR is launched, but after that the relative composition of the basket may change as some firms appreciate and others decrease in value. The number of underlying shares from each company, however, will always remain static. The shareholder has legal ownership of the underlying shares and often receives the prospectuses of the individual companies. When there is a merger, consolidation or spinoff, the HOLDRs trust can now hold the added shares or portions of shares in the trust. Before November of 2000, the trust had been forced to distribute these shares or portions of shares.

It is no surprise that both the primary advantages and disadvantages of HOLDRs surround its lack of rebalancing, or the process by which a fund follows an index by selling the stocks that have dropped out of an index and buying stocks that have been added. Rebalancing involves transaction costs and triggers capital gains taxes, and indeed HOLDRs are quite tax efficient and relatively cheap in terms of maintenance. Rebalancing, on the other hand, allows an investor to maintain assets that accurately reflect the market or portions of a market, that the underlying index represents.

If an investor had bought a HOLDR at the turn of the nineteenth century (not possible, of course as they were introduced in 1999) that represented the largest U.S. companies, he or she would have barely paid any capital gains taxes, but also would have enormous weightings in railroads, buggy whip manufacturers, and women's corsets (or more accurately, the company that bought the remnants of the dated industries).

As a side note, *The Wall Street Journal* published an article in 2000 suggesting that arbitrage traders were pushing up the price of HOLDRs by purchasing underlying stocks ahead of Merrill during its preparation to issue new HOLDRs. According to traders quoted in the article, they were getting wind of and jumping ahead of major buys of the component stocks by Merrill in anticipation of new issuance. Although anyone buying a stock ahead of another investor is going to impact the follower negatively, we do not view this as particularly risk-free activity on the part of arbitrageurs. We generally side with Merrill and doubt *The Wall Street Journal*'s thesis.

Why is this? Only a few key employees at Merrill know the date when the firm will issue new HOLDRs. Merrill chooses fairly random dates, keeps them secret until the close of trading, and disguises the origin of its purchases of stocks for HOLDRs, as it does for its brokerage customers and for other products. Added to this is the fact that the sectors involved are particularly volatile, so any arbitrageur owning possible component stocks on the hope that they will be holding the component stocks on an issuance day could be caught in a downdraft. The trader aiming to front-run the HOLDRs could easily be blindsided by a shifting market.

The stocks also tend to be quite large, so the anticipated impact on a stock of either arbitrageurs or Merrill is generally modest. Nonetheless, in the same way that index rebalance can cause a significant "index effect" as component stocks move in or out of an index, so can the introduction of a HOLDRs cause significant price movement because of the large amount of first-day investment. Thus, the traders may have caused damage to new HOLDRs investors, but it's not clear that the activity is a rational way to pursue sustained profits or that HOLDRs investors will always suffer as a result of the speculative trading. We think that over time arbitrageurs will realize this and the activity will prove insignificant.

For details on the three major types of ETFs in the U.S., please consult Appendix C, which lists each in greater detail.

Other very interesting types of ETFs that have been launched overseas but are not yet available in the U.S. are the fixed income and actively-traded ETFs launched in Canada and Germany, respectively. The Canadian ETFs trade on Canadian Government bonds. The German ETFs are unlike most ETFs in that their NAV is not known in real time. Both are discussed in detail in Chapter 7, and both operate on principles that vary somewhat from those used by equity-holding management investment company funds in the U.S. Many of the most interesting developments in ETFs have occurred abroad. The liquidity crisis in the Malaysian WEBS and the government-sponsored Hong Kong TraHK are two good examples. Both of these are also discussed in Chapter 7.

CHAPTER SIX

THE HISTORY OF ETFs

To understand how exchange-traded funds came about, it is important to be familiar with the history of the stock market, mutual funds, index funds, and the commodities markets. Why the commodities markets? While ETFs may appear similar to closed-ended funds, the genesis of their unique structure originated in the receipt-based commodities markets. As we will discuss, Chairman & President of the iShares, Inc. and iShares Trust, Nate Most's commodities background, coupled with his derivatives work at the American Stock Exchange, ultimately brought about the idea of *index shares*, which have come to be known as exchange-traded funds. For a more personal look at how it all came about, backtrack and read the foreword of this book, which was written by Most himself.

The entire history of the stock market up to the 1970s was all about picking stocks to maximize performance. By the early 1970s, however, all of this began to change. The revolutionary idea that altered the investment landscape was a simple one. Essentially, it was that investors by definition can expect on average to perform the same as the market.

Furthermore, *The Efficient Markets Hypothesis*, first articulated in Eugene Fama's landmark 1965 paper, "Random Walks in Stock Market Prices," essentially held that all available information is priced into the market at any given time. Investors, who by definition *are* the market, are essentially betting against the market's collective wisdom when they try to beat it by stock picking.

Underperformance ultimately creeps in with higher transaction costs. Thus, the best way to equal market performance, Fama's theory holds, is to buy and hold a diversified basket of stocks, minimizing fees, and maximizing tax efficiency.

Institutional investors were the first to take advantage of the new theories. Nobel Prize winner William Sharpe worked with Bill Fouse at Samsonite (later Wells Fargo and today Barclays Global Investors) to open the first index mutual fund in 1971. That fund bore little resemblance to today's mutual funds and was strictly for large institutional investors. In 1976, index funds entered the mainstream. John Bogle, the patron saint of index funds, teamed up with Burton Malkiel of Princeton University to launch the first retail index fund. Bogle opened the Vanguard Group's Vanguard-500 fund, and he has been insistent in preaching the value of low-fee, tax-efficient index investing ever since. Table 6.1 shows a time line of the history of ETFs.

This strategy served Vanguard and investors well, with the Vanguard-500 fund enjoying lofty annual returns that bested those of most of the active mutual funds. In the process, Vanguard quietly built the largest mutual fund in the world, with over $100 billion in assets. Until the advent of ETFs, the Vanguard funds, owing to the company's non-profit structure, had low expense ratios that were untouchable by other mutual fund companies.

So, with investors now buying the baskets of stock and tracking market indexes, only one step remained for ETFs to enter the scene. What was needed was a mechanism for groups of stocks to trade on the market like a single stock. By the early 1980s, it was increasingly common for institutional investors to own large baskets of stocks that tracked indexes and to trade index futures based on those indexes. In addition, there was significant activity on the futures market of the Chicago Mercantile Exchange. These futures and program trades—that bought entire baskets of stocks. Although the best available tools at the time, they were, by today's standards neither cheap nor efficient for retail or even institutional investors to own.

Enter *Cash Index Participations* (CIPs), which began trading on the Philadelphia Stock Exchange in 1989. The American Stock Exchange

TABLE 6.1   A HISTORY OF ETFs

1971	First institutional index fund opened by Wells Fargo
1976	Vanguard launches first retail index fund
Early 1980s	Program trading and futures allow institutional investors to buy and manage large baskets of stocks
1987	Index Participation Shares (IPS) trade on AMEX
1989	Toronto Index Participation Shares (TIPS) begin trading in Canada; first tradable instrument actually tied to underlying shares; TIPS based on TSE-35 Index
1993	SPDRs S&P-500 funds become first U.S.-based ETFs
1996	WEBS become first ETF based on single-country basket
1998	DIAMONDS, HOLDRs and Select Sector SPDRs introduced
1999	QQQ and additional HOLDRs launched
2000	90 new ETFs launched globally
2001	By June 30, 2001, global assets had reached over $95 billion for 169 funds in 10 countries. (over $5 billion of that in HOLDRs and $4 billion in German active funds).

(AMEX) soon followed with *Index Participation Shares* (IPS). More like futures than the ETFs of today, the IPS traded based on a price that was a ratio of the underlying index. From the outset, there was a great deal of interest in the new financial instruments. While they could be bought on margin and loaned out like stocks, the CIPs and IPS essentially behaved like futures in that for every long there was a short and vice versa. They were settled based on cash, and they tracked the index very closely. With rapidly surging popularity posing a threat to futures trading, the SEC, which had aproved the products, was sued by the Chicago Board of Trade (CBOT). With the suit (and the CBOT) in Chicago, a courtroom defeat was certain, jokes ETF inventor Nate Most, who was also familiar with the IPS while he was at the American Stock Exchange. Both the Philadelphia Exchange and AMEX were ultimately forced to shut down the products when a judgment was entered against them.

The IPS gave way to the TIPS. Toronto Stock Exchange Index Participations (TIPS) were warehouse receipt-based instruments designed to track the Toronto-35 index. They were launched on the Toronto Exchange in 1989. Unlike the other tradable instruments like IPS and futures, TIPS were not actually derivatives. Like today's ETFs, TIPS were units of a trust created by the Toronto Stock Exchange. The underlying assets of the trust were actual shares of the 35 constituent companies that made up the TSE-35 Index. These shares were held by the trust in the same proportion as they were reflected in the index, and shares were priced at about $1/10$ the value of the total index by market cap. Later, Toronto-100 Index Participations (HIPS) were introduced. The TIPS and HIPS were wildly successful in Canada, largely because (1) the funds were able to lend securities, and (2) there was a great demand for lent securities in Canada at the time. In March of 2000, the TIPS and HIPS were merged into a single highly-liquid TSE-60 fund (XIU) on the Toronto Exchange managed by Barclays Global Investors. The TSE-60 fund had about $4.6 billion Canadian in assets at the time of the merger. The merger was the end result of a brutal fight between BGI and State Street Global Advisors, who subsequently launched an ETF based on the Dow Jones Canada-40 index.

The origin of the first real ETFs had something to do with the financial distress faced by the American Stock Exchange in the 1980s. Faced with a chronic lack of resources, Nate Most took things in his own hands and came up with a product that he thought could make the AMEX some money. How he came up with the mechanism had as much to do with his background as a commodities trader and his observations about the mutual funds market as it had with anything that he'd previously done at the AMEX.

A physicist by training, Most worked on submarine acoustics for the United States Navy during World War II (cruising in dangerous proximity to Japanese submarines). He spent years traveling throughout India and the far east to sell acoustical material to theaters. More importantly for exchange-traders, however, Most got into the cooking oil business in the 1960s. At that time, Most started working for the Pacific Commodities Exchange.

There, he became accustomed to *warehouse receipts*, "You store a commodity and you get a warehouse receipt and you can finance on that warehouse receipt. You can sell it, do a lot of things with it. Because you don't want to be moving the merchandise back and forth all the time, so you keep it in place and you simply transfer the warehouse receipt."

This spawned the mental spark that ultimately led to the first ETF.

Initially, Most worked with the AMEX on index products like the Major Market Index. This was designed to mirror the Dow Jones Industrial Average, because Dow refused to allow derivatives to be based on its index. However, Most and his derivatives department had a problem. They had no money. The American Stock Exchange was having severe difficulties drawing enough business to be profitable.

"They had a basic volume of about 20 million shares a day and it just stayed there, no matter what they did. They were spending all kinds of money to get new listings, but were unsuccessful. From our side, we needed a lot of money for the things we wanted to do and we couldn't get it. They kept telling us we weren't making enough profit. So I thought—well, maybe I could help the equity side and bring in some money. Well, here I see mutual funds just booming, gaining market fast, without being able to be traded. So I thought—well, why not? I didn't realize at the time all the complications that would be involved."

As it turned out, there were some two years of complications involved. Although the approval process was underway in 1990, the first exchange-traded fund (Standard & Poor's-500 Depositary Receipts, or SPDRs) did not hit the market until January 1993. The process was plagued by seemingly insurmountable regulatory hurdles from SEC, as well as daunting logistical hurdles involved in not knowing exactly how the new investment vehicles would perform or how exactly investors would use them. It was a major accomplishment for AMEX and State Street Global Advisors (SSgA) to bring the ETFs to the market.

The first ETFs were set up as unit investment trusts (UITs) because of the ease and flexibility of running the fund under such an arrangement. UITs were less expensive to run because they didn't require a board of directors. As more funds were released and other benefits (like lack of dividend drag and ability to loan stocks) of open-ended funds were factored in, this cost seemed less important. The introduction of the SPDRs in 1993 was soon followed by the S&P MidCap Fund, managed by the Bank of New York (BNY). Open-ended WEBS were introduced in 1996. They were revolutionary new funds that allowed American investors to buy into foreign stock indexes by purchasing shares on the American Stock Exchange.

In 1998 came the DIAMONDS (SSgA ETFs based on the Dow Jones Industrial Average). In March of 1999, the Nasdaq-100 Trust (BNY), based on the highly volatile and popular Nasdaq-100 index entered the stage in force. By 2000, the floodgates had opened, and in that year 90 new funds were introduced to ETF investors (64 of those in the U.S.). As of June 30, 2001, including the HOLDRs and active German DWS funds, the total of exchange-traded funds available globally had grown to 169, with 103 of those trading on U.S. markets.

At press time, there was no end in site, with the launch of some 50 new funds globally on the immediate horizon. Fund assets have tripled in just three years (through June 2001) and many other financial institutions are seriously looking into the launch of their own ETFs. Most analysts project an astronomical rise in assets under management and number of funds in coming years as ETFs enter many realms of the investment world. This includes, for example, new fixed-income and actively-managed funds.

On the Horizon *(for a complete list of current and future ETFs that trade on non-U.S. markets, please refer to Table 7.2 and Appendix D; for a complete list of all U.S.-traded ETFs, please refer to Appendix C).*

1. Vanguard VIPERs—Nine funds to be based on existing Vanguard funds and proposed for launch in 2001. The launch was delayed considerably by a lawsuit with Standard and Poor's (S&P). Vanguard did launch its first ETF; the Total Stock Market VIPERs on May 31, 2001.

2. Nuveen—Four FITRs (Fixed Income Trust Receipts) and three equity funds proposed for launch in 2001 as well as products proposed for launch in Hong Kong.

3. ProFunds—Enhanced index manager filed with the SEC to launch 30 ETFs based on its existing mutual funds. Like

Vanguard VIPERs, the ProFund launch has also been held up by a lawsuit with S&P.

4. New York Life Investment Management—TechIES Technology Index Equity Shares to be based on Pacific Stock Exchange (PSE) Technology-100 Index.

5. State Street Global Advisors—Continues ETF rollout with more offerings both in country, regional, and sector products, trading both in the U.S. and abroad.

6. Barclays Global Investors—Also planning more global and sector products, as well as a flurry of new country indexes trading both in the U.S. and abroad.

OUTLOOK FOR THE FUTURE

There is a wide range of predictions of what the future of ETFs will hold. One thing seems certain: the number of funds and the level of assets under management globally will continue to rise. How many funds, and what level of assets, seem to be the only questions.

The array of new products will continue to expand the diversity of options available to ETF investors. In addition to an increasing number of sector funds, style funds, and global/regional offerings, the launch of the world's first fixed-income ETFs by iShares in Canada seemed certain to presage the first such funds in the U.S. and Europe (Nuveen and Barclays had already filed with the SEC for launch of fixed-income funds in the United States). Plans for fixed-income ETFs were also being planned in Europe and Asia.

Similarly, the launch of the first actively-managed exchange-traded funds in Germany, while not using the same transparent pricing as other ETFs, seemed to point to a flood of similar offerings in other markets. A broad range of U.S. fund managers were exploring the possibility of squeezing higher margins out of ETFs with value-added, expense-adding, active management and the ability to trade active funds in real time to their offerings. The critical stumbling block in the United States to the launch of actively-managed ETFs was the level of disclosure that fund managers would be forced to give the market. This included how often and to what degree holdings had to be reported to investors, as well as the accuracy and frequency of the reported net asset value. Obviously, active managers have an interest in the market knowing as little as possible about their holdings, with large funds particularly being concerned about the possibility of being front-run by the market. It seemed clear, however, that the SEC would insist on investors having a fairly clear idea of the underlying NAV of the component stocks in real time. They're pretty big on transparency over at the SEC.

Table 6.2 shows a list of funds that were anticipated to be launched in late 2001 or early 2002 and their exchange and manager.

The future isn't quite here yet, as Lee Kranefuss CEO of BGI's Individual Investor Group notes, "Both fixed income and active pose some unique challenges. Different, but unique from both an operational and regulatory perspective, and we're looking at that and we hope to be the first with funds out there. We now have 61 of the 85 funds in the U.S., and we consider ourselves a leader and we'd like to have the first ones out. But it's going to take a lot more work."

TABLE 6.2   COMING SOON

FUND NAME	EXCHANGE	MANAGER
iShares MSCI Brazil	AMEX	BGI
iShares MSCI Greece	AMEX	BGI
iShares MSCI Indonesia	AMEX	BGI
iShares MSCI Portugal	AMEX	BGI
iShares MSCI South Korea	AMEX	BGI
iShares MSCI South Africa	AMEX	BGI
iShares MSCI Taiwan	AMEX	BGI
iShares MSCI Thailand	AMEX	BGI
iShares MSCI Turkey	AMEX	BGI

(continues)

TABLE 6.2   COMING SOON (CONTINUED)

FUND NAME	EXCHANGE	MANAGER
iUnits S&P/TSE Canadian Energy Index Fund	Toronto	BGI
iUnits S&P/TSE Canadian Inform. Tech Index Fund	Toronto	BGI
iUnits S&P/TSE Canadian Gold Index Fund	Toronto	BGI
iUnits S&P/TSE Canadian Financials Index Fund	Toronto	BGI
streetTRACKS Wilshire REIT	AMEX	SSgA
streetTRACKS Straits TIMES Index Fund	Singapore	SSgA
streetTRACKS ASX S&P-200 Index Fund	Australia	SSgA
streetTRACKS AEX Index Fund	Amsterdam	SSgA
streetTRACKS MSCI Pan-Euro Index Fund	Euronext	SSgA
streetTRACKS MSCI Europe Small Cap Index Fund	Euronext	SSgA
streetTRACKS MSCI Europe Consumer Discretionary Index Fund	Euronext	SSgA
streetTRACKS MSCI Europe Consumer Staples Index Fund	Euronext	SSgA
streetTRACKS MSCI Europe Energy Index Fund	Euronext	SSgA
streetTRACKS MSCI Europe Financials Index Fund	Euronext	SSgA
streetTRACKS MSCI Europe Health Care Index Fund	Euronext	SSgA
streetTRACKS MSCI Europe Industrials Index Fund	Euronext	SSgA
streetTRACKS MSCI Europe Information Technology Index Fund	Euronext	SSgA
streetTRACKS MSCI Europe Materials Index Fund	Euronext	SSgA
streetTRACKS MSCI Europe Telecommunication Services Index Fund	Euronext	SSgA
streetTRACKS MSCI Europe Utilities Index Fund	Euronext	SSgA
streetTRACKS MSCI United Kingdom Index Fund	Euronext	SSgA

(continues)

TABLE 6.2   COMING SOON (CONTINUED)

FUND NAME	EXCHANGE	MANAGER
America's Fastest Growing Companies Index Fund	AMEX	Nuveen
INDI SmallCap 500	AMEX	Nuveen
FITRs (Fixed Income Trust Receipts) 4 to be launched	AMEX	Nuveen
TechIES (Pacific Exchange Technology-100 Index Fund)	Pacific & AMEX	New York Life Invest manag.
VIPERs Index Fund	*	Vanguard
VIPERs SmallCap Index Fund	*	Vanguard
VIPERs Growth Index Fund	*	Vanguard
VIPERs Value Index Fund	*	Vanguard
VIPERs Extended Market Index Fund	*	Vanguard

*Not known yet. Still to be determined.

CHAPTER 7

INTERNATIONAL ETFS

J udging by the rapid move of fund managers to launch ETFs in Europe (many of which are tied to STOXX indexes), there is a widespread belief that the international markets will be the next to take part in the ETF boom.

Before there were any ETFs trading in non-U.S. markets, exchange-traded funds radically expanded the opportunities for U.S. investors to invest in international markets. There have been many *World Equity Benchmark Shares* (WEBS—now iShares) single-country ETFs since 1996. Now increasingly, the investors of other countries also have the opportunity to invest in ETFs that trade on their own stock exchanges as well. More importantly, investors are not only given access to other markets, but at generally much-lower expense than with the relatively limited array of existing traditional international mutual funds. Because of the variety of obstacles, including higher trading costs, wider spreads and taxes and regulatory requirements, international investing is generally expensive—and traditional mutual fund have reflected this with their expense ratios. The most expensive international ETFs that trade in the U.S. still have total expense ratios below 1 percent annually (see Table 7.1). Only a handful of international mutual funds have expense ratios this low—though some traditional index funds, particularly those offered by Vanguard, have very competitive expense ratios on their international funds, indeed often lower than the equivalent ETFs.

TABLE 7.1   INTERNATIONAL ETFS TRADING ON U.S. MARKETS

FUND NAME	TICKER	EXPENSE RATIO	NET ASSETS $MM	INCEPTION DATE
streetTRACKS DJ Global Titans	DGT	0.50	21.2	29-Sep-00
iShares S&P Global-100 Index	IOO	0.40	119.8	08-Dec-00
HOLDRs Europe 2001	EKH	*	0	30-Aug-00
iShares MSCI EMU Index	EZU	0.84	80.7	14-Jul-00
iShares S&P Europe-350 Index	IEV	0.60	171.5	25-Jul-00
iShares MSCI Australia Index	EWA	0.84	53.0	18-Mar-96
iShares MSCI Canada Index	EWC	0.84	30.9	18-Mar-96
iShares MSCI Sweden Index	EWD	0.84	11.3	18-Mar-96
iShares MSCI Germany Index	EWG	0.84	129.3	18-Mar-96
iShares MSCI Hong Kong Index	EWH	0.84	59.2	18-Mar-96
iShares MSCI Italy Index	EWI	0.84	35.1	18-Mar-96
iShares MSCI Japan Index	EWJ	0.84	584.3	18-Mar-96
iShares MSCI Belgium Index	EWK	0.84	9.4	18-Mar-96
iShares MSCI Switzerland Index	EWL	0.84	33.6	18-Mar-96
iShares MSCI Malaysia (Free) Index	EWM	0.84	70.0	18-Mar-96
iShares MSCI Netherlands Index	EWN	0.84	25.3	18-Mar-96
iShares MSCI Austria Index	EWO	0.84	10.9	18-Mar-96
iShares MSCI Spain Index	EWP	0.84	27.3	18-Mar-96
iShares MSCI France Index	EWQ	0.84	64.3	18-Mar-96
iShares MSCI Singapore (Free) Index	EWS	0.84	53.6	18-Mar-96
iShares MSCI Taiwan Index	EWT	0.99	99.8	23-Jun-00
iShares MSCI United Kingdom Index	EWU	0.84	122.4	18-Mar-96
iShares MSCI Mexico (Free) Index	EWW	0.84	41.5	18-Mar-96
iShares MSCI South Korea Index	EWY	0.99	25.4	12-May-00
iShares MSCI Brazil (Free) Index	EWZ	0.99	18.0	14-Jul-00
iShares S&P/TSE-60 Index	IKC	0.50	7.0	12-Jun-00

* HOLDRs expense ratio is $8 per 100 shares per year.

Why bother? Nearly every money manager worth listening to will tell you that you reduce your overall risk, rather than increase it, by putting a portion of your portfolio in international investments. Although market strategists at Merrill Lynch and J. P. Morgan, among others, lowered their recommended portfolio allocations of foreign stocks late in 2000, the smallest recommended allocation to overseas investments is 0–5 percent and goes up to 15 or 20 percent. Radical internationalists might even suggest that you allocate the equity part of your portfolio to correspond with the global market, which is at year end 2000 was at about 50 percent U.S. and 50 percent non-U.S. The latest fad in the investment community is to pronounce that correlation benefit of international investing is dead. This gospel is firmly rooted in 10 to 15 years of investment history. If you do choose to buck the consensus and plunk down some earnings overseas anyway, your ETF options are plenty and growing.

There are ETFs for countries, ETFs for regions, and ETFs for top global companies regardless of their country or region. There are also international ETFs specializing in technology and other sectors. Though you might be a gambler, when it comes to international ETFs, there are special risks and questions that require careful consideration before you think of moving your money.

> "It's fascinating to see the huge structural changes going on in Europe. Economic and trade policies have become more similar, and there is a potentially tremendous move toward the equity culture."
>
> **Scott Stark, managing director of STOXX, on the changing international landscape**

WHY USE INTERNATIONAL ETFS?

David Yeske, a certified financial planner in San Francisco, became an early fan of the funds almost by accident when a client moved from the United States to Spain. His client had difficulty investing in traditional U.S. open-ended mutual funds. But because he was a U.S. citizen, he was barred from many foreign mutual funds. The solution? Early versions of the SPDRs and WEBS (World Equity Benchmark Shares). Because they traded like stocks, the client had no problem buying shares. But because they were based on broad indexes, the client got the benefit of low-cost diversification and asset allocation.

After his first client's experience, Yeske says he is likely to recommend international ETFs to nearly all the high net-worth clients he advises. He's unlikely to suggest that a client replace a traditional index mutual fund with an ETF, because of the tax consequences and transaction costs involved in redemption of the traditional fund. But he often suggests that as much as 30 to 40 percent of new money in a portfolio go to ETFs—with 15 to 20 percent of that in international funds. "They've always delivered what we've expected," Yeske says of the international ETFs, where he has been placing significant amounts of client money since mid-1998.

A BRIEF HISTORY OF INTERNATIONAL ETFS

As the first U.S. ETF, the SPDR, was being born on the American Stock Exchange in 1993, Morgan Stanley was experimenting with the concept in Europe. Taking advantage of looser rules for securities in Luxembourg, Morgan Stanley created and listed on the Luxembourg exchange what were called OPALS—*Optimized Portfolios As Listed Securities*. The OPALS tracked a range of prominent indexes, including the S&P 500, FTSE 100, Nikkei 225, and others. They are still a major force in the international ETF market—with some $15 billion in assets. Only the SPDR (SPY) and Cubes (QQQ) among similar products had more assets in 2000.

Some traditional international mutual funds use OPALS as part of their holdings. But they are not sold directly to most investors, and are marketed instead to institutional investors in countries where regulators allow the offerings. "OPALS are securities and not funds. We just add up the bids and offers on the underlying basket of shares. So each OPAL is related to an optimized or fully replicated basket. The prices are updated every 15 seconds to represent the underlying bid/offer spread," says Deborah

Fuhr, vice president and global head of marketing for ETFs and OPALS at Morgan Stanley.

In 1996 after experimenting with new investment management techniques using the OPALS, Morgan Stanley and Barclays Global Investors teamed up to create World Equity Benchmark Shares, or WEBS, that could be sold to retail investors in the United States and listed on the American Stock Exchange (AMEX). There were 17 initial funds, a number that remained constant until the great expansion of exchange-traded funds. In 2000, another eight international ETFs began trading on AMEX, and fund companies began expanding their offerings on international exchanges more rapidly, as well. The original WEBS (since re-branded as the iShares MSCI series) were mostly for developed countries, with 14 of the original 17 tracking national markets represented in Morgan Stanley Capital's Europe/Australasia/Far East Index, or EAFE. Regional index shares followed, and there were plans in 2001 for ETFs tracking the EAFE and cross-border international sector indexes, as well.

Exactly one week before the release of the WEBS, Deutsche Bank launched a line of very similar open-ended ETFs that were know as *Country Baskets*. Since their ignominious departure from the scene in late 1996, they have been known to many ETF insiders as the "country caskets." There were nine Country Baskets covering Financial Times (now FTSE) indexes for nine countries, including Australia, France, Germany, Hong Kong, Italy, Japan, the United Kingdom, and unlike the WEBS, the indexes for both the United States and South Africa. A different product than the WEBs (now iShares), the Country Baskets fully replicated the relevant indexes because the FTSE indexes for those markets were already fully registered investment company (RIC) compliant. RIC rules stipulate that a fund can hold no more than 25 percent in one stock, or to have more than 50 percent invested in stocks with a weighting of greater than 5 percent of the index. Many of the iShares MSCI funds are forced to optimize their holdings in order to be RIC compliant. Since the FTSE indexes were already RIC compliant, the Country Baskets did not need to optimize. The structure, like that of the WEBS, was fully open-ended. The Country Baskets were listed on the New York Stock Exchange, which has only recently reentered the ETF business. So all of that being the case, why did the Country Baskets become the "Country Caskets?"

Herb Blank, who is now the President of QED International, was the Chief Investment Officer of Country Baskets. "The main thing that went wrong, in my opinion, was the lack of long-term corporate commitment to the product. Basically the larger the organization, the larger the politics, and the people who approved and believed in the venture when we started were no longer the decision makers when the plug was pulled. It's that simple."

In addition, Blank had felt that the Financial Times U.S. Basket could have been a legitimate competitor to the SPDR, but "not if your specialist is keeping 75 cent spreads."

Whatever the reasons, the WEBS survived and the Country Baskets are no more. The problems faced by both the WEBS and Country Baskets, however, was small potatoes compared with the regulatory quagmire fund managers and exchanges faced in trying to get European-trading products off the ground.

Regulatory obstacles in Europe (outside of Luxembourg and to some degree Ireland, as many European ETFs are registered for regulatory reasons in Luxembourg) resulted in years of delay before retail-traded ETFs were born there. ETFs, commonly known in Europe as *trackers*, exploded onto the scene once they were finally launched in 2000. A multitude of new funds began to trade on European exchanges, and exchanges started working on plans for true global trading of funds. By the middle of 2001, cross-listed AMEX funds had begun trading in Singapore (5) and Hong Kong (2). The American Stock Exchange also had a similar cross-listing arrangement in the works with the new European exchange, Euronext.

Although ETFs for retail investors really started as an American phenomenon, many of the innovations in the development of ETFs have occurred overseas. One of the first international ETFs that was heavily targeted at retail investors was Hong Kong's TraHK fund, which follows the Hang Seng index. Unlike most ETFs created by financial product developers, the TraHK was created largely because of the need for the Hong Kong government to dispose of its large portfolio, acquired in an attempt to stabilize the Hong Kong market in August 1998. When it came time to divest itself of the shares in 1999, the government, with the management help of State Street Global Advisors, built an ETF product that returned shares to the market and returned billions of dollars to the public treasury. The initial offering of the fund was heavily oversubscribed, with retail demand accounting for well over half of the interest.

With many ETFs allowing international diversification through shares trading on the American Stock Exchange, U.S. investors are well-provided for with international ETFs. Increasingly, however, international investors, particularly in Europe and Asia, have the opportunity to use ETFs to invest both in their home market and internationally. By the end of June 2001, there were over 60 non-U.S.-trading ETFs and rising.

WHY NEW ETFs ARE BORN

Exchange-traded funds, like all other investment products, are developed to make money for the companies that run them. That's the harsh reality of financial life. In free-market systems, products are not necessarily made because they are good for those who buy, but because they can be sold and therefore are good for those who sell. Fortunately, with the right amount of information, both sides of the transaction benefit. Investors won't buy a product unless they think it will make them money—and more money than competing products. Therefore, investment companies have an incentive to create products that are good for those who buy them. Of course, we're assuming here that well-informed investors will be able to cut through all the marketing hype and simplistic media praise that tends to accompany any new fad in investing.

When it comes to creating international ETFs, companies like Barclays Global Investors, State Street Global Advisors, and even the American Stock Exchange look first for demand. Investor interest in particular countries or regions makes a fund or index covering that area much more likely to be offered. But that's just the first step. When investment companies consider developing an international product, they also have to look at practical issues that will affect their costs and returns, and therefore their ability to sell the new product.

Brad Zigler, in charge of iShares education at BGI, notes that liquidity and transparency of a particular equity market is a key consideration. When a portfolio manager has a hard time determining stock prices and values, or when settlement procedures are cumbersome, it's harder to create an ETF or any other kind of fund. That's why the ETF craze started with the usual suspects—a handful of established markets in Canada, the United States, Britain, Germany, Japan and Hong Kong—and only later spread to less developed markets.

YOUR RESULTS MAY VARY

An online discussion between investors and Brad Zigler of BGI carried among its disclosures this warning: "In addition to the normal risks associated with equity investing, investments in smaller companies or single nations typically exhibit higher volatility. International investments may involve risk of capital loss from unfavorable fluctuations in currency values, from differences in generally accepted accounting procedures, or from economic or political instability in other nations. Investments in emerging markets or concentrated in a single country are subject, in addition to the normal risks associated with international investing, to greater risk of loss and volatility."

Mercer Bullard, a former assistant chief counsel in the SEC's Division of Investment Management, now runs Fund Democracy to provide investors with information about mutual funds and advocate for fund shareholder rights. He generally likes the idea of ETFs, but feels there is a good chance of investors being misled into believing that an ETF trades like a mutual fund—particularly the mistaken belief that international ETFs will trade at net asset value. "As the data demonstrate, ETFs can trade at significant discounts or premiums for extended periods," Bullard wrote in a request for a SEC hearing on the funds in early 2000. "The risk of discounts and premiums is particularly acute for ETFs that invest in foreign securities." Bullard later withdrew his request for a hearing after BGI agreed to make it easier for investors to compare ETF share prices and the fund's underlying NAV, but he says investors need to realize they aren't buying a traditional mutual fund when they're trading ETFs. They are buying shares at a trading value that can vary significantly from the actual value of its underlying stocks.

In addition, international ETFs are subject to problems common to any international investment. These include currency fluctuation, varying degrees of regulation (and therefore potential corruption of foreign markets), political decisions that are not always based on good economic sense and the potential for a lack of liquidity. A Securities and Exchange Commission report noted that single-country funds can "often contain a large percentage of securities that are thinly traded or are considered to be illiquid for other reasons."

According to Rafael Garcia Romero, who is heading up an effort by Serfiex to launch ETFs in Spain, only four of the 35 stocks in the Spanish IBEX-35 index trade with much liquidity.

The liquidity problems are especially acute in less developed countries with smaller stock markets, slower and more complex settlement procedures, currency restrictions, and a relative lack of information to value securities. Liquidity is lacking in developing markets in the best of times, and the problem could be much worse in a market crisis. Clearly, it is possible for local market turmoil and volatility to overwhelm the low fees and tax benefits of an ETF or, for that matter, any financial instrument.

In the midst of the Asian market crisis of 1998, the Malaysian government imposed currency restrictions that prevented most investors from converting proceeds from securities sales into foreign currencies. Because of the currency restrictions, Malaysia WEBS announced it would not be able to honor redemptions of creation units in currency other than Malaysian ringgito. The AMEX halted trading in shares of Malaysia WEBS, and when trading resumed, the fund's discount to NAV almost doubled from 10.26 percent to 19.25 percent, according to a study commissioned by Fund Democracy. From September 1998 to April 2000, fund analysts Wiesenberger/Thompson Financial found that the Malaysia WEBS traded at discounts or premiums of more than 200 basis points for 265 rolling four-day periods. The discount or premium was more than 10 percent for 127 four-day periods and over 30 percent for four rolling four-day periods. While ETF proponents say Malaysia is an exception to the theory that ETFs will trade at close to NAV, the events of September 1998 should serve as a warning to investors. It may not be likely, but there is nothing to say it could not happen again. While they may appear to be inherently liquid instruments, special circumstances, and certainly any illiquid underlying equities, can make this feature meaningless.

Scary? You bet. The fault of the ETF? Nope. Steven Schoenfeld, who is head of international equity management of the Global Index and Markets Group at Barclays Global Investors, notes that during the Malaysian crisis, "...the WEBS from Malaysia were basically the only vehicle in town. So it provided an enormously useful tool, despite the discount..."

Schoenfeld makes a fine point that is often overlooked in discussions about ETFs. Generally speaking, ETFs are just as good as their underlying components. Essentially, they use the gravity of market forces to keep prices in line with supply and demand. In fact they can actually have a benefit over the local market, and Malaysia is an excellent illustration of this point. Even when there was no trading going on in Malaysia, iShares holders were able to sell their shares to those who were willing to take advantage of potentially large discounts to the NAV. Essentially ETF structure will always assure that there is a balance between the degree of liquidity of the underlying stocks, and the market's perception of risk and reward. If the underlying components of an ETF can be hedged off adequately, competition will ensure that the markets are tight.

BENEFITS AND RISKS OF THE ARBITRAGE FACTOR

The fund companies, and those who invented and research ETFs, believe arbitrage by institutional investors will keep the fund share prices on a close track to the NAV of the underlying basket of stocks and the index that serves as the fund's benchmark. It makes sense: institutions will see any significant premium or discount of fund prices as an opportunity to make money by creating or liquidating creation units. It has generally worked that way. But, as in Malaysia, there is no guarantee that the arbitrage process will occur efficiently. The fund companies and retail investors have no control over the investment decisions of institutions or, of course, the performance and liquidity of the underlying markets and stocks. This potential problem is somewhat more pronounced with international ETFs, owing in part to issues of market stability and transparency.

In the case of international ETFs whose shares trade in North America on AMEX, even determining the exact NAV at any moment can be difficult. That's because the underlying stocks are traded on a foreign exchange, which trades in a different time zone and at different trading hours. That means, at times, you are trading your ETF shares when the underlying stocks are not trading, and the price of the underlying stocks is fluctuating during the local trading day when you aren't necessarily able to trade your ETF shares on AMEX. ETFs that track U.S. and some global indexes have three primary tickers, and therefore three prices: one for the share price, one for the current estimated NAV and one for the end-of-day NAV. But those figures have been more difficult for retail investors to come by in the case of most international ETFs, although the information may move more into the public domain as the funds mature. The actual pricing of the NAVs is a difficult business, as it must factor in not only currency market movement, but also whatever futures trading seems to indicate market direction. Even if you know the share price and are served a relatively accurate NAV, it will be difficult for individuals to compete with the institutions and their international trading desks to take advantage of premiums or discounts.

Then there is the whole question of how much ETF investors can count on the institutions. There is no guarantee that the brokerage houses and specialists will step forward to fill the arbitrage role. "Experience shows that [fund promoters'] faith in the ability of arbitrageurs to 'discipline' market prices is unjustified," says Mercer Bullard of Fund Democracy. At his request, in early 2000, the fund analysis company Wiesenberger/Thompson Financial analyzed closing prices of 30 ETFs trading on AMEX and compared them with the same day net asset values. The study found that 21 ETFs traded at discounts or premiums to NAV in excess of 50 basis points for a total of 2,921 rolling four-day periods from inception of the fund through April 26, 2000. Twenty-eight of the funds traded at a discount or premium in excess of 200 basis points at least once in its history. In addition, the largest premiums or discounts were noted in the international funds. Calculating premiums and discounts, however, is not an easy business. Often, and particularly with lightly-traded funds (as many of the international funds are), there may be many ETFs that didn't trade for much of the day. A premium and discount analysis, for example, could compare the 4:00 P.M. NAV to the last trade that may have occurred at 11:00 A.M., hardly a fair comparison. ETF fund managers complain that for this reason, premium/discount calculations based on the NAV are often misleading.

> "On internationals, where large NAV discrepancies are reported, remember that you're dealing with stale prices in many cases. So let's take a Japan fund as an example. At 4:00 today an NAV will be cut on the iShares MSCI Japan. That's based on closing market prices in Japan, which will have been approximately 16 hours earlier. In reality, the trading price is likely to be much closer to the fair value of the underlying equities than the NAV."
>
> **Lee Kranefuss, CEO of U.S. Individual Investor Business at Barclays Global Investors**

Because most ETFs are so new, it will take some time before we can determine at what level of discount or premium to the NAV the specialists and securities firms will step in. Because of increased trading costs and uncertainty of information and regulation involved in international markets, the level is bound to be higher internationally than for U.S. funds. There is also the question of how the big institutions, and therefore the funds, would react in the case of a sharp turn in international markets. Nobody can say for sure that institutional investors faced with a widespread market crisis would react by immediately turning to arbitrage to keep iShares Malaysia, for example, trading near the fund's NAV. For more on the premium/discount issue, please refer to Chapter 9.

WATCH ALL THE COSTS

As with any investment, it's important not to focus solely on returns for ETFs without considering the costs. In the bull-market '90s, many investors lost sight of the true costs of their choices because they seemed insignificant when compared to the overall returns. That is not the case in slower times, and is certainly not the case with ETFs. One of the big advantages of an ETF is generally lower costs than other investments—but make sure you know that's true when you're buying.

Expense ratios may be lower for an ETF than most mutual funds, even the low-cost index funds. But expense ratios for international ETFs are generally higher than those of domestic funds, because it's generally more expensive to trade in foreign markets. Settlement costs alone can boost international ETF expenses. Settlement for French equity transactions, for example, takes place 30 days after trade date. Imagine the financing headaches endured waiting a month to get sale proceeds. You should also remember that single-country or sector funds are likely to have higher expenses than regional or global funds. That is partly due to higher turnover rates and more extensive research needs.

Even if international ETF expense ratios are higher than those for U.S. exchange-traded funds, they still might beat traditional international mutual funds. But make sure you calculate all the other costs. With the international ETFs, there is the question of discount or premium to NAV, as we've already discussed. There is also the prospect of a wider bid-ask spread than with domestic funds. Be sure to calculate your total cost including brokerage commissions as well—and consider your trading or investment style and how it will affect those costs in the long run. In the end, the ETF may come out ahead, but it's a decision you can only make if you know all the variables and risks.

THE QUESTION OF CURRENCY

When you buy into a country or a region as an investment, you have to remember you're taking a double risk (with correspondent potential for reward). You assume the risk that the prices of the equities that make up your underlying index could lose some or all of their value. But even if the stocks, and the companies that they represent, remain strong, your investment can disappear because of a fluctuation in foreign currency. An investment in the best, fastest growing, most profitable companies in Thailand isn't worth much if the baht collapses. On the other hand, there is potential for gains because of currency fluctuations as well—and sometimes those gains can dwarf any increased real value in the underlying shares.

How to Evaluate
International ETFs

Because the early international ETFs were single-country funds, they were most useful to institutional investors or high net-worth individuals who wanted exposure to a specific market as part of their portfolio. But the increased risk of single-market funds make them more difficult to sell to most retail investors, who might be interested in diversifying overseas but want broad international exposure. It would probably be unwise for a small investor in the United States to put the international portion of a portfolio in only one country, and likewise, a small investor would be unlikely to buy bits of 17 different country funds to get broader international exposure. The newer regional and global funds, therefore, are likely to be more attractive to the small individual investor, although if they are actively inclined, they might use the country funds as well to make a bet on the Brazilian market, for instance.

For institutional investors interested in creating and redeeming ETF shares in local markets, there are some issues to keep in mind. As with all other ETFs that trade in U.S. markets, creations and redemptions can only be executed through members of the Depository Trust Corporation/ National Stock Clearing Corp., which posts creation and redemption baskets, and guarantees secondary market trades. A non-U.S. entity *can* effect creations and redemptions through a correspondent relationship with an authorized participant. As with U.S.-based ETFs, creations and redemptions in ETFs based in international markets are effected when the U.S. market is closed.

Because ETFs in general, and most international ETFs in particular, are such a new phenomenon, it's difficult to come up with meaningful evaluations. Every economist contacted for this chapter said the data was insufficient for a proper academic study of international ETFs. The academics can point to aspects of international ETFs in theory that might be encouraging or of concern to investors—but it's too early for the studies that are common on more mature investment products.

Brad Zigler of BGI acknowledged in his chat with *Morningstar* readers that you would need at least a full year, and perhaps more, to gauge the tax efficiency and perhaps the overall costs of new ETFs. He said meaningful medium-term performance statistics would require at least two years of data—and *Morningstar* itself looks for 36 months of data to generate portfolio statistics like R-squared, alpha, and beta for funds.

One statistic that can be evaluated, to some extent, is the "tracking error" of international ETFs versus their underlying index. In a study of WEBS from inception in 1996 to September 1999, William Bernstein of Efficient Frontier found that the ETF shares returned an average of 1.81 percent less than their benchmark indexes on an annual basis. He also found a correlation between WEBS with high turnover, like Belgium, to higher tracking error. In the case of Belgium WEBS, turnover for the period of the study was 34.13 percent and the shares under performed the index by 4.63 percent. United Kingdom WEBS, on the other hand, had an annualized turnover of 4.48 percent and the return was just 0.65 percent below the underlying index. In your own evaluation, consider whether lower ETF expense ratios compared with traditional international index funds is counteracted by potentially more significant tracking error. Bear in mind as well, that because many of the iShares MSCI country funds are optimized, that the index return is not always a fully accurate guage for the fund's return. By and large, traditional mutual funds face most of the same issues that ETFs do. And the secondary market can actually *add* an extra layer of liquidity for investors, as the Malaysian iShares demonstrated.

WHAT'S NEXT FOR INTERNATIONAL ETFs?

The last half of 2000 and the beginning of 2001 brought a flurry of activity in the international ETF market. New funds were launched, plans for even more were finalized, and fund companies began a marketing push for the older ETFs. As the number of international ETFs listed on American exchanges increased, so too did the number of international exchanges on which new ETF products were launched. And work was continuing on links between the U.S. and international market-listed funds to move closer to the dream of truly global trading.

The fund companies expect the biggest growth in regional and global funds, and in multiple-country sector funds. Those would track global or European technology indexes, for instance. If an international index exists, you can be sure an ETF product is being considered to track it. And don't be surprised as new or little-known international indexes spring up as the basis for ETFs—if the fund companies feel there is demand for the investment vehicle.

Perhaps the most interesting experiment on the international ETF scene is the formation of the world's first actively-traded ETF in Germany. Like many other ETF innovations, it's being attempted in an international market before the United States. Because of certain disclosure issues, and the fact that during market hours investors do no have access to the funds NAV. Most ETF experts do not consider the German active funds (managed by Die Wertpapier Spezialisten [DWS], an arm of Deutsche Bank Gruppe) to be "true ETFs." The concept of an active ETF does, however, raise many interesting questions, which are addressed in Chapter 9. Table 7.1 shows a list of international ETFs being traded on U.S. markets, and Table 7.2 shows those being traded on foreign markets.

TABLE 7.2   ETFS TRADING ON FOREIGN MARKETS

FUND NAME	SYMBOL	EXCHANGE	FEE (%)	NET ASSETS	INCEPTION DATE
streetTRACKS AEX Index Fund	AEXT	Amsterdam	0.30	$9,822,930	30-May-01
EuroSTOXX-50 Ex Anteile	SX5EEX GY	Deutsche Börse	0.50	0	27-Dec-00
DAX Ex Anteile	DAXEX GY	Deutsche Börse	0.50	$205,301,350	27-Dec-00
DJ Euro STOXX-50 LDRS		Deutsche Börse	0.50	$563,265,075	29-Jun-01
DJ Euro STOXX Banks Ex	SX7EEX GY	Deutsche Börse	0.50	$1,706,115	4-May-01

(continues)

TABLE 7.2   ETFs TRADING ON FOREIGN
               MARKETS (CONTINUED)

FUND NAME	SYMBOL	EXCHANGE	FEE (%)	NET ASSETS	INCEPTION DATE
DJ Euro STOXX Healthcare Ex	SXDEEX GY	Deutsche Börse	0.50	$2,087,444	4-May-01
DJ Euro STOXX Technology Ex	SX8EEX GY	Deutsche Börse	0.50	$1,927,594	4-May-01
DJ Euro STOXX Telecommunications	SXKEEX GY	Deutsche Börse	0.50	$6,479,526	4-May-01
DJ STOXX-50 LDRS		Deutsche Börse	0.50	$165,937,926	29-Jun-01
DJ STOXX-600 Banks Ex	SX7PEX GY	Deutsche Börse	0.50	$1,386,118	4-May-01
DJ STOXX-600 Healthcare Ex	SXDPEX GY	Deutsche Börse	0.50	$2,572,686	4-May-01
DJ STOXX-600 Technology Ex	SX8PEX GY	Deutsche Börse	0.50	$6,533,482	4-May-01
DJ STOXX-600 Telecommunications	SXKPEX GY	Deutsche Börse	0.50	$2,442,000	4-May-01
Dow Jones Euro STOXX-50 Ex		Deutsche Börse	0.50	$113,006,117	29-Jun-01
Dow Jones STOXX-50 Ex		Deutsche Börse	0.50	$77,891,168	29-Jun-01
DW3 ASIATISCHE		Deutsche Börse	1.50	$224,460,000	29-Jun-01
DWS BIOTECH-AKTIEN		Deutsche Börse	1.50	$1,852,440,000	29-Jun-01
DWS DT. AKT.TYP O		Deutsche Börse	1.25	$598,560,000	29-Jun-01
DWS EUROPAEISCHE		Deutsche Börse	1.50	$750,780,000	29-Jun-01
DWS GOLDMINENAKTIEN		Deutsche Börse	1.50	$35,260,000	29-Jun-01
DWS INTERNAT-AKTIEN		Deutsche Börse	1.50	$73,960,000	29-Jun-01
DWS INTERNET-AKTIEN		Deutsche Börse	1.50	$291,540,000	29-Jun-01
DWS NEW MARKETS		Deutsche Börse	1.50	$83,420,000	29-Jun-01

(continues)

TABLE 7.2   ETFs Trading on Foreign Markets (CONTINUED)

FUND NAME	SYMBOL	EXCHANGE	FEE (%)	NET ASSETS	INCEPTION DATE
DWS PHARMA-AKTIEN		Deutsche Börse	1.50	$378,400,000	29-Jun-01
DWS US AKTIEN		Deutsche Börse	1.50	$26,660,000	29-Jun-01
DWS US TECHNOAKTIEN		Deutsche Börse	1.50	$509,980,000	29-Jun-01
MDAX Ex	MDAXEX GY	Deutsche Börse	0.50	$8,127,041	25-Apr-01
Nemax 50	NMKXEX GY	Deutsche Börse	0.50	$28,704,305	11-Apr-01
SATRIX 40	STX40 SJ	Deutsche Börse	0.30	0	9-Nov-00
SMI Ex Anteile	SMIEX GY	Deutsche Börse	0.50	$6,135,165	22-Mar-01
STOXX-50 Ex Anteile	SX5PEX GY	Deutsche Börse	0.50	0	27-Dec-00
STOXX-50 LDRs	EUN1	Euronext (Paris & Amsterdam)	0.50	0	11-Apr-01
streetTRACKS Pan-Euro	ERO	Euronext (Paris)	0.50	$21,700,440	19-Jun-01
EuroSTOXX-50 LDRs - Amsterdam	EUN2	Euronext Amsterdam	0.50	$563,265,075	11-Apr-01
iBloomberg European Financials	IBEF	Euronext Amsterdam	0.50	$56,017,517	12-Feb-01
iBloomberg European Pharmaceuticals	IBEP	Euronext Amsterdam	0.50	$61,703,797	12-Feb-01
iBloomberg European Technology	IBQQ	Euronext Amsterdam	0.50	$39,125,119	12-Feb-01
iBloomberg European Telecoms	IBET	Euronext Amsterdam	0.50	$35,594,823	12-Feb-01
EasyETF EURO STOXX 50	ETE FP	Euronext Paris	1.00	$32,495,036	25-Apr-01
EasyETF Global Titans 50	ETT FP	Euronext Paris	1.00	$26,468,249	25-Apr-01
EasyETF STOXX 50	ETN FP	Euronext Paris	1.00	$32,865,481	25-Apr-01
EuroSTOXX-50 LDRs - Paris	EUN2	Euronext Paris	0.50	$563,265,075	11-Apr-01

(continues)

TABLE 7.2   ETFS TRADING ON FOREIGN
                MARKETS (CONTINUED)

FUND NAME	SYMBOL	EXCHANGE	FEE (%)	NET ASSETS	INCEPTION DATE
Master DJ Euro STOXX 50	MSE FP	Euronext Paris	0.40	$199,313,527	19-Mar-01
Master Dow Jones	DJE FP	Euronext Paris	0.50	$169,738,225	17-May-01
Master Share CAC 40	CAC FP	Euronext Paris	0.30	$327,377,302	22-Jan-01
Tracker Fund of Hong Kong (TraHK)	2800.hk	Hong Kong	0.10	$3,645,590,137	12-Nov-99
iShares FTSE ExUK-100 Index Fund	IEUR LN	London	0.50	$23,969,945	18-Dec-00
iShares FTSE TMT Index Fund	ITMT LN	London	0.50	$17,376,558	17-Oct-00
iShares FTSE-100 Index Fund	ISF LN	London	0.35	$183,646,752	27-Apr-00
XACTOMX	XACTOMX SS	Stockholm	0.30	0	27-Dec-00
Xmtch	XMSMI SW	SWX (Swiss Exchange)	0.35	0	15-Mar-01
TALI 25	TALI IT	TASE (Tel Aviv)	0.80	0	28-May-00
Dow Jones Canada-40 Index Fund	DJF CN	Toronto	0.08	$146,901,957	3-Oct-00
iUnits Government of Canada 10 year Bond Fund	XGX CN	Toronto	0.25	$47,546,721	23-Nov-00
iUnits Government of Canada 5 year Bond Fund	XGV CN	Toronto	0.25	$50,188,206	23-Nov-00
iUnits S&P-500 Index RSP Fund	XSP CN	Toronto	0.30	$12,547,051	29-May-01
iUnits S&P/TSE-60 Index Fund	XIU CN	Toronto	0.17	$2,994,783,068	4-Oct-99
iUnits S&P/TSE Canadian Energy Index Fund	XEG CN	Toronto	0.55	$26,414,845	22-Mar-01
iUnits S&P/TSE Canadian Financials Index Fund	XFN CN	Toronto	0.55	$27,735,587	29-Mar-01

(continues)

TABLE 7.2   ETFs Trading on Foreign
                Markets (CONTINUED)

Fund Name	Symbol	Exchange	Fee (%)	Net Assets	Inception Date
iUnits S&P/TSE Canadian Gold Index Fund	XGD CN	Toronto	0.55	$33,678,928	29-Mar-01
iUnits S&P/TSE Canadian Inform. Tech Index Fund	XIT CN	Toronto	0.55	$12,547,051	22-Mar-01
iUnits S&P/TSE Canadian MidCap Index Fund	XMD CN	Toronto	0.55	$48,867,464	8-Mar-01
iUnits S&P/TSE Capped-60 Index Fund	XIC CN	Toronto	0.17	$173,677,607	22-Feb-01
TSE-300 Capped Index Fund	TCF CN	Toronto	0.25	$56,134,437	23-Feb-01
TSE-300 Index Fund	TTF CN	Toronto	0.25	$115,991,675	23-Feb-01

CHAPTER EIGHT

DAY TRADING WITH ETFs

> "Never look behind you, somethin' might be gainin' on you."
>
> **Satchel Paige**

ETFs give day traders the ability to buy or short entire markets or market sectors. They have given short-term investors a tool to make rapid-fire macro bets in ways never before possible. Popular legends would have us believe that day traders either strike it rich or lose their entire fortune with a few clicks. For the day-trading rank and file, this activity is both less dramatic and more engrossing. This is particularly true for those betting on ETFs, which because they represent a group of stocks, are inherently less volatile than individual equities.

For professional traders at hedge funds, day trading is just another investment tool. For such investors, ETFs, and index funds in general, have opened up some perceived opportunities to front-run large funds which are forced to buy and sell equities based on the composition of the index they track. While large hedge funds have always engaged in day trading to some degree, this activity is a fairly recent phenomenon at the retail level. A unique set of circumstances converged to make day trading possible for the non-professional investor. Highly visible and volatile ETFs, most notably the QQQ (or Cubes), have proved to be the perfect tool for short-term technology wagers, both for retail and institutional traders.

> "I think QQQs fit a very unique pattern in the most successful ETFs in that it's got appeal to both retail and institutional investors. And its emergence as an excellent vehicle for arbitrage I think is what fuels the volume in the product."
>
> **Joe Keenan, vice president in charge of exchange-traded products at The Bank of New York.**

The infrastructure for day trading was in place before ETFs even came into existence. For day traders to initiate and close out positions quickly and efficiently, there had to be an infrastructure in place for them to connect to markets. The first electronic communications network (ECN) was promoted by a specialist on the Pacific Stock Exchange, Bill Lupien, in 1983. The original purpose of this ECN, called Instinet, was to match trades among institutions without involving brokers or dealers. As Instinet evolved, it allowed brokers and dealers to participate. Despite high telecommunications costs and 300-baud modems, Instinet grew over 75 percent a year and was bought out by Reuters in 1988.

A SHORT HISTORY OF DAY TRADING

Instinet was not perfect. It was slow and expensive, and it denied access to those it considered undesirable. To this day, their order book cannot be seen by the retail investor. Datek, a day-trading firm that was denied access to Instinet, designed its own ECN in 1992. Its creation, Island, made direct-access trading possible for individuals—who were now allowed to see all standing orders waiting to be filled. This electronic execution technology paved the way for individuals to participate directly in the 1990s bull market. Island overtook Instinet by the end of 1998 in terms of trading volume.

Online brokers, observing this demand, started competing madly for these traders in 1995. Web brokers such as Waterhouse and E*Trade multiplied like rabbits, forcing drastic reductions in commission fees to the point where some brokers started offering free trades (sometimes accompanied by fees described in very fine print). As trading costs became cheaper, many investors took a shorter-term view of their holdings. It was hard to hang onto 50 percent profits made in a month or even a day without cashing in the position, especially if the trade took place in a tax-free retirement account such as a Keough, a 401(k), or an IRA.

Day-trading firms also grew in number, with over 100 companies opening offices across the U.S. in the 1990s. However, as high-speed Internet access became available in homes, some day traders found it just as worthwhile to conduct transactions from the family computer. By using technology platforms being developed by a new breed of brokerages, they offered direct access to the financial marketplace for their clients.

These direct-access brokers, including Tradescape, TradeCast, and CyBerCorp, allowed individual investors to hook up directly with ECNs and Nasdaq's SelectNet system for instantaneous executions and confirmations (in theory). SelectNet showed all the market makers for a specific equity, allowing traders to direct their orders to the market maker of their choice. Day trading had now begun in earnest across the U.S.

RETAIL TRADERS

There are two distinct groups of retail day traders. Many high-volume day traders conduct intraday trading at a firm that provides real-time access to the major stock exchanges and the Nasdaq market. This group executes many intraday trades to take advantage of small price movements in stocks ($\frac{1}{16}$–$\frac{1}{8}$ of a point per trade). Such activity is sometimes referred to as *scalping*. As the number of trades increases per day, so do commission costs. Figure 8.1 shows the profits required to break even after fees.

Profit generation must be very high to cover these costs. There are an estimated 7,000 of these high-volume retail day traders in the U.S. Many of these traders opt for pure plays on individual stocks, although ETFs are finding favor in this group, especially given their ability to be shorted on a downtick. These high-volume traders affect markets, particularly Nasdaq, in ways greater than their numbers would suggest. Their trading activity generates up to 15 percent of the daily Nasdaq volume.

ETF Trading Volumes—A High Volume Day at the AMEX Top 5 ETFs trading on March 9, 2001

1. Nasdaq-100 Index Tracking Stock (QQQ)—79,990,900 shares

2. Standard & Poor's Depositary Receipts—SPDRs (SPY)—10,020,300 shares

3. DIAMONDS Trust Series 1 (DIA)—3,106,100 shares

4. iShares S&P-500 Index Fund (IVV)—2,122,400 shares

5. MidCap SPDRs (MDY)—1,318,700 shares

Online day traders who operate from their homes and offices comprise a much larger group, estimated at up to 100,000 individuals. These less frenetic traders are part of the more than 10 million retail investors who use the Internet for brokerage services. This group has mushroomed in numbers over the past few years due to the availability of high-speed Internet access; reduced commission costs and direct access to financial

FIGURE 8.1   **COMPARATIVE ANALYSIS OF PROFIT REQUIRED PER MONTH TO BREAK EVEN**

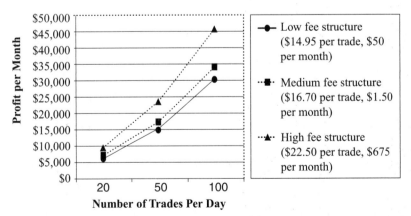

markets; the tax advantages of frequent trading in retirement accounts; and the proliferation of financial information on the Internet.

These traders have embraced ETFs as a trading vehicle. Gail Bateson, a health educator in the San Francisco Bay Area and occasional day trader, finds QQQ and SPY particularly appealing. "I can check how they're doing in after-hours, go short to protect my core holdings, and not worry about getting stuck at the exit. Plus, it's easy to look at their intraday charts and get an idea of how they'll move the next day. I feel comfortable holding Cubes and Spiders overnight and turning a day trade into a swing trade," says Bateson.

ROLE OF ETFS IN DAY TRADING

ETFs present unique advantages to the short-term trader. They offer the tradability of a stock and the diversification of an index fund. For anyone who has been caught in a downdraft of a stock on the heels of bad news during the trading day, the diversification factor provides a great deal of comfort (see Emulex story later in this chapter). ETFs are priced continuously throughout market hours, can be bought on margin, and can be sold short on a downtick. This flexibility and relative safety makes some ETFs very attractive vehicles for short-term trading. The sector ETFs provide a way for traders to obtain exposure to desired areas while avoiding others.

Freude Bartlett, a California advertising copywriter, likes to form paired trades with ETFs. In the fall of 2000, she wanted to take advantage of market weakness without overexposure to the technology sector. "I was scared of tech exposure, even though there had been a washout in the sector. But I did want to buy on general market weakness. So I bought SPY and sold short XLK. Since SPY is about 40 percent technology, I bought 10 SPY shares for every four XLK shares. That was a trade that was good for several days," notes Bartlett. Thanks to her tight stop on the XLK short, she did not suffer when the tech sector rallied at the end of that week.

Like day traders of individual stocks, ETF day traders look for high liquidity, high volume (of the underlying shares), and reasonable volatility in their trading vehicles. The majority of ETFs do not fill these require-

TABLE 8.1   ETFs SUITABLE FOR DAY TRADING

ETF	VOLUME[a]	TOTAL SHARES OUTSTANDING	BETA[b]
QQQ	57,112,500	308,750,000	1.82
SPY	7,587,200	173,025,000	1.00
BBH	1,085,100	N/A	1.64
XLK	890,600	24,550,000	1.45
SMH	762,000	N/A	2.68
TBH	704,000	N/A	1.58
HHH	682,200	N/A	1.85
XLF	408,600	12,950,000	1.10

[a] on 12/1/00

[b] based on S&P 500

ments. Some do not trade for several days in a row, and others have very low volatility. While excellent long-term investments, ETFs with these qualities are not appropriate for day trading. Table 8.1 is a list of the ETFs with beta equal to or greater than one and volume or total shares outstanding greater than 500,000. The Nasdaq-100, QQQ, is by far the most popular ETF for day trading, as evidenced by its daily volume.

TOOLS OF THE TRADE

Technical analysis is the foundation of day trading. There are numerous excellent resources for technical information on stock trading. Nearly every financial Web site offers some sort of charting capability. Popular Web sites for technical analysis of stocks include BigCharts.com and StockCharts.com.

Kevin Eagle, a full-time day trader in Orlando, Florida, develops his daily game plan based on charts of equities and indexes that are overbought or oversold. He uses fast and slow stochastics, MACD, OBV, and RSI, as his primary measuring sticks for these conditions. As Eagle puts it, "You have to trust the charts. They don't lie." *Stochastics* is a momentum indicator that measures the price of a security relative to the high/low range over a given time period. Readings below 20 using the "fast" stochastic indicate oversold, while readings above 80 indicate overbought. *MACD* stands for *moving average convergence/divergence indicator*. By using moving averages, MACD can provide information on trends. *OBV* refers to *on balance volume*. The concept behind this indicator is that volume precedes price. *RSI* is a *relative strength indicator*. Like most experienced traders, Eagle sells out or goes short when the RSI kicks over 80. He goes long on an equity or an ETF when the RSI creeps up to 32, sometimes maintaining the position for several days if all the indicators are pointing north. Eagle generally avoids ETFs. "They just don't move fast enough for day traders," he notes. The exception to this rule is QQQ. "I like the Cubes for several reasons," says Eagle. "First, I almost always trade them on overextended Nasdaq days (either overbought or oversold), usually about a half-hour after the market opens, since this is when an apex frequently occurs. Then there is a fairly consistent pattern of reversal for the next half-hour, but it behooves the trader to watch the numbers. I especially like Cubes because I can short them on a downtick," explains Eagle. There are few other ways to easily initiate a short position in a down market. The following chart (Figure 8.2) shows trading for QQQ on July 10, 2001 and displays typical action for this ETF. Following the morning activity, midday is generally quiet. After-

FIGURE 8.2   A TYPICAL DAY OF QQQ TRADING

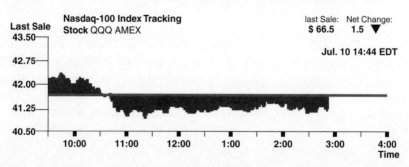

noons offer more trading opportunities. There is adequate trading range in QQQ to capture a few points without undue volatility. That is why the Cubes are a favored instrument of day traders who study the charts.

THE ART OF EXECUTION

Eagle has two brokers. His primary broker, CyBerCorp, offers direct access to ECNs and, through SelectNet, to market makers. Ameritrade is his Web broker. There are advantages and disadvantages to each. Web brokers will generally get an order filled, although not always at the best price or fastest speed. Direct access brokers allow for immediate execution and confirmation, but a fill is not guaranteed. "The market makers are not required to fill your order, so if I want to get in or out of a position in a really volatile market, that can cause problems," says Eagle. "And since the ECNs are auction houses, nothing is guaranteed there either. If you see the shares on an ECN, you can have them if you get there before someone else. So sometimes it makes sense to go with my Web broker instead of direct access. That way I'll at least get my trade," notes Eagle.

Many traders believe that a large part of successful trading lies in execution. Sometimes ECNs or SelectNet offer the best opportunities for a day trade, but sometimes a Web broker can be the most efficient conduit for a trade. There is no substitute for experience in this regard. "That's why paper trades don't always provide accurate experience in day trading," suggests Eagle. He feels that during less volatile times, direct access works well for ETFs such as Cubes, but when markets are frantic, Web brokers might offer better service.

Risk Management for Day Traders

Until an investment disaster strikes, most traders pay little heed to risk management. The rational course of action is to develop a plan to reduce risks before money is lost. This is especially pertinent when engaging in high-risk activities such as day trading. Eagle inadvertently became a player in one of the biggest financial hoaxes of the century when day trading a momentum stock, Emulex. He had noticed that the stock was overextended, so he shorted the stock at 110 at market open on the morning that Emulex made headlines across the news wires.

> "I don't care so much about the return on my money as I do the return of my money."
>
> **Will Rogers**

EMULEX: A CAUTIONARY TALE

As the trading day of August 25, 2000 began, most participants expected a ho-hum day with little activity on the horizon. Fridays in August are traditionally sleepy times for financial markets because everybody is off to the beaches or mountains. It was the perfect day for a hoax. Just as the stock market was opening, the Internet Wire, a Los Angeles-based corporate news service, distributed a bogus press release on Emulex. It said that the company was restating its most recent quarterly earnings as a loss and that the CEO had resigned.

The fake release was picked up by Bloomberg and other news organizations shortly after 10 A.M. EST. By the time trading in Emulex stock was halted around 10:30 A.M., it had fallen from its opening price of 110 to a low of 43. This was an eye-opener even for the most jaded of market watchers—a 60 percent loss in a stock in less than 30 minutes! For day traders with long positions in Emulex and related companies such as QLogic, it was one huge, stomach-churning freefall into financial disaster. Since short positions on individual stocks can be initiated only on upticks, and upticks don't happen during market meltdowns, there was no way for day traders on the long side to hedge their bets.

As Eagle watched his Emulex 110 short position, he was ebullient. As the stock price plummeted, Eagle learned about the press release. Since it had come out on Bloomberg, he assumed it was reliable information. Further, Eagle realized that most stocks that take a 50 percent haircut in one day continue to fall over the next few days. It seemed prudent to let profits run, at least for a little while. Unfortunately, trading in Emulex was halted at that point. Eagle had no recourse. When trading resumed a few hours later, it began at 130. What had started as a remarkably profitable trade for Eagle ended as a wash, as Emulex subsided to slightly below the opening price and Eagle's short entry.

It was little comfort to learn a week later that the bogus press release had been written by a 23-year-old former employee of Internet Wire by the name of Mark Jakob. He e-mailed the press release from a library computer at El Camino Community College to his former employer. A few weeks earlier, Jakob had sold short 3,000 shares of Emulex. Once the shares began their plunge, he covered his short positions and went long 3,500 shares. He made about $250,000, which was confiscated by the SEC upon his arrest a few days later.

Jakob was charged with securities and wire fraud and faces 15 years in prison, hopefully without Internet access.

Despite the numerous and glittering red flags indicated by this event, news organizations are pushing forward in their rush to provide instantaneous data. *Business Wire*, an issuer of corporate press releases, announced on September 18, 2000 that it would end the policy of keeping financial news portals and Web sites, waiting 15 minutes after wire services receive press releases. Those 15 minutes afforded journalists the chance to check the veracity of press releases with corporate offices. This push to provide raw press releases ensures more frequent hoaxes along the lines of the Emulex fiasco, with individual stocks at the mercy of cyber-manipulation.

KEEPING LOSSES AT BAY

The Emulex scenario will not play itself out in the portfolio of ETF holders. By their very nature, ETFs sidestep pure play disasters. But today's market drags down entire sectors when one participant takes a wrong step. It is still necessary to maintain a defensive stance to protect principal. The following are suggestions offered by experienced day traders to minimize the risks of day trading.

- **Rules of Thumb: USE STOPS**—Whether trading ETFs or individual stocks, keeping losses to a minimum is the primary rule of successful day traders. One way to accomplish this is through the use of stops. Bartlett is a fervent believer in their use. "Always, always, always trade with stops. They don't limit your upside. And they prevent huge losses, which have ruined my portfolio performance a lot more than exiting with small profits,"

explains Bartlett. This is of even greater import for a short position, which can create losses greater than an initial investment.

- **Check Transaction Costs**—There are transaction costs related to
  ETFs that must be considered in order to minimize the risks of
  day trading them. ETFs sometimes trade at a premium or discount
  to their NAVs. Intraday NAVs are available and should always be
  consulted prior to initiating a day trading position. Further, as with
  individual stocks, the bid/ask spread can affect the profit of a day
  trade. The trader is advised to be aware of this erosion factor. See
  Chapter 9 for a more detailed explanation of these issues.

- **Don't Risk Everything**—Common sense plays a major role in
  managing the risks of day trading, as it does in every aspect of
  daily life. Risking everything is never a reasonable proposition.

- **Watch Out with Margin**—Margin exponentially increases risk,
  so it is imperative to use caution in direct proportion to margin
  levels. Make sure short-, medium-, and long-term trends are all
  in the same direction of a trade executed on margin.

- **Know the Market**—Awareness of general market conditions and
  sector-specific events is necessary to maintain a profitable record
  with ETF day trades. It can be a painful experience to have
  unknowingly entered a position moments before a leading economic indicator is announced. Aside from general market events,
  earnings season can also produce exceptional volatility. Successful
  traders know which companies will be reporting earnings on a
  given week in the sector they will be trading. They will study the
  probability of a company failing to meet earnings estimates
  before formulating a trading strategy.

INSTITUTIONAL HEDGE FUNDS— A BRIEF REVIEW

The move toward index investing has opened up a whole new industry in
the hedge fund world. Because of the increasing amount of money track-

ing indexes, some of it in ETFs, hedge funds can make bets on stock movement tied to actions index fund managers are forced to make. For example, every time an index provider like Standard & Poor's decides that it is
time for one stock to enter an index and for another to leave, the managers of funds tied to that index must sell one stock and buy another. The
effect of the actual action, as well as the anticipation of this buying and
selling, can cause a rise or fall in the price to the stocks. A hedge manager's aim is to front-run this movement and make a quick profit.

The most significant example occurred when Morgan Stanley Capital International (MSCI) announced that it would be switching to free-
float weighting over an extended period in two stages (in June 2001 and
May 2002). *Free-float weighting* essentially adjusts the amount of shares
of a stock in an index based on the amount of publicly available stock in
that company. So if a company's ownership was 80 percent private, its
weighting in the index would be based only on the 20 percent of shares
available to the public. In any case, with $200 billion directly tracking MSCI
indexes, and perhaps as much as $3 trillion more or less benchmarked and
in the neighborhood of 25 percent turnover expected, the effect on prices
moving in or out of the indexes was expected to be significant. While index
fund managers were given a fighting chance to minimize price damage
over an extended period of time, hedge fund managers hovered overhead,
hoping to buy low and sell high based on this forced movement of the
underlying stocks.

Gaming indexes, however, is not as simple as it might seem. Despite
the fact that:

1. most major indexes have switched to the free-float system
   because it squeezed stock prices and hurt index returns and

2. a very large number of institutional investors were forced to buy
   and sell stocks as the indexes rebalance.

Provisional indexes that were set up to game the MSCI indexes had actually been beaten through June of 2001, because:

1. if you rebalance in advance of the "real" rebalance, you are not
   only making a bet on the index effect, you are also making huge

collateral side bets on sectors or countries...side bets that have turned out badly for EAFE gamers, and

2. the fact that many other hedge fund managers and other assorted profiteers are attempting the same trick ensures that the hedge fund manager who is trying to beat index changes is clearly earning his or her money.

ADVANCED TOPICS

HOW ETFS MANAGE A TAX-EFFICIENCY EDGE OVER TRADITIONAL MUTUAL FUNDS

For all the talk that ETFs are more tax-efficient, there's rarely a detailed explanation of exactly why this is so. As a result, many investors do not truly understand the tax benefits and liabilities of ETFs. It's important to emphasize that ETFs are not a magic potion that will lay Uncle Sam to rest in a field of poppies. There are tax consequences to investing in ETFs, both for the fund and for the individual. Essentially, for an investor who buys and sells individual ETF shares, the tax consequences are identical to those he or she would suffer in buying and selling ordinary stock. If you sell less than a year after you buy, the gain in price of the ETF shares will be taxed as ordinary income. When you sell after more than a year, you'll be taxed at a lower capital gains rate (10 percent or 20 percent currently, depending on your tax bracket). If the fund loses value, you can write off the loss against other capital gains (and up to $3000 annually of ordinary income) when you sell.

   The simplest way to look at the tax *benefits* of ETFs is to regard them as a trade. Where ETFs often have nontaxable trades of ETF shares for underlying stock and vice versa, traditional mutual funds generally have sales events, which trigger tax consequences.

Because most ETFs *are* mutual funds, you are also subject to many of the tax liabilities that apply to mutual funds. That is, when a fund is forced to sell stock to change its composition, for example when an index rebalances, the *fundholders* have to pay capital gains on whatever the gain was of the stock that is sold. Here's where it gets tricky, though. ETFs have the potential to make that gain smaller than it might be in a traditional mutual fund. How? Simple. Because ETFs are created and redeemed with stock that is traded *in-kind*—it is possible to raise the overall cost-basis of the stock that underlies the fund. Whenever a basket of stock is redeemed, the fund gives the redeemer the lowest cost-basis underlying stock. It doesn't matter to the redeemer. He pays based on his individual cost-basis regardless. The net result is that the fund is holding higher cost-basis stock, making the exposure to capital gains less when a particular stock must be sold in rebalancing.

Traditional open-ended mutual funds operate in the opposite manner. When redemptions come in, they sell off their higher cost-basis stock to lower immediate gains, leaving the fund exposed to ever-widening capital gains. This leads us to the other, more widely understood, tax advantage of ETFs. They are not exposed to capital gains that result *after* redemptions, as traditional mutual funds are. With a traditional mutual fund, when an investor cashes in his or her investment, the fund is often forced to sell underlying stock to pay him or her cash. This results in capital gains to the fund that must be picked up by all shareholders. ETF investors are never subject to this, because nothing in the underlying portfolio changes when an investor buys or sells individual ETF shares. And when an authorized participant *does* redeem ETF shares, it is actually to the collective *benefit* of the remaining shareholders.

The degree to which ETFs hold an advantage over traditional mutual funds depends on two factors. The first of these is the extent to which there are net redemptions on the traditional funds. The more fund shareholders want out of the traditional fund, the more it will cost the remaining shareholders. The second factor is the level of creations and redemptions that occur in the ETF. Of course the more redemptions there are, the more opportunity there is for the fund to slough off its low-cost-basis stock. Let's take a look at a couple of recent scenarios to give you an idea of how murky tax analysis can be.

Brian Mattes, principal at the Vanguard Group, notes, "Barclays was making all this noise about how they were more tax efficient than the Vanguard-500 fund, saying that would protect people from taxes. Not only did they not do it (iShares-500 fund made capital gains distributions in 2000), but we did protect people from taxes" (Vanguard paid out zero capital gains distributions on its 500 fund). Mattes feels that if someone is really concerned about taxes, tax-managed funds are the way to go because they have a variety of tax-management tools available to them that the passive ETFs do not. Mattes is also quick to point out that mutual funds are often protected from making significant distributions when shareholders are redeeming shares, because this often occurs when the market is falling and the fund is holding losses to offset gains.

It is possible, however, to analyze much of the data for most ETFs, since they've been in existence for such a short time. Of the 44-cent-per-share Barclays 500 fund distributed, about 7 cents was in brutal short-term gains. Barclays maintains that special circumstances and the fund's rapid growth were responsible. Tom Taggart, principal at BGI, says the short-term capital gain for the iShares S&P 500 was due to the new fund experiencing heavy creation/redemption activity as a result of recent significant contributions. In less than a year, BGI's 9.45-basis-point 500 fund went from inception to over $2 billion in assets under management.

In the interest of fairness, it should also be noted that the iShares Russell-2000 fund experienced total distributions of about 43 cents per share (about 0.50% of value) in 2000, while the Vanguard-SmallCap Index fund was estimated to have total year-end distributions of $2.81 per share (over 13% of value). The reason for *this* is simple. The Russell 2000 is notorious for high turnover. The new iShares Russell-2000 fund had very little in the way of gains, while the Vanguard fund, which has been around for many years, gets hit hard by all those accumulated gains when it is forced to rebalance.

Unfortunately, there is not a lot of historical ETF data to look at, but there does happen to be a very good test case we can examine. One hard cold fact that bears examination is that the granddaddy of ETFs, the SPDRs trust, has paid out one single 9 cent long-term capital gains distribution in its entire 1993—2000 history (and that, it is rumored, owed itself to a mistake in the management of the fund), and no short-term gains. The Vanguard 500, the granddaddy of all index funds, while it didn't pay out any capital gains distributions *last year*, over the same time period had capital gains ranging from 21 cents to 55 cents total (topping out at about 0.40% of value). That occurred with no net redemption and a relatively low-turnover index. One must grant that the Vanguard fund has had more time to accumulate gains...but the preliminaries for the higer-redemption level ETF, like SPDRs, show decided tax-efficiency advantage. Ah, if it were only so simple though. Over the five year 1995–2000 time period, the Vanguard 500 had a higher total return (*not* tax-adjusted) than the SPDR—15.54 to 15.39 percent—probably owing to more creative index fund management. If you had your investment in a taxable account, it appeared to practically be a wash. The tax advantage of ETFs over traditional mutual funds, though, especially given significant redemption activity (in either the ETF or in the mutual fund you are comparing it to) and higher turnover indexes, is real.

PREMIUMS AND DISCOUNTS

With ETFs, unlike mutual funds, you can trade in or out of the fund in real time. This benefit does not come without a price, however. Traditional mutual funds can be bought or sold at the calculated NAV. Thus, the investor is assured that he is paying what the stocks in the fund are worth. ETF prices are not guaranteed to match the underlying value of the stocks in the portfolio. Investors, therefore, can find themselves paying a premium to buy ETF shares, or they may be selling them at a discount.

With many ETFs the variations are negligible. But some of the funds trade at prices that can vary considerably from the correspondent NAV at the time of the trade. In such cases, an investor who inadvertently buys an ETF at a premium to its underlying value is exposed to natural corrective forces (namely savvy traders who exploit the difference between the trading price and the NAV).

The risk of price variation is greatest with ETFs containing illiquid underlying stocks, namely international, sector, and style funds.

In an article written by Karen Damato and Aaron Lucchetti for the *Wall Street Journal*, various ETF supporters responded to the charges. Lee Kranefuss of Barclays Global Investors said his firm had fully disclosed the mechanics and risks of ETFs. Even so, Barclays, threatened with a regulatory hearing, later agreed to provide additional information on its ETF Web site about the daily premiums and discounts of some of its iShares.

Presently, many of the ETFs that trade on the American Stock Exchange have three ticker symbols: one shows the trading value, another shows the estimated NAV of the underlying stocks, and the third shows the official NAV of the underlying stocks at the previous day's close. For many of the funds, there are up to seven tickers, detailing everything from cash level to dividend payouts.

Unfortunately, this information is presently only available for U.S.-based ETFs. The same information is not readily available to most retail investors trading in low-volume international funds. With the recent attention that has been paid to the premium/discount issue, however, look for this information to appear soon.

Gus Fleites, director of ETFs at State Street Global Advisors, agreed that price variation can be significant for some funds and may not always be explained clearly. Regarding ETFs that track international-stock indexes or lightly traded U.S. industry sectors, he noted, "Retail investors, beware...."

Fund specialists, including Mercer Bullard, a former SEC regulator who founded Fund Democracy, an investor advocate organization, have praised ETFs not only for allowing intraday trading, but also for their ability to feature lower operating expenses and greater tax efficiency. Bullard has also been critical of funds trading at high premiums and discounts to the NAV, however, and has successfully pushed for increased disclosure. Expect the transparency of trading/NAV differentials to fall increasingly into the public domain. Traders, not fund managers, gain from the premiums and discounts.

With Barclays already voluntarily posting the information, it seems likely the problem will soon be largely resolved. Aside from increased transparency cutting down the gap, one expects that the increased attention to the issue will also help narrow the premiums that are exploited by traders. In the meantime, let the buyer beware.

TABLE 9.1   PREMIUM/DISCOUNT STUDY OVERVIEW

	INTRADAY VALUE VS. BID	INTRADAY VALUE VS. MIDPOINT	INTRADAY VALUE VS. ASK
AVERAGE	−0.167%	0.014%	0.196%
CAP-WEIGHTED AVERAGE	−0.039%	0.028%	0.094%
MAXIMUM	0.246%	0.667%	1.108%
MINIMUM	−1.481%	−1.167%	−0.853%

Source: Salomon Smith Barney

From the Table 9.1 it can be deduced that the average ETF had a bid price that was at a 0.167 percent discount to actual intraday net asset value. The cap-weighted average was a 0.039 percent discount (on occasion, however, ETFs experience real-time discounts of over 1 percent to their NAV, and premiums of over 0.5 percent).

EXAMINING ETF LIQUIDITY

The same forces that keep price spreads and discounts/premiums to the NAV fairly tight on ETFs are also responsible for ensuring liquidity in the funds. As long as the underlying stocks are liquid, the ETFs should theoretically, trade with high liquidity. The reason for this is that, even in funds that trade very lightly, when an investor wants to make a trade, there will be a specialist posting the price who is fully willing and able to guarantee that price and step in to take advantage of the tight premium or discount that the order engenders.

Salomon Smith Barney conducted a premium/discount study with ETFs that emphasizes the point that traditional liquidity measures for equities do not pertain to ETFs. The main characteristic of ETFs that limits premiums and discounts is their creation/redemption feature. A specialist or other authorized participant can create or redeem ETFs daily through "creation units"—creating new shares to meet demand or terminating shares to quell supply on a daily basis. If the specialist is not keeping the price reasonably close to the underlying net asset value, other authorized participants can arbitrage any inefficiencies.

Lee Kranefuss of Barclays Global Investors recently pointed out that comparing last trade and closing NAVs for ETFs can be misleading because many ETFs trade infrequently, or when the markets for their underlying shares are closed. In some cases, the last trade could have been hours or even days before the NAV was calculated, or vice versa when foreign markets are closed while the ETFs trade in the U.S. The Solomon study seems to confirm this assertion. The issue of how prices are set when underlying foreign markets are closed is discussed in greater detail in the specialists section of this chapter.

To test how well the creation/redemption process works, Salomon analysts took random "snapshots" of U.S. ETFs for the month of September, 2000 (no international ETFs were included in the study). They compared the bid price, ask price, and midpoint between bid/ask to the intraday value. Intraday value is an estimated NAV calculated for ETFs every 15 seconds and is available from several quote services.

In general, the study concluded that the creation/redemption process is working, and that in 91 percent of the sample, ETF intraday values were in-between the bid and ask prices.

Table 9.2 shows the average bid/ask spread and sizes found for all of the ETF "snapshots" in the study.

TABLE 9.2   LIQUIDITY MEASURES IN ETFS

AVERAGE BID	83,795 shares
AVERAGE ASK	87,438 shares
AVERAGE SPREAD	$0.21
AVERAGE SPREAD PERCENTAGE	0.36%
CAP-WEIGHTED AVERAGE SPREAD	$0.13
CAP-WEIGHTED AVERAGE SPREAD PERCENTAGE	0.13%

Source: Salomon Smith Barney

PREMIUMS AND DISCOUNTS
FOR INTERNATIONAL AND
LIGHTLY-TRADED ETFS

Well, you may say, it's easy enough to trade with fairly tight pricing on highly liquid funds like the QQQs and the SPDRs. How do very lightly-traded funds, and funds based on stock markets that are closed while the ETFs trade on U.S. markets, fare? Morgan Stanley Dean Witter conducted a study on July 5, 2000 following after-dark hours price movements in U.S. markets of iShares MSCI Japan ETF and after-hours Nikkei 225 futures contracts—two instruments representing the same Japanese stock index. *Futures contracts* are contracts giving the investor various payoffs depending on the behavior of an index, commodity, or other asset. Since ETF specialists may use them to make markets on ETFs, they follow the ETF closely.

The study started at the close of Tokyo's exchange, when the official end-of-day NAV was recorded and Japanese traders went to bed. The ETF and futures soon began to trade in New York and meandered throughout the day, incorporating changes in investor sentiment, interest rates, and a myriad of other news. The ETFs and futures remained nearly in lockstep, moving inexorably away from the official end-of-day NAV. Lo and behold, when the Japanese stock traders arrived for business the next day, NAV at the opening resumed almost exactly where ETFs and U.S. futures left off, and far from the previous day's official NAV. All of this is consistent with basic trading theory.

A similar situation occurs with a U.S. ETF replication U.S. small-cap stocks. Both types of instruments trade during the same hours, but they certainly don't all trade as frequently. Many small stocks have relatively few interested investors and trades are separated by hours so that NAV figures, on average, represent relatively old information. ETFs, on the other hand, tend to trade by the minute, if not the second.

In such cases, bid-ask spreads of the small stocks tell more about where the next trade is likely to take place than the last trades used to construct official NAV figures.

In summary, because of their structure, as long as the underlying stocks can trade, it is highly unlikely that significant premiums/discounts to the underlying NAV will develop, because specialists and other large traders will take advantage of those anomalies.

TRADING COSTS

The point is often raised that, because they are created with stock that is traded in-kind, ETFs are not only more tax efficient, but they suffer from none of the trading costs that dog stock traders. Of course, we know that there is no free lunch in the market, and that someone must pay the transaction fees. It is true that for ETFs, the fund itself does not pay these costs in the way that a traditional mutual fund does when it buys stock for the fund. However, the individual or institutional investor does, whether he or she is the creator of the ETF creation unit or the buyer of ETF shares.

An authorized participant who creates a basket of 50,000 ETF shares, for example, had to pay trading costs on all the stocks that he or she bought before trading them for ETF shares. The individual or institutional investor who buys ETF shares pays trading costs in the form of commissions, losses to the ask/bid spread, etc., when purchasing those shares.

How does a small investor know he or she is getting the best price when he or she buys or sells an exchange-traded fund? The truth is that brokers may quite legally complete a trade at less-than-optimal prices, and the investor may never be the wiser.

How does that happen?

Brokers often buy equity positions to trade, becoming market makers or dealers. In essence this puts them in competition with their own customers. Essentially, the brokers hold inside knowledge of trades in the hopper, and this can lead to handsome profits. Brokers can also route trades to third parties who profit from completing transactions and who offer cash rebates called "payment for order flow." There is no assurance in either case that the customer has received the best possible deal.

At the center of these issues is the *bid-ask spread*, or the difference between the lowest price a seller offers and the highest price a buyer will pay. This difference, or spread, is what gives incentive to middlemen to complete the trade for everyone's benefit. In the era of computer networking, no one believes this spread has to be large for very liquid stocks. At the same time, no one believes it will go away completely. A problem common to all stock transactions, the ask/bid issue is a separate one from the trading/net asset value premium discount issue we discussed in a February 22, 2001 IndexFunds.com article.

The bid-ask spread often costs 1 percent or more to the investor, acting much like a "load" in a mutual fund and dragging down long-term profits. It is one of the primary drains on the small investor's final returns. The good news is that the ease with which middlemen can abuse their positions is dropping for a variety of reasons, including greater competition among brokers, better technology, and stricter regulatory controls. A bit of vigilance on the part of the investor is the main ingredient to getting a fair trade.

One strategy to avoid having a trade executed at an unexpectedly low price is to issue limit orders, or orders that set a maximum buy-price or minimum sell price for a trade, as opposed to market orders, which are placed at the "best price." This removes flexibility from the broker—flexibility that can be lead to a lower-than-expected price.

There is a misconception that indexers need only worry about bid-ask spreads with exchange-traded funds bought or sold midday through a brokerage. Not true. Mutual funds also face bid-ask spread costs because they also trade securities. In addition, funds are exposed to the danger of injecting volatility with big orders that may swing the market. Partial remedies exist for funds to help mitigate both of these trading costs. For instance, Instinet, Reuters' institutional trading system, boasts that it ensures anonymity, never holds positions in competition against its customers, and more rigorously seeks the best possible price.

Downward pressure on bid-ask spreads is expected now that stock markets have "decimalized" stock quotes, effectively allowing spreads to shrink to one penny. While stocks were once priced in 1/16 of a dollar, decimilazation now allows them to be quoted in pennies.

Pressure on the bid-ask spread is also coming from numerous electronic exchanges and discount brokers that market their ability to more methodically seek out the best possible price for investors. The ones who don't are being singled out in the media and by word-of-mouth.

Lastly, the Securities and Exchange Commission continues to apply pressure on market participants to decrease spreads.

Perhaps the most controversial aspect of the bid-ask spread is the so-called payment for order flow. This occurs when a broker directs large amounts of orders to an independent market maker, a firm whose specialty is bringing buyers and sellers together and takes the spread as profit. Such market makers return stock brokers a cash rebate called payment for order flow. Critics decry it as a crude kickback.

"We have come out fairly strongly against that practice in the past. A broker-dealer who accepts payment for order flow is advantaging one set of customers over another," says Deborah Mittelman, a vice president in execution services at Instinet Corp., "They also have a free look at orders before they go to the market."

The SEC barely tolerates payments for order flow, as can be seen from an announcement on the subject in July of 2000:

> *Since its growth in the 1980s in the equities markets, the Commission has made clear its concern about the practice of payment for order flow. It has repeatedly recognized that the practice constitutes a potential conflict for brokers handling customer orders, and that it may present a threat to aggressive quote competition.*
>
> *At the same time, we have acknowledged that payment for order flow is not necessarily inconsistent with a broker's duty of best execution, and that it has become a feature of competition among our equity market centers. The Commission decided not to ban payment for order flow in the early 1990s. In considering the arrangements, the Commission noted that payment for order flow is, in substance, the economic equivalent of internalization.*

Indeed, research by the Federal Reserve suggests that payment for order flow may actually *lower* bid-ask spreads.

Kenneth D. Pasternak, CEO of Knight Trading Group, a major independent market maker that pays for order flow, defended the practice before the Subcommittee on Securities of the U.S. Senate Committee on Banking, Housing and Urban Affairs, April 26, 2000:

"It has been the subject of incessant debate because it obviously poses a potential conflict: if a market center like ours gives brokers cash rebates or other inducements, how can the investor be sure than an order will receive the best possible execution?"

"...Last year, we rebated nearly $139 million to our broker-dealer clients who sent us their order flow. What our client firms did with that money is a question best answered by them, but no doubt they would tell you that, because of those rebates, their customers paid lower commissions, received more free real-time market data, and more free technical and fundamental analysis of more and more securities."

Payment for order flow may seem like a conflict of interest, he admits, but "the securities industry is rife with conflicts." For instance, firms underwrite and recommend securities at the same time. He advocates full and fair disclosure as the main solution to all such potential conflicts of interest.

REGULATORY AND TAX COMPLICATIONS

Many of the early developers of ETFs say that it took a miraculous convergence of determination and circumstance to ultimately garner the approval of the SEC and get the new products off the ground. The basic structure of ETFs runs counter to some important SEC regulations. Therefore, every time a new ETF hits the market, it has to seek special exceptions from the SEC to these regulations.

DOWN TO THE NITTY GRITTY

Here is how the complicated process goes from a legal standpoint, from conception of a fund to its launch on a stock exchange.

While much of the trail has already been blazed by the early ETFs, every prospective fund still has to go through a series of organizational and regulatory procedures before it can be launched. Briefly, here are the legal tasks that must be dealt with before a fund can begin trading.

- The firm that wants to launch the ETF must set up an investment company in the same way you would with an ordinary mutual fund.

- The ETF organizer must file an exemptive order with the SEC's Division of Investment Management to ask for exemptive relief from certain sections (details follow) of the 1940 act.

- The ETF organizer must file an exemption request for the 1934 act to the SEC Division of Market Regulation to allow trading exemptions (details also follow).

- For a domestic fund, the exchange that the ETF will trade on must have current rules that allow the operation of that specific type of ETF. If the rules do not already exist, the exchange must apply on the fund's behalf to a different section of the SEC's Division of Market Regulation to approve the rule changes.

- Relief must be applied for to the National Association of Securities Dealers (NASD) to make sure that the shares trading on the secondary market are permitted to trade at a price other than the NAV.

- Typically, no special IRS relief is required under a typical investment company structure.

- The fund advisor must set up relationships with the Depository Trust and Clearing Corporation (DTCC-NSCC/DTC) so that the logistics of ETF trading are possible.

"Prospectus delivery relief was a huge point of discussion. Another was certainly the concept of secondary market shares trading differently than NAV, how different they would trade from NAV, and would the arbitrage mechanism work. We had to meet with the SEC staff and explain to them why we thought hypothetically it ought to work."

Kathleen Moriarty, partner at Carter, Ledyard & Milburn

LAWS FROM WHICH ETF MANAGERS MUST SEEK EXEMPTIVE RELIEF

The following is an outline of the exemptions that must be obtained from the SEC in order to launch an ETF. It comes courtesy of Kathleen Moriarty, partner at Carter, Ledyard & Milburn, who was involved in gaining regulatory approval for SPDRs, and has also served as legal counsel for DIAMONDS, WEBS, MidCap SPDRs, QQQs, iShares, and the VIPERs and forthcoming Nuveen ETFs.

Exemptive Relief under the 1940 Act

- Typical requests for an ETF structured as a UIT or as an open-end fund include: relief from Sections 2(a)(32) and 5(a)(1) , to permit ETFs to redeem shares only in creation unit size; Section 22d and Rule 22c-1 to permit trading of shares to take place at prices other than NAV; Sections 17(a) and 17(b), to permit affiliates to deposit securities into, and receive portfolio securities from, the ETF; Section 26(a)(2), to permit certain expenses associated with the creation and maintenance of the trust to be borne by the trust rather than its sponsor; Section 14(a), to exempt the sponsor from the $100,000 seed capital requirement; and Section 17(d) and Rule 17d-2, to permit certain affiliated transactions.

- Other requests may include relief from Section 24(d), to permit exemption from prospectus delivery requirements in connection with secondary market trading activity; Section 22(e), to permit satisfaction of redemption requests to be made in excess of the statutory 7-calendar day requirement under certain circumstances; Sections 18(f)(l) and 18(i) to permit the addition of an exchange-traded fund class to an existing multi-class structure; Section 12(d)(1), to permit a "fund of funds" structure; and other Section 17 relief if the structure of the fund and relationship with its participants and service providers necessitates relief.

Exemptive, Interpretive and No-Action Relief from the 1934 Act

- Exemptive, interpretive and no-action requests for relief from various 1934 act trading restrictions include: relief from Rule 10a-1 ("uptick rule") with respect to short sales of ETFs; relief from Rule 101 of Reg M and Rule 14e-5, to permit broker-dealers and others to bid for, purchase, redeem or engage in other secondary market transactions for ETF units/shares and portfolio securities during a distribution, or tender offer for portfolio securities; relief from Rule 102 of Reg M, to permit ETFs to redeem their units/shares in creation units during their continuous offering of ETF units/shares; relief from Rule 10b-10, to permit broker-dealers and other persons to deposit portfolio securities and to receive portfolio securities without providing their customers with a statement of the number, identity and price of each individual portfolio security; relief from Rules 11(d)1-1 and 11(d)1-2, to permit margining of ETF units/shares without a thirty-day restriction under certain circumstances.

- Section 19b and Rule 19b-4 rule changes are required to permit the primary listing exchange to list ETFs. Note that certain generic ETF listing standards may already have been adopted by an exchange (see for example, AMEX Rules 1000 and 1000A).

- No-action relief has also been sought for the officers and directors of the ETF and owners of more than 10 percent of the ETF's units/shares so that such persons do not have to comply with reporting requirements imposed by Sections 16(a) and 13(d).

HISTORY OF REGULATORY APPROVAL FOR VARIOUS ETFS

1. Standard & Poor's Depositary Receipts (SPDRs)—Unit Investment Trust

   - application first filed: June 25, 1990

- application amended four (4) times: 2/2/91; 2/28/92; 6/8/92 and 8/7/92

- notice published: September 17, 1992

- Commission review

- order granted: October 26, 1992

  <u>Total elapsed time</u>: 28 months

2. MidCap SPDRs—Unit Investment Trust

- application first filed: May 28, 1993

- application amended twice: July 13, 1994 and January 18, 1995

- notice published: December 23, 1994

- Commission review

- order granted: January 18, 1995

  <u>Total elapsed time</u>: 20 months

3. DIAMONDS—Unit Investment Trust

- application first filed: June 17, 1997

- application amended: December 3, 1997

- notice published: December 5, 1997

- delegated authority, no Commission review

- order granted: December 30, 1997

  <u>Total elapsed time</u>: 6 months

4. Country Baskets—Open-end mutual fund

- application first filed: August 19, 1994

- application amended five (5) times: 10/28/94; 11/30/94; 1/10/95; 3/30/95 and 6/30/95

- notice published: February 6, 1996
- Commission review
- order granted: March 5, 1996

  Total elapsed time: 19 months

5. WEBS (now iShares MSCI)—Open-end mutual fund
   - application first filed: September 19, 1994
   - application amended four (4) times: 12/23/94; 5/19/95; 1/17/96 and 2/28/96
   - notice published: February 6, 1996
   - delegated authority, no Commission review
   - order granted: March 5, 1996

     Total elapsed time: 18 months

6. Select Sector SPDRS—Open-end mutual fund
   - application first filed: May 13, 1997
   - application amended twice: September 4 and November 8, 1998
   - notice published: October 20, 1998
   - delegated authority, no Commission review
   - order granted: November 13, 1998

     Total elapsed time: 18 months

7. QQQs—Unit Investment Trust
   - application first filed: August 19, 1998
   - application amended: February 18, 1999
   - notice published: January 27, 1999
   - delegated authority, no Commission review

- order granted: February 22, 1999

  Total elapsed time: 6 months

8. iShares—Open-end fund structure
   - applications first filed: April 30, 1999
   - applications amended twice: May 2 and May 11, 2000
   - notice published: April 17, 2000
   - delegated authority, no Commission review
   - order granted: May 12, 2000

     Total elapsed time: 12.5 months

9. VIPERs—Open-end mutual fund
   - application first filed: May 12, 2000
   - application amended: July 12, 2000
   - notice published: October 6, 2000
   - hearing request filed: October 31, 2000
   - Commission review to grant or deny hearing request
   - Hearing request denied and order granted: December 12, 2000

     Total elapsed time: 7 months

Although ETFs are able to achieve tax efficiencies that traditional open-ended mutual funds do not enjoy, no landmark IRS decision was required to launch the new products. The fact is, existing funds are allowed to trade equities in-kind, but very rarely do, as most investors are looking for cash when they redeem their investments. Because tax must ultimately be paid on all gains, the in-kind process does not provide a legal hurdle. It is just an interesting (and unforeseen, according to the early developers of the SPDRs) benefit of ETF structure. As Nate Most, president and chairman of iShares Trust said, "We did not consider the tax advantages of the structure while we were developing it, that only became clear later."

OPTIMIZATION AND TRACKING ISSUES

As discussed in Chapter 7, there is no guarantee that ETFs will track their underlying indexes. Already, in the case of Malaysia, the WEBS (now iShares) that was based there traded at a vastly discounted price to its underlying net-asset value owing to extraordinary market turmoil.

In addition, recently, some international and smaller sector funds have been dogged by diversification problems that have forced unwieldy and costly optimization of funds. In the U.S., for example, mutual funds covered by registered investment company (RIC) diversification rules are not allowed to have the fund invested at more than 25 percent in one stock, or have the sum total of all stocks that have over 5 percent weighting add up to over 50 percent. As a result, when one stock reaches representation of over 25 percent, the fund is forced to sell off shares of the fund. In 2000, investors in the Canadian and Swedish iShares, for example, took huge distributions of over 20 percent in one shot (and therefore significant tax hits as the result of this process).

In an index like the Dow Jones Energy, which has Exxon represented at over 40 percent of the index, the fund must constantly hold an optimized position that attempts to replicate the performance of the problem stock by buying others that should theoretically duplicate it. Obviously, this can cause not only tax problems, but also significant tracking error.

MARKET MAKERS—WHAT *IS* AN AP?

Known formally as authorized participants (APs), market makers do just what their name suggests…they ultimately make much of the market in ETFs. The market maker is the firm who actually orders the creation of ETF shares. When an AP wants ETF shares, it gathers enough of the underlying shares of stock to form some multiple of (usually 50,000) ETF shares, also known as a *creation unit*. It then approaches the fund managers

(State Street, Barclays Global or the Bank of New York, for example) and asks to exchange those shares for ETF shares. The actual underlying shares are deposited by the fund manager and cleared in the U.S. by the National Securities and Clearing Corporation (NSCC) and deposited by the Depository Trust and Clearing Company (DTCC)—which owns the NSCC and makes a tiny fee on each clearing transaction. The NSCC clears virtually every equity and bond trade in the U.S.—over $70 trillion in annual transactions a year. Creations and redemptions are done at NAV when the market that trades the ETF shares is closed.

Why create or redeem ETF units? One reason, of course, is to meet shareholder demand. The other, and the reason that the spreads on ETFs are so tight and the trading price's variance from the NAV generally so slim, is that market makers and specialists will step in to profit from very slim premiums or discounts to the underlying net asset value, and immediately create or redeem ETF shares as appropriate, potentially selling the ETF shares or underlying stocks for a quick profit. To protect the prices, these institutions use derivatives such as futures to hedge off price movement and guarantee the profit.

HOW SPECIALISTS AND MARKET MAKERS PRICE AND TRADE ETFS

Critical to the success of ETFs are the specialists. Specialists set prices and ensure the liquidity of ETF offerings. These companies, which count Spear, Leeds & Kellogg, Susquehanna Investment Group, Wolverine Trading, Bear Hunter and Hull Trading among their number, are critical in guaranteeing tight price spreads and liquidity for ETF issues.

In many ways, the role specialists play in pricing ETFs is very similar to how they make a market on ordinary equities. One of the biggest differences, of course, is that ETFs trade largely based on a known underlying NAV, whereas ordinary equities are not linked to anything but supply and demand. Therein lies the magic of ETF liquidity and its immunity to any sort of price squeeze as an instrument. Because the value of the underlying ETF components is known, and the risk in price movement is generally hedgeable, they are almost always guaranteed to trade near their underlying net asset value (NAV). Why? Because there's money to be made. If the difference between the value of the underlying stock and the trading price gets too large, specialists or market makers will step in to take advantage of the discount or premium.

Because of their role in guaranteeing ETF markets that are both tight and deep, and their trading expertise and ability to see the entire playing field, most ETF creations and redemptions are effected by specialists. It should be noted that creations and redemptions are also sometimes effected by large market makers (authorized participants) who are not specialists, such as Merrill Lynch, Morgan Stanley, Lehman Brothers, Salomon Smith Barney, and Goldman Sachs. These APs step in to create or redeem shares, particularly when one of their clients places a large order. Between the specialists and large brokerage houses, the competition is fierce, and the trading margins are thin. The high-volume ETFs trade with a spread of only five or ten cents on a $100 share, and the specialist can handle your million-share order at the drop of a hat.

This trend has only strengthened over time as ETF awareness has increased. As Jay Baker, vice president responsible for index shares marketing at Spear, Leeds & Kellogg notes, "As more and more people have understood these things, they've become more efficient, and they're not as profitable as they used to be."

Because all of this competition is in place, the only limitation on ETF liquidity is the liquidity of its underlying stock. This issue is one on which you find ETF fund managers largely mute. How, for example, will the pricing and trading look in a market crash or in exceptional market circumstances? You would be hard-pressed to find an institutional player to buy into an ETF at near NAV if he or she can't sell the underlying stock for cash or hedge his or her position. This is particularly true in the more unpredictable international markets. The perfect case in point is WEBS (now iShares) Malaysia, which during the Asian crisis of 1998 to 1999, traded at discounts of over 30 percent to its NAV. The only way to cash out of the fund was to accept payment in ringgits, apparently not a very appetizing option to many institutional investors. For a more detailed analysis of the Malaysian crisis, please refer to Chapter 7.

It is with these international funds that the most interesting and unique challenges are posed to specialists. How, for example, do you price an ETF when the market on which the underlying shares trade is closed? The answer almost always lies in the futures market. Correspondingly, the ETFs' price moves to reflect both currency rate fluctuations and the movement in the perceived value of the underlying stock, which takes into account information in real time. For this reason, the closing price of the ETF in the U.S. is often closer to the market opening of the underlying securities than the closing NAV (which is used to calculate the premium/discount).

Specialists are selected based on their expertise. Most of the single-country iShares, for example, are handled by Spear, Leeds & Kellogg, while Hull Trading makes a market on many small-cap funds. Goldman Sachs, the investment-banking goliath, now owns both companies. Table 9.3 is a list of American Stock Exchange specialists for ETFs.

TABLE 9.3   SPECIALISTS FOR ALL U.S.-TRADING ETFs

Fund Name	Symbol	Manager	Specialist
DIAMONDS Trust Series I	DIA	SSgA	Spear, Leeds & Kellogg
FORTUNE e-50 Index Fund	FEF	SSgA	Bear Hunter LLC.
FORTUNE-500 Index Fund	FFF	SSgA	Bear Hunter LLC.
iShares MSCI-Australia Index Fund	EWA	BGI	AIM Securities, Inc.
iShares MSCI Canada Index Fund	EWC	BGI	AIM Securities, Inc.
iShares MSCI-Sweden Index Fund	EWD	BGI	Spear, Leeds & Kellogg
iShares MSCI-Germany Index Fund	EWG	BGI	AIM Securities, Inc.
iShares MSCI-Hong Kong Index Fund	EWH	BGI	Spear, Leeds & Kellogg
iShares MSCI-Italy Index Fund	EWI	BGI	AIM Securities, Inc.
iShares MSCI-Japan Index Fund	EWJ	BGI	AIM Securities, Inc.
iShares MSCI-Belgium Index Fund	EWK	BGI	Spear, Leeds & Kellogg
iShares MSCI-Switzerland Index Fund	EWL	BGI	Spear, Leeds & Kellogg
iShares MSCI-Malaysia Index Fund	EWM	BGI	AIM Securities, Inc.
iShares MSCI-Netherlands Index Fund	EWN	BGI	Spear, Leeds & Kellogg
iShares MSCI-Austria Index Fund	EWO	BGI	AIM Securities, Inc.
iShares MSCI-Spain Index Fund	EWP	BGI	Spear, Leeds & Kellogg
iShares MSCI-France Index Fund	EWQ	BGI	AIM Securities, Inc.

(continues)

TABLE 9.3   SPECIALISTS FOR ALL U.S.-TRADING ETFS (CONTINUED)

FUND NAME	SYMBOL	MANAGER	SPECIALIST
iShares MSCI-Singapore Index Fund	EWS	BGI	Spear, Leeds & Kellogg
iShares MSCI-Taiwan Index Fund	EWT	BGI	Susquehanna
iShares MSCI-U.K. Index Fund	EWU	BGI	Spear, Leeds & Kellogg
iShares MSCI-Mexico Index Fund	EWW	BGI	Spear, Leeds & Kellogg
iShares MSCI-South Korea Index Fund	EWY	BGI	Susquehanna
iShares MSCI-Brazil Index Fund	EWZ	BGI	Susquehanna
iShares MSCI-EMU Index Fund	EZU	BGI	Susquehanna
iShares Nasdaq Biotechnology Index Fund	IBB	BGI	Hull Trading Co.
iShares Cohen & Steers Realty Majors Index Fund	ICF	BGI	Bear Hunter
iShares DJ US Utilities Index Fund	IDU	BGI	Spear, Leeds & Kellogg
iShares S&P-100 Index Fund	OEF	BGI	Wolverine Trading L.P.
iShares S&P Europe-350 Index Fund	IEV	BGI	Susquehanna
iShares S&P MidCap-400 Index Fund	IJH	BGI	Hull Trading Co.
iShares S&P MidCap-400/BARRA Value Index Fund	IJJ	BGI	Hull Trading Co.
iShares S&P MidCap-400/BARRA Growth Index Fund	IJK	BGI	Hull Trading Co.
iShares S&P SmallCap-600 Index Fund	IJR	BGI	Hull Trading Co.
iShares S&P SmallCap-600/BARRA Value Index Fund	IJS	BGI	Hull Trading Co.
iShares S&P SmallCap-600/BARRA Growth Index Fund	IJT	BGI	Hull Trading Co.
iShares S&P/TSE-60 Index Fund	IKC	BGI	Susquehanna
iShares S&P Global-100 Index Fund	IOO	BGI	Susquehanna
iShares S&P-500/BARRA Value Index Fund	IVE	BGI	Hull Trading Co.
iShares S&P-500 Index Fund	IVV	BGI	Hull Trading Co.
iShares S&P-500/BARRA Growth Index Fund	IVW	BGI	Hull Trading Co.
iShares Russell-1000 Index Fund	IWB	BGI	Hull Trading Co.

(continues)

TABLE 9.3   SPECIALISTS FOR ALL U.S.-TRADING
ETFS (CONTINUED)

FUND NAME	SYMBOL	MANAGER	SPECIALIST
iShares Russell-1000 Value Index Fund	IWD	BGI	Hull Trading Co.
iShares Russell-1000 Growth Index Fund	IWF	BGI	Hull Trading Co.
iShares Russell-2000 Index Fund	IWM	BGI	Susquehanna
iShares Russell-2000 Value Index Fund	IWN	BGI	Susquehanna
iShares Russell-2000 Growth Index Fund	IWO	BGI	Susquehanna
iShares Russell-3000 Index Fund	IWV	BGI	Hull Trading Co.
iShares Russell-3000 Value Index Fund	IWW	BGI	Hull Trading Co.
iShares Russell-3000 Growth Index Fund	IWZ	BGI	Hull Trading Co.
iShares DJ US Consumer Cyclical Index Fund	IYC	BGI	Spear, Leeds & Kellogg
iShares DJ US Chemicals Index Fund	IYD	BGI	Spear, Leeds & Kellogg
iShares DJ US Energy Index Fund	IYE	BGI	Spear, Leeds & Kellogg
iShares DJ US Financial Sector	IYF	BGI	Susquehanna
iShares DJ US Financial Services	IYG	BGI	Susquehanna
iShares DJ US Healthcare Index Fund	IYH	BGI	Spear, Leeds & Kellogg
iShares DJ US Industrial Index Fund	IYJ	BGI	Spear, Leeds & Kellogg
iShares DJ US Non-Consumer Cyclical Index Fund	IYK	BGI	Spear, Leeds & Kellogg
iShares DJ US Basic Materials Index Fund	IYM	BGI	Spear, Leeds & Kellogg
iShares DJ US Real Estate Index Fund	IYR	BGI	Spear, Leeds & Kellogg
iShares DJ US Internet Index Fund	IYV	BGI	Spear, Leeds & Kellogg
iShares DJ US Technology Index Fund	IYW	BGI	Susquehanna
iShares DJ US Total Market Index Fund	IYY	BGI	Hull Trading Co.
iShares DJ US Telecommunications Index Fund	IYZ	BGI	Spear, Leeds & Kellogg
MidCap SPDRs	MDY	BNY	Susquehanna
Nasdaq-100 Index Tracking Stock	QQQ	BNY	Susquehanna
streetTRACKS Dow Jones US Small Cap Growth Index Fund	DSG	SSgA	Bear Hunter

(continues)

TABLE 9.3   SPECIALISTS FOR ALL U.S.-TRADING
ETFS (CONTINUED)

FUND NAME	SYMBOL	MANAGER	SPECIALIST
streetTRACKS Dow Jones US Small Cap Value Index Fund	DSV	SSgA	Wolverine Trading
streetTRACKS Dow Jones US Large Cap Growth Index Fund	ELG	SSgA	Wolverine Trading
streetTRACKS Dow Jones US Large Cap Value Index Fund	ELV	SSgA	Bear Hunter
streetTRACKS Morgan Stanley Internet Index	MII	SSgA	Wolverine Trading
streetTRACKS Morgan Stanley High Tech 35 Index	MTK	SSgA	Bear Hunter
streetTRACKS Dow Jones Global Titans Index Fund	DGT	SSgA	Bear Hunter
Select Sector SPDR-Basic Industries Fund	XLB	SSgA	Bear Hunter
Select Sector SPDR-Energy Fund	XLE	SSgA	Susquehanna
Select Sector SPDR-Financial Fund	XLF	SSgA	Spear, Leeds & Kellogg
Select Sector SPDR-Industrial Fund	XLI	SSgA	AGS/STR/OTA
Select Sector SPDR-Technology Fund	XLK	SSgA	Susquehanna
Select Sector SPDR-Consumer Staples Fund	XLP	SSgA	Bear Hunter
Select Sector SPDR-Utilities Fund	XLU	SSgA	AGS/STR/OTA
Select Sector SPDR-Consumer Services Fund	XLV	SSgA	Spear, Leeds & Kellogg
Select Sector SPDR-Cyclical/ Transportation Fund	XLY	SSgA	Spear, Leeds & Kellogg
SPDRs	SPY	SSgA	Spear, Leeds & Kellogg

ETF Assets
1993–2000

AMEX LISTED INDEX SHARES & HOLDRs	ASSETS 12/31/1993	ASSETS 12/31/1994	ASSETS 12/31/1995
	$461,270,700	$419,173,362	$1,053,498,984
	ASSETS 12/31/1996	ASSETS 12/31/1997	ASSETS 12/31/1998
	$2,410,008,663	$6,709,447,821	$15,615,131,287
	ASSETS 12/31/1999	ASSETS 12/31/2000	
	$35,889,911,748	$70,316,552,223	
INDEX SHARES ONLY	ASSETS 12/31/1993	ASSETS 12/31/1994	ASSETS 12/31/1995
	$461,270,700	$419,173,362	$1,053,498,984
	ASSETS 12/31/1996	ASSETS 12/31/1997	ASSETS 12/31/1998
	$2,410,008,663	$6,709,447,821	$15,615,131,287
	ASSETS 12/31/1999	ASSETS 12/31/2000	
	$33,908,072,660	$65,257,789,213	
ISHARES MSCI	ASSETS 12/31/1996	ASSETS 12/31/1997	ASSETS 12/31/1998
	$258,377,920	$507,221,415	$1,026,162,858
	ASSETS 12/31/1999	ASSETS 12/31/2000	
	$1,992,469,362	$1,798,615,360	
	ASSETS 12/31/1998	ASSETS 12/31/1999	ASSETS 12/31/2000
Select SPDRs	$482,595,050	$2,580,141,928	$2,397,139,214
HOLDRS	—	$1,981,839,088	$5,058,763,010
iShares S&P	—	—	$3,319,937,000
iShares Russell	—	—	$1,517,261,000
iShares Dow Jones	—	—	$504,537,000
streetTRACKS Dow Jones	—	—	$154,094,212
streetTRACKS Morgan Stanley	—	—	$96,255,515
INDIVIDUAL ETFs *AMEX-LISTED ETFs*			
S&P 500 SPDR (SPY)	ASSETS 12/31/1993	ASSETS 12/31/1994	ASSETS 12/31/1995
	$461,270,700	$419,173,362	$999,182,578
	ASSETS 12/31/1996	ASSETS 12/31/1997	ASSETS 12/31/1998
	$2,001,756,375	$5,514,411,813	$12,203,868,188
	ASSETS 12/31/1999	ASSETS 12/31/2000	
	$19,806,669,709	$25,480,978,991	
S&P 400 MIDCAP SPDR (MDY)	ASSETS 12/31/1995	ASSETS 12/31/1996	ASSETS 12/31/1997
	$54,316,406	$149,874,368	$687,814,594
	ASSETS 12/31/1998	ASSETS 12/31/1999	ASSETS 12/31/2000
	$1,457,837,250	$2,346,862,344	$3,946,825,420

	Assets 12/31/1998	Assets 12/31/1999	Assets 12/31/2000
DJIA DIAMONDS (DIA)	$444,667,941	$1,293,672,358	$2,339,638,014
Nasdaq-100 Trust (QQQ)	N/A	$5,888,256,960	$23,560,371,266
iShares MSCI Series	Assets 12/31/1998	Assets 12/31/1999	Assets 12/31/2000
Australia (EWA)	$43,056,000	$65,651,103	$58,466,000
Austria (EWO)	$9,750,000	$12,134,191	$10,794,000
Belgium (EWK)	$16,960,000	$13,538,883	$11,563,200
Brazil (EWZ)	N/A	N/A	$15,561,000
Canada (EWC)	$12,914,000	$11,553,117	$17,303,000
EMU (EZU)	N/A	N/A	$40,271,000
France (EWQ)	$51,885,610	$82,021,520	$94,150,770
Germany (EWG)	$79,402,050	$156,978,553	$164,575,590
Hong Kong (EWH)	$67,885,080	$88,850,976	$70,451,740
Italy (EWI)	$81,810,000	$60,105,439	$54,024,000
Japan (EWJ)	$307,210,240	$978,551,099	$650,105,170
Malaysia (EWM)	$70,143,000	$103,193,462	$88,452,000
Mexico (EWW)	$11,407,000	$27,010,566	$30,981,000
Netherland (EWN)	$24,497,760	$28,855,640	$38,952,900
Singapore (EWS)	$90,280,000	$131,270,656	$69,113,000
South Korea (EWY)	N/A	N/A	$17,443,500
Spain (EWP)	$31,300,500	$42,141,988	$40,296,000
Sweden (EWD)	$14,302,500	$24,180,091	$24,624,000
Switzerland (EWL)	$40,463,280	$42,241,378	$50,610,000
Taiwan (EWT)	N/A	N/A	$70,959,500
U.K. (EWU)	$85,532,360	$124,190,700	$179,917,990
Select Sector SPDRs	Assets 12/31/1998	Assets 12/31/1999	Assets 12/31/2000
Basic Industries (XLB)	$10,780,000	$110,985,239	$78,201,725
Consumer Services (XLV)	$39,897,000	$117,632,002	$77,848,423
Consumer Staples (XLP)	$77,776,500	$266,559,574	$205,651,325
Cyclical/Transportation (XLY)	$18,277,000	$166,929,903	$67,721,224
Energy (XLE)	$48,972,000	$228,292,915	$262,844,882
Financial (XLF)	$62,593,000	$342,108,580	$504,451,659
Industrial (XLI)	$16,968,000	$133,094,390	$53,197,680
Technology (XLK)	$156,480,000	$1,091,977,384	$1,074,375,436
Utilities (XLU)	$51,510,000	$122,561,942	$72,846,862
iShares Dow Jones	Assets 12/31/1998	Assets 12/31/1999	Assets 12/31/2000
US Basic Materials (IYM)	N/A	N/A	$9,632,500
US Chemicals (IYD)	N/A	N/A	$17,088,000
US Consumer Cyclical (IYC)	N/A	N/A	$13,842,500
US Energy (IYE)	N/A	N/A	$40,972,500

(continues)

iSHARES DOW JONES	ASSETS 12/31/1998	ASSETS 12/31/1999	ASSETS 12/31/2000
US Financial Sector (IYF)	N/A	N/A	$21,750,000
US Financial Services (IYG)	N/A	N/A	$24,615,000
US Healthcare (IYH)	N/A	N/A	$57,416,000
US Industrial (IYJ)	N/A	N/A	$22,576,000
US Internet (IYV)	N/A	N/A	$18,546,000
US Non-Consumer Cyclical (IYK)	N/A	N/A	$15,099,000
US Real Estate (IYR)	N/A	N/A	$34,101,000
US Technology (IYW)	N/A	N/A	$111,855,000
US Telecommunications (IYZ)	N/A	N/A	$44,631,500
US Total Market (IYY)	N/A	N/A	$36,852,000
US Utilities (IDU)	N/A	N/A	$35,560,000
iSHARES RUSSELL	ASSETS 12/31/1998	ASSETS 12/31/1999	ASSETS 12/31/2000
Russell 1000 (IWB)	N/A	N/A	$238,170,000
Russell 1000 Growth (IWF)	N/A	N/A	$106,458,000
Russell 1000 Value (IWD)	N/A	N/A	$152,694,000
Russell 2000 (IWM)	N/A	N/A	$394,748,000
Russell 2000 Growth (IWO)	N/A	N/A	$106,045,500
Russell 2000 Value (IWN)	N/A	N/A	$162,148,000
Russell 3000 (IWV)	N/A	N/A	$312,395,000
Russell 3000 Growth (IWZ)	N/A	N/A	$25,615,000
Russell 3000 Value (IWW)	N/A	N/A	$18,987,500
iSHARES S&P	ASSETS 12/31/1998	ASSETS 12/31/1999	ASSETS 12/31/2000
S&P 500 (IVV)	N/A	N/A	$2,319,057,000
S&P 500/BARRA Growth (IVW)	N/A	N/A	$130,473,000
S&P 500/BARRA Value (IVE)	N/A	N/A	$229,068,000
S&P Europe 350 Index (IEV)	N/A	N/A	$86,353,500
MidCap 400 (IJH)	N/A	N/A	$216,552,000
MidCap 400/BAR. Growth (IJK)	N/A	N/A	$92,917,500
MidCap 400/BARRA Value (IJJ)	N/A	N/A	$42,685,000
SmallCap 600 (IJR)	N/A	N/A	$125,120,000
SmallCap 600/BAR. Growth (IJT)	N/A	N/A	$31,296,000
SmallCap 600/BAR. Value (IJS)	N/A	N/A	$38,360,000
S&P/TSE 60 (IKC)	N/A	N/A	$8,055,000
streetTRACKS	ASSETS 12/31/1998	ASSETS 12/31/1999	ASSETS 12/31/2000
Dow Jones Global Titans (DGT)	N/A	N/A	$30,786,018
DJ US Large Cap Growth (ELG)	N/A	N/A	$28,788,134
DJ US Large Cap Value (ELV)	N/A	N/A	$54,618,972
DJ US Small Cap Growth (DSG)	N/A	N/A	$16,078,993
DJ US Small Cap Value (DSV)	N/A	N/A	$23,822,094

*street*TRACKS	ASSETS 12/31/1998	ASSETS 12/31/1999	ASSETS 12/31/2000
DJ MS High Tech (MTK)	N/A	N/A	$60,526,653
DJ MS Internet (MII)	N/A	N/A	$35,728,861
FORTUNE INDEXES	ASSETS 12/31/1998	ASSETS 12/31/1999	ASSETS 12/31/2000
Fortune 500 (FFF)	N/A	N/A	$92,418,417
Fortune e-50 (FEF)	N/A	N/A	$49,717,804
HOLDRs	ASSETS 12/31/1998	ASSETS 12/31/1999	ASSETS 12/31/2000
Biotech (BBH)	N/A	$763,405,650	$1,675,857,969
Broadband (BDH)	N/A	N/A	$299,710,125
Internet Architecture (IAH)	N/A	N/A	$199,402,256
Internet Bus. to Bus. (BHH)	N/A	N/A	$259,344,825
Internet (HHH)	N/A	$1,218,433,438	$255,839,125
Internet Infrastructure (IIH)	N/A	N/A	$164,145,000
Market + 2000 (MKH)	N/A	N/A	$365,034,313
Pharmaceutical (PPH)	N/A	N/A	$786,759,775
Regional Bank (RKH)	N/A	N/A	$90,600,000
Semiconductor (SMH)	N/A	N/A	$315,603,810
Software (SWH)	N/A	N/A	$75,330,656
Telecommunications (TTH)	N/A	N/A	$369,541,813
Utilities (UTH)	N/A	N/A	$74,843,344
Wireless (WMH)	N/A	N/A	$126,750,000
NYSE-LISTED	ASSETS 12/31/1998	ASSETS 12/31/1999	ASSETS 12/31/2000
iShares S&P 100 Global (IOO)	N/A	N/A	$118,422,000
CHICAGO-LISTED	ASSETS 12/31/1998	ASSETS 12/31/1999	ASSETS 12/31/2000
iShares S&P 100 U.S. (OEF)	N/A	N/A	$181,975,500

Source: AMEX data as of 12/31/2000.

ETF SHARE VOLUME 1993–2000

AMEX LISTED INDEX SHARES & HOLDRs	1993 TOTAL	AVERAGE DAILY	
	53,012,800	226,550	
	1994 TOTAL	**AVERAGE DAILY**	
	102,025,600	404,863	
	1995 TOTAL	**AVERAGE DAILY**	
	82,199,100	331,979	
	1996 TOTAL	**AVERAGE DAILY**	
	293,819,800	1,208,300	
	1997 TOTAL	**AVERAGE DAILY**	
	933,991,758	3,691,667	
	1998 TOTAL	**AVERAGE DAILY**	
	2,380,790,600	9,884,702	
	1999 TOTAL	**AVERAGE DAILY**	
	4,382,435,800	19,382,780	
	2000 TOTAL	**AVERAGE DAILY**	
	11,257,067,113	45,752,750	
TOTAL ANNUAL SHARE VOLUME iSHARES MSCI	**VOLUME 1996**	**VOLUME 1997**	**VOLUME 1998**
	49,637,100	99,129,920	254,528,700
	VOLUME 1999	**VOLUME 2000**	
	282,926,100	277,746,500	
SELECT SPDRs	**VOLUME 1998**	**VOLUME 1999**	**VOLUME 2000**
Select SPDRs	2,952,800	347,748,200	550,498,700
HOLDRS	—	59,585,600	800,672,213
iShares S&P	—	—	72,609,600
iShares Russell	—	—	49,572,400
iShares Dow Jones	—	—	27,056,300
streetTRACKS Morgan Stanley	—	—	6,930,700
streetTRACKS Dow Jones	—	—	664,800
INDIVIDUAL ETFs *TOTAL ANNUAL SHARE VOLUME*			
S&P 500 SPDR (SPY)	**1993 VOLUME**	**1994 VOLUME**	**1995 VOLUME**
	53,012,800	102,025,600	79,280,100
	1996 VOLUME	**1997 VOLUME**	**1998 VOLUME**
	229,181,900	805,674,238	1,873,277,500
	1999 VOLUME	**2000 VOLUME**	
	1,824,143,200	1,932,970,300	

S&P 400 MidCap SPDR (MDY)	1995 Volume	1996 Volume	1997 Volume
	2,919,000	15,000,800	29,187,600
	1998 Volume	**1999 Volume**	**2000 Volume**
	100,909,800	213,182,000	212,466,000
	1998 Volume	**1999 Volume**	**2000 Volume**
DJIA DIAMONDS (DIA)	149,121,800	222,885,200	351,403,900
Nasdaq-100 Trust (QQQ)	—	1,431,965,500	6,972,864,800
iShares MSCI Series	**1998 Volume**	**1999 Volume**	**2000 Volume**
Australia (EWA)	5,328,300	5,424,800	4,974,500
Austria (EWO)	2,334,700	2,204,200	2,473,300
Belgium (EWK)	2,779,700	1,789,800	1,842,600
Brazil (EWZ)	—	—	445,600
Canada (EWC)	2,545,300	2,454,000	5,966,200
EMU (EZU)	—	—	1,596,500
France (EWQ)	6,479,800	6,946,500	10,384,400
Germany (EWG)	9,449,100	16,033,300	21,050,700
Hong Kong (EWH)	29,291,500	18,344,800	15,523,600
Italy (EWI)	9,651,500	4,851,700	4,823,200
Japan (EWJ)	75,115,300	127,226,400	112,165,800
Malaysia (EWM)	52,018,100	36,388,700	24,851,600
Mexico (EWW)	4,103,100	8,276,000	7,886,800
Netherland (EWN)	2,072,100	2,087,700	2,925,600
Singapore (EWS)	36,241,400	27,672,200	20,610,300
South Korea (EWY)	—	—	2,499,200
Spain (EWP)	3,590,400	2,596,500	2,544,300
Sweden (EWD)	1,301,200	1,470,200	2,162,100
Switzerland (EWL)	4,187,300	4,801,000	6,185,300
Taiwan (EWT)	—	—	8,790,900
U.K. (EWU)	8,039,900	14,358,300	18,044,000
Select Sector SPDRs	**1998 Volume**	**1999 Volume**	**2000 Volume**
Basic Industries (XLB)	10,800	17,891,500	23,593,400
Consumer Services (XLV)	73,400	8,015,600	12,684,300
Consumer Staples (XLP)	465,200	21,297,700	44,699,100
Cyclical/Transportation (XLY)	91,100	8,307,700	35,286,500
Energy (XLE)	165,600	44,071,600	87,438,200
Financial (XLF)	447,800	58,173,200	132,079,500
Industrial (XLI)	47,600	11,595,800	16,190,800
Technology (XLK)	1,488,400	170,130,800	169,306,900
Utilities (XLU)	162,900	8,264,300	29,220,000

(continues)

iSHARES DOW JONES	1998 VOLUME	1999 VOLUME	2000 VOLUME
US Basic Materials (IYM)	—	—	332,600
US Chemicals (IYD)	—	—	97,400
US Consumer Cyclical (IYC)	—	—	240,400
US Energy (IYE)	—	—	3,950,900
US Financial Sector (IYF)	—	—	3,999,300
US Financial Services (IYG)	—	—	773,900
US Healthcare (IYH)	—	—	3,027,600
US Industrial (IYJ)	—	—	203,500
US Internet (IYV)	—	—	3,140,900
US Non-Consumer Cyclical (IYK)	—	—	321,000
US Real Estate (IYR)	—	—	2,426,300
US Technology (IYW)	—	—	3,346,500
US Telecommunications (IYZ)	—	—	1,869,800
US Total Market (IYY)	—	—	1,760,800
US Utilities (IDU)	—	—	1,565,400
iSHARES RUSSELL	**1998 VOLUME**	**1999 VOLUME**	**2000 VOLUME**
Russell 1000 (IWB)	—	—	3,497,800
Russell 1000 Growth (IWF)	—	—	4,819,100
Russell 1000 Value (IWD)	—	—	8,568,900
Russell 2000 (IWM)	—	—	17,219,900
Russell 2000 Growth (IWO)	—	—	5,203,300
Russell 2000 Value (IWN)	—	—	2,267,600
Russell 3000 (IWV)	—	—	7,233,800
Russell 3000 Growth (IWZ)	—	—	318,400
Russell 3000 Value (IWW)	—	—	443,600
iSHARES S&P	**1998 VOLUME**	**1999 VOLUME**	**2000 VOLUME**
S&P 500 (IVV)	—	—	33,234,900
S&P 500/BARRA Growth (IVW)	—	—	5,057,100
S&P 500/BARRA Value (IVE)	—	—	6,893,500
S&P Europe 350 Index (IEV)	—	—	2,121,700
MidCap 400 (IJH)	—	—	14,234,800
MidCap 400/BAR. Growth (IJK)	—	—	1,942,900
MidCap 400/BARRA Value (IJJ)	—	—	1,245,000
SmallCap 600 (IJR)	—	—	5,828,000
SmallCap 600/BAR. Growth (IJT)	—	—	714,100
SmallCap 600/BAR. Value (IJS)	—	—	1,293,200
S&P/TSE 60 (IKC)	—	—	44,400

STREET**TRACKS**	1998 VOLUME	1999 VOLUME	2000 VOLUME
Dow Jones Global Titans (DGT)	—	—	199,400
DJ US Large Cap Growth (ELG)	—	—	94,100
DJ US Large Cap Value (ELV)	—	—	285,600
DJ US Small Cap Growth (DSG)	—	—	77,800
DJ US Small Cap Value (DSV)	—	—	7,900
DJ MS High Tech (MTK)	—	—	5,746,100
DJ MS Internet (MII)	—	—	1,184,600
FORTUNE INDEXES	1998 VOLUME	1999 VOLUME	2000 VOLUME
Fortune 500 (FFF)	—	—	1,070,400
Fortune e-50 (FEF)	—	—	540,500
HOLDRs	1998 VOLUME	1999 VOLUME	2000 VOLUME
Biotech (BBH)	—	6,245,100	191,395,900
Broadband (BDH)	—	—	38,489,200
Internet Architecture (IAH)	—	—	18,762,200
Internet Bus. to Bus. (BHH)	—	—	104,944,300
Internet (HHH)	—	53,340,500	224,810,700
Internet Infrastructure (IIH)	—	—	47,153,119
Market + 2000 (MKH)	—	—	3,444,800
Pharmaceutical (PPH)	—	—	36,422,400
Regional Bank (RKH)	—	—	4,535,300
Semiconductor (SMH)	—	—	92,513,400
Software (SWH)	—	—	2,937,900
Telecommunications (TTH)	—	—	30,613,594
Utilities (UTH)	—	—	3,571,000
Wireless (WMH)	—	—	1,078,400

Source: AMEX data as of 12/31/2000.

ETFs Trading on U.S. Markets

BROAD-BASED DOMESTIC ETFs (INCLUDING SIZE AND STYLE-BASED ETFs)

SPDRs (SPY)

FUND INFORMATION

Expense Ratio:	0.17%
Total Net Assets:	$30,035,380,000
Structure:	Unit Inv Trust
Benchmark:	S&P 500
Options:	Yes
Initial Divisor:	1/10
Min. Investment:	1 Share
Date of Inception:	29-Jan–93
52 Week Range:	108.04–153.59
2000 Total Dist.:	1.51

FUNDAMENTALS

Med Mkt Cap:	$60,768,000,000
P/E Ratio:	28.60
P/B Ratio:	6.70
P/C Ratio:	19.90
Standard Dev:	19.77
Sharpe Ratio:	−0.09
Alpha:	−0.10
Beta:	1.00
3 Yr Earn Gr:	16.90
1 Yr Fwd Gr:	4.70
12 Month Yield:	1.18

PREMIUM/DISCOUNT (6/29/2001)

P/D Close:	N/A
P/D Midpoint:	0.3%

TICKERS

Symbol:	SPY	ECash:	SXV.EU
NAV:	SXV	TCash:	SXV.TC
Close:	SXV.NV	Div:	SXV.DP
Shares:	SXV.SO	Index:	SPX

TOP 10 HOLDINGS

1) General Electric Co	3.98%
2) Microsoft Corp	2.80%
3) ExxonMobil Corp	2.70%
4) Pfizer Inc	2.48%
5) Citigroup Inc	2.16%
6) Wal-Mart Stores	2.16%
7) AIG Inc	1.79%
8) Intel Corp	1.70%
9) Merck & Co Inc	1.68%
10) AOL Time Warner	1.66%

SECTOR BREAKDOWN

Utilities:	3.30%
Energy:	7.50%
Financials:	17.80%
Industrial Cyclicals:	12.10%
Consumer Durables:	1.80%
Consumer Staples:	6.40%
Services:	11.70%
Retail:	6.50%
Health:	12.90%
Technology:	19.90%

FUND MANAGEMENT

Manager:	State Street Global
Web Site:	http://www.amex.com/
Telephone:	800–843–2639
Specialist:	Spear, Leeds
Distributor:	ALPS Mutual Funds
Administrator:	N/A
Sponsor:	PDR Services, LLC
Exchange:	AMEX

1 Yr	3 Yr	5 Yr	2000	1999	1998	1997
−14.19	4.01	14.44	−9.73	20.39	28.69	33.48

Source: AMEX and Morningstar data as of 6/30/2001.

MidCap SPDRs (MDY)

Fund Information

Expense Ratio:	0.25%
Total Net Assets:	$4,188,800,000
Structure:	Unit Inv Trust
Benchmark:	S&P MidCap 400
Options:	Yes
Initial Divisor:	1/5
Min. Investment:	1 Share
Date of Inception:	04-May-95
52 Week Range:	79.00–101.12
2000 Total Dist.:	0.78

Fundamentals

Med Mkt Cap:	$2,661,000,000
P/E Ratio:	24.80
P/B Ratio:	4.20
P/C Ratio:	18.00
Standard Dev:	26.12
Sharpe Ratio:	0.36
Alpha:	10.02
Beta:	1.03
3 Yr Earn Gr:	14.20
1 Yr Fwd Gr:	10.00
12 Month Yield:	0.60

Premium/Discount (6/29/2001)

P/D Close:	0.07%
P/D Midpoint:	0%

Tickers

Symbol:	MDY	ECash:	MXV.EU
NAV:	MXV	TCash:	MXV.TC
Close:	MXV.NV	Div:	MXV.DP
Shares:	MXV.SO	Index:	MID

Top 10 Holdings

1) Genzyme Corp	1.11%
2) Electronic Arts Inc	0.94%
3) M & T Bank Corp	0.88%
4) SunGuard Data Syst	0.85%
5) Millennium Pharma	0.84%
6) DST Systems Inc	0.78%
7) Waters Corp	0.78%
8) BJ Services Corp	0.76%
9) IDEC Pharma Corp	0.74%
10) RJ Reynolds	0.74%

Sector Breakdown

Utilities:	8.10%
Energy:	7.70%
Financials:	16.20%
Industrial Cyclicals:	10.60%
Consumer Durables:	4.00%
Consumer Staples:	4.10%
Services:	15.40%
Retail:	4.30%
Health:	12.10%
Technology:	17.70%

Fund Management

Manager:	Bank of New York
Web Site:	http://www.amex.com/
Telephone:	800–843–2639
Specialist:	Susquehanna
Distributor:	ALPS Mutual Funds
Administrator:	PDR Services LLC
Sponsor:	N/A
Exchange:	AMEX

1 Yr	3 Yr	5 Yr	2000	1999	1998	1997
7.97	13.79	18.25	17.31	15.51	17.32	31.88

Source: AMEX and Morningstar data as of 6/30/2001.

NASDAQ 100 TRUST SHARES (QQQ)

FUND INFORMATION

Expense Ratio:	0.18%
Total Net Assets:	$24,226,460,000
Structure:	Unit Inv Trust
Benchmark:	Nasdaq–100
Options:	Yes
Initial Divisor:	1/40
Min. Investment:	1 Share
Date of Inception:	10-Mar–99
52 Week Range:	33.60–103.51
2000 Total Dist.:	0.00

FUNDAMENTALS

Med Mkt Cap:	$18,361,000,000
P/E Ratio:	42.60
P/B Ratio:	7.90
P/C Ratio:	28.40
Standard Dev:	N/A
Sharpe Ratio:	N/A
Alpha:	N/A
Beta:	N/A
3 Yr Earn Gr:	37.10
1 Yr Fwd Gr:	−2.60
12 Month Yield:	N/A

PREMIUM/DISCOUNT (6/29/2001)

P/D Close:	0.19%
P/D Midpoint:	0.96%

TICKERS

Symbol:	QQQ	ECash:	QXV.EU
NAV:	QXV	TCash:	QXV.TC
Close:	QXV.NV	Div:	QXV.DP
Shares:	QXV.SO	Index:	NDX

TOP 10 HOLDINGS

1) Microsoft Corp	9.48%
2) Intel Corp	5.85%
3) QUALCOMM Inc	4.86%
4) Cisco Sytems	3.84%
5) Oracle Corp	3.29%
6) Amgen	2.76%
7) VoiceStream Wireless	2.42%
8) JDS Uniphase Corp	2.34%
9) Dell Computer Corp	2.31%
10) Sun Microsystems	2.06%

SECTOR BREAKDOWN

Utilities:	0.00%
Energy:	0.00%
Financials:	0.90%
Industrial Cyclicals:	1.30%
Consumer Durables:	0.00%
Consumer Staples:	0.00%
Services:	15.30%
Retail:	3.50%
Health:	10.50%
Technology:	68.50%

FUND MANAGEMENT

Manager:	Bank of New York
Web Site:	http://www.amex.com/
Telephone:	800–843–2639
Specialist:	Susquehanna
Distributor:	ALPS Mutual Funds
Administrator:	N/A
Sponsor:	Nasdaq Investment
Exchange:	AMEX

1 Yr	3 Yr	5 Yr	2000	1999	1998	1997
−50.76	—	—	−36.12	—	—	—

Source: AMEX and Morningstar data as of 6/30/2001.

DIAMONDS Trust Series I (DIA)

Fund Information

Expense Ratio:	0.18%
Total Net Assets:	$2,696,180,000
Structure:	Unit Inv Trust
Benchmark:	DJ Ind. Ave.
Options:	No
Initial Divisor:	1/100
Min. Investment:	1 Share
Date of Inception:	20-Jan–98
52 Week Range:	91.00–114.09
2000 Total Dist.:	1.05

Fundamentals

Med Mkt Cap:	$93,598,000,000
P/E Ratio:	24.40
P/B Ratio:	5.80
P/C Ratio:	16.50
Standard Dev:	19.84
Sharpe Ratio:	0.10
Alpha:	2.98
Beta:	0.87
3 Yr Earn Gr:	12.30
1 Yr Fwd Gr:	0.10
12 Month Yield:	1.54

Premium/Discount (6/29/2001)

P/D Close:	0.09%
P/D Midpoint:	0.13%

Tickers

Symbol:	DIA	ECash:	DXV.EU
NAV:	DXV	TCash:	DXV.TC
Close:	DXV.NV	Div:	DXV.DP
Shares:	DXV.SO	Index:	INDU

Top 10 Holdings

1) Minnesota Mining	6.82%
2) IBM	6.32%
3) Johnson & Johnson	5.74%
4) ExxonMobil Corp	5.32%
5) Merck & Co Inc	4.98%
6) United Technologies	4.81%
7) Procter & Gamble	4.11%
8) Boeing Co	3.66%
9) Microsoft Corp	3.59%
10) General Motors Co	3.40%

Sector Breakdown

Utilities:	0.00%
Energy:	5.30%
Financials:	8.50%
Industrial Cyclicals:	32.40%
Consumer Durables:	6.30%
Consumer Staples:	9.70%
Services:	7.50%
Retail:	6.00%
Health:	10.10%
Technology:	14.20%

Fund Management

Manager:	State Street Global
Web Site:	http://www.amex.com/
Telephone:	800–843–2639
Specialist:	Spear, Leeds
Distributor:	ALPS Mutual Funds
Administrator:	N/A
Sponsor:	PDR Services, LLC
Exchange:	AMEX

1 Yr	3 Yr	5 Yr	2000	1999	1998	1997
2.38	7.00	—	−5.92	27.56	—	—

Source: AMEX and Morningstar data as of 6/30/2001.

iSHARES S&P 500 INDEX (IVV)

FUND INFORMATION

Expense Ratio:	0.09%
Total Net Assets:	$2,576,280,000
Structure:	Open-Ended
Benchmark:	S&P 500
Options:	No
Initial Divisor:	1/10
Min. Investment:	1 Share
Date of Inception:	15-May–00
52 Week Range:	108.38–153.47
2000 Total Dist.:	0.84

FUNDAMENTALS

Med Mkt Cap:	$60,833,000,000
P/E Ratio:	28.60
P/B Ratio:	6.70
P/C Ratio:	20.00
Standard Dev:	N/A
Sharpe Ratio:	N/A
Alpha:	N/A
Beta:	N/A
3 Yr Earn Gr:	17.00
1 Yr Fwd Gr:	4.70
12 Month Yield:	N/A

PREMIUM/DISCOUNT (6/29/2001)

P/D Close:	0.02%
P/D Midpoint:	0.37%

TICKERS

Symbol: IVV		ECash:	NNV.EU
NAV:	NNV	TCash:	NNV.TC
Close:	NNV.NV	Div:	NNV.DP
Shares:	NNV.SO	Index:	SPX

TOP 10 HOLDINGS

1) General Electric Co	3.99%
2) Microsoft Corp	2.81%
3) ExxonMobil Corp	2.71%
4) Pfizer Inc	2.49%
5) Wal-Mart Stores	2.17%
6) Citigroup Inc	2.17%
7) AIG Inc	1.80%
8) Intel Corp	1.70%
9) Merck & Co Inc	1.68%
10) AOL Time Warner	1.67%

SECTOR BREAKDOWN

Utilities:	3.30%
Energy:	7.50%
Financials:	17.80%
Industrial Cyclicals:	12.10%
Consumer Durables:	1.80%
Consumer Staples:	6.40%
Services:	11.70%
Retail:	6.50%
Health:	13.00%
Technology:	20.00%

FUND MANAGEMENT

Manager:	Barclays Global
Web Site:	http://www.ishares.com/
Telephone:	800–474–2737
Specialist:	Hull Trading Co.
Distributor:	SEI Investments
Administrator:	Investors Bank & Trust
Sponsor:	N/A
Exchange:	AMEX

1 Yr	3 Yr	5 Yr	2000	1999	1998	1997
−14.53	—	—	—	—	—	—

Source: AMEX and Morningstar data as of 6/30/2001.

VIPERs Total Market Index Fund (VTI)

Fund Information

Expense Ratio:	0.15%
Total Net Assets:	$63,060,000
Structure:	Open-Ended
Benchmark:	Wishire 5000
Options:	No
Initial Divisor:	1/100
Min. Investment:	1 Share
Date of Inception:	31-May-01
52 Week Range:	109.00–118.00
2000 Total Dist.:	—

Fundamentals

Med Mkt Cap:	$36,795,000,000
P/E Ratio:	28.00
P/B Ratio:	6.20
P/C Ratio:	19.90
Standard Dev:	N/A
Sharpe Ratio:	N/A
Alpha:	N/A
Beta:	N/A
3 Yr Earn Gr:	16.80
1 Yr Fwd Gr:	5.10
12 Month Yield:	N/A

Premium/Discount (6/29/2001)

P/D Close:	N/A
P/D Midpoint:	N/A

Tickers

Symbol:	VTI	ECash:	TSJ.EU
NAV:	TSJ	TCash:	TSJ.TC
Close:	TSJ.NV	Div:	TSJ.DP
Shares:	TSJ.SO	Index:	TMW

Top 10 Holdings

1) General Electric Co	0.00%
2) Microsoft Corp	0.00%
3) ExxonMobil Corp	0.00%
4) Pfizer Inc	0.00%
5) Citigroup, Inc	0.00%
6) Wal-Mart Stores	0.00%
7) AIG	0.00%
8) Intel Corp	0.00%
9) Merck & Co Inc	0.00%
10) AOL Time Warner	0.00%

Sector Breakdown

Utilities:	3.60%
Energy:	6.30%
Financials:	19.50%
Industrial Cyclicals:	10.40%
Consumer Durables:	2.10%
Consumer Staples:	5.80%
Services:	13.60%
Retail:	6.30%
Health:	13.30%
Technology:	19.20%

Fund Management

Manager:	The Vanguard Group
Web Site:	http://www.vanguard.com/
Telephone:	866–499–8473
Specialist:	Spear, Leeds
Distributor:	Vanguard Marketing
Administrator:	JP Morgan
Sponsor:	N/A
Exchange:	AMEX

1 Yr	3 Yr	5 Yr	2000	1999	1998	1997
—	—	—	—	—	—	—

Source: AMEX and Morningstar data as of 6/30/2001.

iShares Dow Jones US Total Market Ind (IYY)

Fund Information

Expense Ratio:	0.20%
Total Net Assets:	$65,580,000
Structure:	Open-Ended
Benchmark:	DJ US Tot. Market
Options:	No
Initial Divisor:	1/5
Min. Investment:	1 Share
Date of Inception:	12-Jun-00
52 Week Range:	50.00–71.97
2000 Total Dist.:	0.25

Fundamentals

Med Mkt Cap:	$43,576,000,000
P/E Ratio:	28.40
P/B Ratio:	6.40
P/C Ratio:	20.20
Standard Dev:	N/A
Sharpe Ratio:	N/A
Alpha:	N/A
Beta:	N/A
3 Yr Earn Gr:	17.10
1 Yr Fwd Gr:	5.90
12 Month Yield:	N/A

Premium/Discount (6/29/2001)

P/D Close:	0.47%
P/D Midpoint:	0.34%

Tickers

Symbol:	IYY	ECash:	NLA.EU
NAV:	NLA	TCash:	NLA.TC
Close:	NLA.NV	Div:	NLA.DP
Shares:	NLA.SO	Index:	DJUS

Top 10 Holdings

1) General Electric Co	3.68%
2) ExxonMobil Corp	2.49%
3) Pfizer Inc	2.29%
4) Microsoft Corp	2.23%
5) Citigroup Inc	2.02%
6) Merck & Co Inc	1.55%
7) AOL Time Warner	1.48%
8) Intel Corp	1.48%
9) IBM	1.48%
10) AIG Inc	1.42%

Sector Breakdown

Utilities:	3.50%
Energy:	6.50%
Financials:	18.50%
Industrial Cyclicals:	11.70%
Consumer Durables:	2.00%
Consumer Staples:	5.50%
Services:	13.00%
Retail:	5.60%
Health:	13.40%
Technology:	20.30%

Fund Management

Manager:	Barclays Global
Web Site:	http://www.ishares.com/
Telephone:	800–474–2737
Specialist:	Hull Trading Co.
Distributor:	SEI Investments
Administrator:	Investors Bank & Trust
Sponsor:	N/A
Exchange:	AMEX

1 Yr	3 Yr	5 Yr	2000	1999	1998	1997
−14.10	—	—	—	—	—	—

Source: AMEX and Morningstar data as of 6/30/2001.

iShares S&P 100 Index (OEF)

Fund Information

Expense Ratio:	0.20%
Total Net Assets:	$244,090,000
Structure:	Open-Ended
Benchmark:	S&P 100
Options:	Yes
Initial Divisor:	—
Min. Investment:	1 Share
Date of Inception:	27-Oct-00
52 Week Range:	54.79–76.13
2000 Total Dist.:	0.15

Fundamentals

Med Mkt Cap:	$145,365,000,000
P/E Ratio:	30.30
P/B Ratio:	7.60
P/C Ratio:	21.70
Standard Dev:	N/A
Sharpe Ratio:	N/A
Alpha:	N/A
Beta:	N/A
3 Yr Earn Gr:	17.50
1 Yr Fwd Gr:	6.70
12 Month Yield:	N/A

Premium/Discount (6/29/2001)

P/D Close:	N/A
P/D Midpoint:	N/A

Tickers

Symbol: OEF	ECash:	—
NAV: —	TCash:	—
Close: —	Div:	—
Shares: —	Index:	N/A

Top 10 Holdings

1) General Electric Co	7.26%
2) ExxonMobil Corp	4.62%
3) Pfizer Inc	4.44%
4) Cisco Sytems	4.20%
5) Citigroup Inc	3.92%
6) Wal-Mart Stores	3.63%
7) Microsoft Corp	3.53%
8) American Intl Grp	3.50%
9) Merck & Co Inc	3.30%
10) Intel Corp	3.09%

Sector Breakdown

Utilities:	2.30%
Energy:	6.80%
Financials:	16.60%
Industrial Cyclicals:	14.50%
Consumer Durables:	2.00%
Consumer Staples:	6.10%
Services:	7.00%
Retail:	6.10%
Health:	14.10%
Technology:	24.40%

Fund Management

Manager:	Barclays Global
Web Site:	http://www.ishares.com/
Telephone:	800–474–2737
Specialist:	Wolverine Trading
Distributor:	N/A
Administrator:	N/A
Sponsor:	N/A
Exchange:	CBOE

1 Yr	3 Yr	5 Yr	2000	1999	1998	1997
—	—	—	—	—	—	—

Source: AMEX and Morningstar data as of 6/30/2001.

Fortune 500 Index (FFF)

Fund Information

Expense Ratio:	0.20%
Total Net Assets:	$47,930,000
Structure:	Open-Ended
Benchmark:	Fortune 500
Options:	Yes
Initial Divisor:	1/10
Min. Investment:	1 Share
Date of Inception:	10-Oct–00
52 Week Range:	77.05–98.91
2000 Total Dist.:	—

Fundamentals

Med Mkt Cap:	$64,990,000,000
P/E Ratio:	27.90
P/B Ratio:	6.60
P/C Ratio:	19.60
Standard Dev:	N/A
Sharpe Ratio:	N/A
Alpha:	N/A
Beta:	N/A
3 Yr Earn Gr:	16.90
1 Yr Fwd Gr:	3.40
12 Month Yield:	N/A

Premium/Discount (6/29/2001)

P/D Close:	0.94%
P/D Midpoint:	0.25%

Tickers

Symbol:	FFF	ECash:	FFY.EU
NAV:	FFY	TCash:	FFY.TC
Close:	FFY.NV	Div:	FFY.DP
Shares:	FFY.SO	Index:	FFX

Top 10 Holdings

1) General Electric Co	4.40%
2) Microsoft Corp	3.09%
3) XOMA Corp	2.98%
4) Pfizer Inc	2.74%
5) Citigroup Inc	2.40%
6) Wal-Mart Stores	2.39%
7) AIG Inc	1.99%
8) Intel Corp	1.88%
9) Merck & Co Inc	1.85%
10) AOL Time Warner	1.85%

Sector Breakdown

Utilities:	3.60%
Energy:	6.10%
Financials:	18.80%
Industrial Cyclicals:	11.40%
Consumer Durables:	1.90%
Consumer Staples:	6.60%
Services:	13.80%
Retail:	7.00%
Health:	12.90%
Technology:	18.00%

Fund Management

Manager:	State Street Global
Web Site:	http://www.amex.com/
Telephone:	866-787-2257
Specialist:	KV Executions Services
Distributor:	State Street Gl Cap
Administrator:	State Street Gl B&T
Sponsor:	N/A
Exchange:	AMEX

1 Yr	3 Yr	5 Yr	2000	1999	1998	1997
—	—	—	—	—	—	—

Source: AMEX and Morningstar data as of 6/30/2001.

iSHARES S&P 500/BARRA GROWTH INDEX (IVW)

FUND INFORMATION

Expense Ratio:	0.18%
Total Net Assets:	$228,380,000
Structure:	Open-Ended
Benchmark:	S&P 500/BARRA Gr
Options:	No
Initial Divisor:	1/10
Min. Investment:	1 Share
Date of Inception:	22-May–00
52 Week Range:	52.88–94.25
2000 Total Dist.:	0.27

FUNDAMENTALS

Med Mkt Cap:	$126,686,000,000
P/E Ratio:	36.20
P/B Ratio:	10.40
P/C Ratio:	25.50
Standard Dev:	N/A
Sharpe Ratio:	N/A
Alpha:	N/A
Beta:	N/A
3 Yr Earn Gr:	19.80
1 Yr Fwd Gr:	10.10
12 Month Yield:	N/A

PREMIUM/DISCOUNT (6/29/2001)

P/D Close:	0.65%
P/D Midpoint:	0.5%

TICKERS

Symbol: IVW		ECash:	NJG.EU
NAV:	NJG	TCash:	NJG.TC
Close:	NJG.NV	Div:	NJG.DP
Shares:	NJG.SO	Index:	SGX

TOP 10 HOLDINGS

1) General Electric Co	8.71%
2) Microsoft Corp	6.13%
3) Pfizer Inc	5.43%
4) Wal-Mart Stores	4.74%
5) AIG Inc	3.94%
6) Intel Corp	3.72%
7) Merck & Co Inc	3.68%
8) AOL Time Warner	3.65%
9) IBM	3.54%
10) Johnson & Johnson	2.55%

SECTOR BREAKDOWN

Utilities:	0.40%
Energy:	0.00%
Financials:	8.30%
Industrial Cyclicals:	10.70%
Consumer Durables:	0.30%
Consumer Staples:	9.80%
Services:	3.40%
Retail:	9.30%
Health:	25.60%
Technology:	32.20%

FUND MANAGEMENT

Manager:	Barclays Global
Web Site:	http://www.ishares.com/
Telephone:	800–474–2737
Specialist:	Hull Trading Co.
Distributor:	SEI Investments
Administrator:	Investors Bank & Trust
Sponsor:	N/A
Exchange:	AMEX

1 Yr	3 Yr	5 Yr	2000	1999	1998	1997
−30.93	—	—	—	—	—	—

Source: AMEX and Morningstar data as of 6/30/2001.

iSHARES S&P 500/BARRA VALUE INDEX (IVE)

FUND INFORMATION

Expense Ratio:	0.18%
Total Net Assets:	$447,110,000
Structure:	Open-Ended
Benchmark:	S&P 500/BARRA Val
Options:	No
Initial Divisor:	1/10
Min. Investment:	1 Share
Date of Inception:	22-May–00
52 Week Range:	55.00–67.00
2000 Total Dist.:	0.60

FUNDAMENTALS

Med Mkt Cap:	$33,598,000,000
P/E Ratio:	21.70
P/B Ratio:	3.40
P/C Ratio:	13.70
Standard Dev:	N/A
Sharpe Ratio:	N/A
Alpha:	N/A
Beta:	N/A
3 Yr Earn Gr:	14.50
1 Yr Fwd Gr:	−0.30
12 Month Yield:	N/A

PREMIUM/DISCOUNT (6/29/2001)

P/D Close:	0.24%
P/D Midpoint:	0.09%

TICKERS

Symbol:	IVE	ECash:	NME.EU
NAV:	NME	TCash:	NME.TC
Close:	NME.NV	Div:	NME.DP
Shares:	NME.SO	Index:	SVX

TOP 10 HOLDINGS

1) ExxonMobil Corp	5.00%
2) Citigroup Inc	4.01%
3) SBC Communications	2.68%
4) Verizon Comm	2.36%
5) Royal Dutch Petrol Co	2.10%
6) Philip Morris Co Inc	1.87%
7) BankAmerica Corp	1.58%
8) JP Morgan Chase & Co	1.52%
9) Wells Fargo & Co	1.50%
10) Fannie Mae	1.42%

SECTOR BREAKDOWN

Utilities:	5.90%
Energy:	14.00%
Financials:	25.90%
Industrial Cyclicals:	13.20%
Consumer Durables:	3.10%
Consumer Staples:	3.50%
Services:	18.80%
Retail:	4.10%
Health:	2.00%
Technology:	9.50%

FUND MANAGEMENT

Manager:	Barclays Global
Web Site:	http://www.ishares.com/
Telephone:	800–474–2737
Specialist:	Hull Trading Co.
Distributor:	SEI Investments
Administrator:	Investors Bank & Trust
Sponsor:	N/A
Exchange:	AMEX

1 Yr	3 Yr	5 Yr	2000	1999	1998	1997
7.20	—	—	—	—	—	—

Source: AMEX and Morningstar data as of 6/30/2001.

iShares Russell 3000 Index (IWV)

Fund Information

Expense Ratio:	0.20%
Total Net Assets:	$760,370,000
Structure:	Open-Ended
Benchmark:	Russell 3000
Options:	No
Initial Divisor:	1/10
Min. Investment:	1 Share
Date of Inception:	22-May–00
52 Week Range:	59.44–84.69
2000 Total Dist.:	0.36

Fundamentals

Med Mkt Cap:	$42,222,000,000
P/E Ratio:	28.20
P/B Ratio:	6.30
P/C Ratio:	20.10
Standard Dev:	N/A
Sharpe Ratio:	N/A
Alpha:	N/A
Beta:	N/A
3 Yr Earn Gr:	17.20
1 Yr Fwd Gr:	4.80
12 Month Yield:	N/A

Premium/Discount (6/29/2001)

P/D Close:	0.39%
P/D Midpoint:	0.26%

Tickers

Symbol: IWV		ECash:	NMV.EU
NAV:	NMV	TCash:	NMV.TC
Close:	NMV.NV	Div:	NMV.DP
Shares:	NMV.SO	Index:	RRY

Top 10 Holdings

1) General Electric Co	3.69%
2) ExxonMobil Corp	2.50%
3) Pfizer Inc	2.30%
4) Citigroup Inc	2.01%
5) Microsoft Corp	1.93%
6) Intel Corp	1.57%
7) Merck & Co Inc	1.56%
8) IBM	1.50%
9) AIG Inc	1.44%
10) AOL Time Warner	1.42%

Sector Breakdown

Utilities:	3.70%
Energy:	6.30%
Financials:	18.60%
Industrial Cyclicals:	11.20%
Consumer Durables:	2.10%
Consumer Staples:	5.50%
Services:	12.90%
Retail:	5.50%
Health:	13.60%
Technology:	20.60%

Fund Management

Manager:	Barclays Global
Web Site:	http://www.ishares.com/
Telephone:	800–474–2737
Specialist:	Hull Trading Co.
Distributor:	SEI Investments
Administrator:	Investors Bank & Trust
Sponsor:	N/A
Exchange:	AMEX

1 Yr	3 Yr	5 Yr	2000	1999	1998	1997
−13.01	—	—	—	—	—	—

Source: AMEX and Morningstar data as of 6/30/2001.

iSHARES RUSSELL 3000 GROWTH INDEX (IWZ)

FUND INFORMATION

Expense Ratio:	0.25%
Total Net Assets:	$22,190,000
Structure:	Open-Ended
Benchmark:	Russell 3000 Growth
Options:	No
Initial Divisor:	1/10
Min. Investment:	1 Share
Date of Inception:	24-Jul-00
52 Week Range:	25.00–71.97
2000 Total Dist.:	0.03

FUNDAMENTALS

Med Mkt Cap:	$65,990,000,000
P/E Ratio:	36.80
P/B Ratio:	9.10
P/C Ratio:	25.60
Standard Dev:	N/A
Sharpe Ratio:	N/A
Alpha:	N/A
Beta:	N/A
3 Yr Earn Gr:	24.10
1 Yr Fwd Gr:	6.20
12 Month Yield:	N/A

PREMIUM/DISCOUNT (6/29/2001)

P/D Close:	1.12%
P/D Midpoint:	0.66%

TICKERS

Symbol:	IWZ	ECash:	NBE.EU
NAV:	NBE	TCash:	NBE.TC
Close:	NBE.NV	Div:	NBE.DP
Shares:	NBE.SO	Index:	RAG

TOP 10 HOLDINGS

1) General Electric Co	8.29%
2) Pfizer Inc	5.67%
3) Microsoft Corp	4.76%
4) Intel Corp	3.89%
5) AOL Time Warner	3.23%
6) Wal-Mart Stores	2.75%
7) IBM	2.74%
8) Cisco Systems	2.50%
9) Home Depot Inc	2.20%
10) Merck & Co Inc	1.92%

SECTOR BREAKDOWN

Utilities:	0.70%
Energy:	2.10%
Financials:	2.70%
Industrial Cyclicals:	10.50%
Consumer Durables:	0.80%
Consumer Staples:	3.30%
Services:	7.50%
Retail:	8.60%
Health:	20.80%
Technology:	43.10%

FUND MANAGEMENT

Manager:	Barclays Global
Web Site:	http://www.ishares.com/
Telephone:	800–474–2737
Specialist:	Hull Trading Co.
Distributor:	SEI Investments
Administrator:	Investors Bank & Trust
Sponsor:	N/A
Exchange:	AMEX

1 Yr	3 Yr	5 Yr	2000	1999	1998	1997
—	—	—	—	—	—	—

Source: AMEX and Morningstar data as of 6/30/2001.

iShares Russell 3000 Value Index (IWW)

Fund Information

Expense Ratio:	0.25%
Total Net Assets:	$33,790,000
Structure:	Open-Ended
Benchmark:	Russell 3000 Value
Options:	No
Initial Divisor:	1/10
Min. Investment:	1 Share
Date of Inception:	24-Jul–00
52 Week Range:	36.00–78.53
2000 Total Dist.:	0.64

Top 10 Holdings

1) ExxonMobil Corp	4.20%
2) Citigroup Inc	3.38%
3) AIG Inc	2.41%
4) SBC Communications	2.25%
5) Verizon Comm	1.99%
6) Johnson & Johnson	1.71%
7) Philip Morris Co Inc	1.57%
8) BankAmerica Corp	1.34%
9) Merck & Co Inc	1.31%
10) JP Morgan Chase & Co	1.27%

Fundamentals

Med Mkt Cap:	$32,677,000,000
P/E Ratio:	22.20
P/B Ratio:	4.30
P/C Ratio:	14.60
Standard Dev:	N/A
Sharpe Ratio:	N/A
Alpha:	N/A
Beta:	N/A
3 Yr Earn Gr:	13.00
1 Yr Fwd Gr:	4.10
12 Month Yield:	N/A

Sector Breakdown

Utilities:	5.80%
Energy:	9.10%
Financials:	30.70%
Industrial Cyclicals:	11.80%
Consumer Durables:	2.90%
Consumer Staples:	7.30%
Services:	16.80%
Retail:	3.30%
Health:	8.20%
Technology:	4.00%

Premium/Discount (6/29/2001)

P/D Close:	0.01%
P/D Midpoint:	N/A

Tickers

Symbol: IWW		ECash:	NNW.EU
NAV:	NNW	TCash:	NNW.TC
Close:	NNW.NV	Div:	NNW.DP
Shares:	NNW.SO	Index:	RAV

Fund Management

Manager:	Barclays Global
Web Site:	http://www.ishares.com/
Telephone:	800–474–2737
Specialist:	Hull Trading Co.
Distributor:	SEI Investments
Administrator:	Investors Bank & Trust
Sponsor:	N/A
Exchange:	AMEX

1 Yr	3 Yr	5 Yr	2000	1999	1998	1997
—	—	—	—	—	—	—

Source: AMEX and Morningstar data as of 6/30/2001.

iShares Russell 1000 Index (IWB)

Fund Information

Expense Ratio:	0.15%
Total Net Assets:	$281,750,000
Structure:	Open-Ended
Benchmark:	Russell 1000
Options:	No
Initial Divisor:	1/10
Min. Investment:	1 Share
Date of Inception:	15-May–00
52 Week Range:	56.98–81.78
2000 Total Dist.:	0.45

Fundamentals

Med Mkt Cap:	$49,602,000,000
P/E Ratio:	28.60
P/B Ratio:	6.50
P/C Ratio:	20.30
Standard Dev:	N/A
Sharpe Ratio:	N/A
Alpha:	N/A
Beta:	N/A
3 Yr Earn Gr:	17.30
1 Yr Fwd Gr:	4.40
12 Month Yield:	N/A

Premium/Discount (6/29/2001)

P/D Close:	0.27%
P/D Midpoint:	0.3%

Tickers

Symbol:	IWB	ECash:	NJB.EU
NAV:	NJB	TCash:	NJB.TC
Close:	NJB.NV	Div:	NJB.DP
Shares:	NJB.SO	Index:	RIY

Top 10 Holdings

1) General Electric Co	3.97%
2) ExxonMobil Corp	2.70%
3) Pfizer Inc	2.47%
4) Citigroup Inc	2.16%
5) Microsoft Corp	2.08%
6) Intel Corp	1.70%
7) Merck & Co Inc	1.68%
8) IBM	1.62%
9) AIG Inc	1.55%
10) AOL Time Warner	1.53%

Sector Breakdown

Utilities:	3.60%
Energy:	6.40%
Financials:	18.40%
Industrial Cyclicals:	10.70%
Consumer Durables:	1.90%
Consumer Staples:	5.70%
Services:	12.90%
Retail:	5.60%
Health:	13.60%
Technology:	21.20%

Fund Management

Manager:	Barclays Global
Web Site:	http://www.ishares.com/
Telephone:	800–474–2737
Specialist:	Hull Trading Co.
Distributor:	SEI Investments
Administrator:	Investors Bank & Trust
Sponsor:	N/A
Exchange:	AMEX

1 Yr	3 Yr	5 Yr	2000	1999	1998	1997
−14.51	—	—	—	—	—	—

Source: AMEX and Morningstar data as of 6/30/2001.

iSHARES RUSSELL 1000 GROWTH INDEX (IWF)

FUND INFORMATION

Expense Ratio:	0.20%
Total Net Assets:	$353,600,000
Structure:	Open-Ended
Benchmark:	Russell 1000 Growth
Options:	No
Initial Divisor:	1/10
Min. Investment:	1 Share
Date of Inception:	22-May–00
52 Week Range:	46.66–92.33
2000 Total Dist.:	0.20

FUNDAMENTALS

Med Mkt Cap:	$78,485,000,000
P/E Ratio:	37.40
P/B Ratio:	9.40
P/C Ratio:	25.90
Standard Dev:	N/A
Sharpe Ratio:	N/A
Alpha:	N/A
Beta:	N/A
3 Yr Earn Gr:	24.00
1 Yr Fwd Gr:	6.20
12 Month Yield:	N/A

PREMIUM/DISCOUNT (6/29/2001)

P/D Close:	1.01%
P/D Midpoint:	0.87%

TICKERS

Symbol:	IWF	ECash:	NBF.EU
NAV:	NBF	TCash:	NBF.TC
Close:	NBF.NV	Div:	NBF.DP
Shares:	NBF.SO	Index:	RLG

TOP 10 HOLDINGS

1) General Electric Co	8.96%
2) Pfizer Inc	6.13%
3) Microsoft Corp	5.14%
4) Intel Corp	4.20%
5) AOL Time Warner	3.49%
6) Wal-Mart Stores	2.96%
7) IBM	2.95%
8) Cisco Systems	2.70%
9) Home Depot Inc	2.37%
10) Merck & Co Inc	2.07%

SECTOR BREAKDOWN

Utilities:	0.70%
Energy:	1.80%
Financials:	2.20%
Industrial Cyclicals:	10.40%
Consumer Durables:	0.60%
Consumer Staples:	3.40%
Services:	6.80%
Retail:	8.80%
Health:	20.80%
Technology:	44.50%

FUND MANAGEMENT

Manager:	Barclays Global
Web Site:	http://www.ishares.com/
Telephone:	800–474–2737
Specialist:	Hull Trading Co.
Distributor:	SEI Investments
Administrator:	Investors Bank & Trust
Sponsor:	N/A
Exchange:	AMEX

1 Yr	3 Yr	5 Yr	2000	1999	1998	1997
−35.28	—	—	—	—	—	—

Source: AMEX and Morningstar data as of 6/30/2001.

ISHARES RUSSELL 1000 VALUE INDEX (IWD)

FUND INFORMATION

Expense Ratio:	0.20%
Total Net Assets:	$323,020,000
Structure:	Open-Ended
Benchmark:	Russell 1000 Value
Options:	No
Initial Divisor:	1/10
Min. Investment:	1 Share
Date of Inception:	22-May–00
52 Week Range:	51.70–61.62
2000 Total Dist.:	0.44

FUNDAMENTALS

Med Mkt Cap:	$38,031,000,000
P/E Ratio:	22.50
P/B Ratio:	4.50
P/C Ratio:	14.70
Standard Dev:	N/A
Sharpe Ratio:	N/A
Alpha:	N/A
Beta:	N/A
3 Yr Earn Gr:	13.10
1 Yr Fwd Gr:	3.20
12 Month Yield:	N/A

PREMIUM/DISCOUNT (6/29/2001)

P/D Close:	N/A
P/D Midpoint:	N/A

TICKERS

Symbol: IWD	ECash:	NJU.EU
NAV: NJU	TCash:	NJU.TC
Close: NJU.NV	Div:	NJU.DP
Shares: NJU.SO	Index:	RLV

TOP 10 HOLDINGS

1) ExxonMobil Corp	4.52%
2) Citigroup Inc	3.63%
3) AIG Inc	2.60%
4) SBC Communications	2.42%
5) Verizon Comm	2.14%
6) Johnson & Johnson	1.84%
7) Philip Morris Co Inc	1.69%
8) BankAmerica Corp	1.45%
9) Merck & Co Inc	1.41%
10) JP Morgan Chase & Co	1.37%

SECTOR BREAKDOWN

Utilities:	5.80%
Energy:	9.80%
Financials:	30.20%
Industrial Cyclicals:	10.90%
Consumer Durables:	2.90%
Consumer Staples:	7.40%
Services:	17.30%
Retail:	3.20%
Health:	8.40%
Technology:	4.20%

FUND MANAGEMENT

Manager:	Barclays Global
Web Site:	http://www.ishares.com/
Telephone:	800–474–2737
Specialist:	Hull Trading Co.
Distributor:	SEI Investments
Administrator:	Investors Bank & Trust
Sponsor:	N/A
Exchange:	AMEX

1 Yr	3 Yr	5 Yr	2000	1999	1998	1997
8.50	—	—	—	—	—	—

Source: AMEX and Morningstar data as of 6/30/2001.

iShares Russell 2000 Index (IWM)

Fund Information

Expense Ratio:	0.20%
Total Net Assets:	$970,240,000
Structure:	Open-Ended
Benchmark:	Russell 2000
Options:	Yes
Initial Divisor:	1/5
Min. Investment:	1 Share
Date of Inception:	22-May–00
52 Week Range:	83.15–109.19
2000 Total Dist.:	0.85

Fundamentals

Med Mkt Cap:	$988,000,000
P/E Ratio:	22.80
P/B Ratio:	3.50
P/C Ratio:	16.00
Standard Dev:	N/A
Sharpe Ratio:	N/A
Alpha:	N/A
Beta:	N/A
3 Yr Earn Gr:	14.80
1 Yr Fwd Gr:	10.30
12 Month Yield:	N/A

Premium/Discount (6/29/2001)

P/D Close:	N/A
P/D Midpoint:	N/A

Tickers

Symbol: IWM		ECash:	NJM.EU
NAV:	NJM	TCash:	NJM.TC
Close:	NJM.NV	Div:	NJM.DP
Shares:	NJM.SO	Index:	RTY

Top 10 Holdings

1) Caremark Rx Inc	0.37%
2) Abercrombie & Fitch	0.37%
3) AmeriSource Health Corp	0.32%
4) AmeriCredit Corp	0.31%
5) Centex Corp	0.31%
6) Astoria Financial	0.30%
7) MDU Resources	0.29%
8) Bergen Brunswig Corp	0.28%
9) Gallagher A J & Co	0.27%
10) Health Net Inc	0.27%

Sector Breakdown

Utilities:	4.60%
Energy:	4.20%
Financials:	21.10%
Industrial Cyclicals:	17.50%
Consumer Durables:	4.00%
Consumer Staples:	3.10%
Services:	14.00%
Retail:	5.20%
Health:	13.00%
Technology:	13.20%

Fund Management

Manager:	Barclays Global
Web Site:	http://www.ishares.com/
Telephone:	800–474–2737
Specialist:	Susquehanna
Distributor:	SEI Investments
Administrator:	Investors Bank & Trust
Sponsor:	N/A
Exchange:	AMEX

1 Yr	3 Yr	5 Yr	2000	1999	1998	1997
−0.64	—	—	—	—	—	—

Source: AMEX and Morningstar data as of 6/30/2001.

iShares Russell 2000 Growth Index (IWO)

Fund Information

Expense Ratio:	0.25%
Total Net Assets:	$227,520,000
Structure:	Open-Ended
Benchmark:	Russell 2000 Growth
Options:	No
Initial Divisor:	1/5
Min. Investment:	1 Share
Date of Inception:	24-Jul–00
52 Week Range:	49.45–86.50
2000 Total Dist.:	0.06

Top 10 Holdings

1) Caremark Rx Inc	0.89%
2) Abercrombie & Fitch	0.89%
3) AmeriSource Health Corp	0.77%
4) AmeriCredit Corp	0.75%
5) Lincare Holdings Inc	0.63%
6) Laboratory Corp of Am	0.63%
7) Varian Medical Syst	0.59%
8) Enzon Inc	0.59%
9) Investors Finl Services	0.54%
10) Eaton Vance Corp	0.54%

Fundamentals

Med Mkt Cap:	$930,000,000
P/E Ratio:	27.80
P/B Ratio:	5.10
P/C Ratio:	21.00
Standard Dev:	N/A
Sharpe Ratio:	N/A
Alpha:	N/A
Beta:	N/A
3 Yr Earn Gr:	25.70
1 Yr Fwd Gr:	5.70
12 Month Yield:	N/A

Sector Breakdown

Utilities:	0.20%
Energy:	5.80%
Financials:	8.70%
Industrial Cyclicals:	11.70%
Consumer Durables:	2.80%
Consumer Staples:	1.80%
Services:	16.60%
Retail:	5.60%
Health:	20.90%
Technology:	26.00%

Premium/Discount (6/29/2001)

P/D Close:	N/A
P/D Midpoint:	N/A

Tickers

Symbol: IWO		ECash:	NLO.EU
NAV:	NLO	TCash:	NLO.TC
Close:	NLO.NV	Div:	NLO.DP
Shares:	NLO.SO	Index:	RUO

Fund Management

Manager:	Barclays Global
Web Site:	http://www.ishares.com/
Telephone:	800–474–2737
Specialist:	Susquehanna
Distributor:	SEI Investments
Administrator:	Investors Bank & Trust
Sponsor:	N/A
Exchange:	AMEX

1 Yr	3 Yr	5 Yr	2000	1999	1998	1997
—	—	—	—	—	—	—

Source: AMEX and Morningstar data as of 6/30/2001.

ISHARES RUSSELL 2000 VALUE INDEX (IWN)

FUND INFORMATION

Expense Ratio:	0.25%
Total Net Assets:	$407,230,000
Structure:	Open-Ended
Benchmark:	Russell 2000 Value
Options:	No
Initial Divisor:	1/5
Min. Investment:	1 Share
Date of Inception:	24-Jul–00
52 Week Range:	99.50–129.20
2000 Total Dist.:	0.89

FUNDAMENTALS

Med Mkt Cap:	$1,028,000,000
P/E Ratio:	19.20
P/B Ratio:	2.20
P/C Ratio:	11.40
Standard Dev:	N/A
Sharpe Ratio:	N/A
Alpha:	N/A
Beta:	N/A
3 Yr Earn Gr:	9.20
1 Yr Fwd Gr:	12.80
12 Month Yield:	N/A

PREMIUM/DISCOUNT (6/29/2001)

P/D Close:	N/A
P/D Midpoint:	N/A

TICKERS

Symbol:	IWN	ECash:	NAJ.EU
NAV:	NAJ	TCash:	NAJ.TC
Close:	NAJ.NV	Div:	NAJ.DP
Shares:	NAJ.SO	Index:	RUJ

TOP 10 HOLDINGS

1) Centex Corp	0.53%
2) Astoria Financial	0.51%
3) MDU Resources	0.49%
4) Bergen Brunswig Corp	0.48%
5) Health Net Inc	0.46%
6) INMC Mort REIT	0.42%
7) Allete	0.42%
8) Conectiv Inc	0.41%
9) Pactiv Corp	0.41%
10) Venator Group Inc	0.41%

SECTOR BREAKDOWN

Utilities:	8.10%
Energy:	3.00%
Financials:	30.80%
Industrial Cyclicals:	22.40%
Consumer Durables:	5.00%
Consumer Staples:	4.10%
Services:	11.90%
Retail:	4.80%
Health:	6.00%
Technology:	3.80%

FUND MANAGEMENT

Manager:	Barclays Global
Web Site:	http://www.ishares.com/
Telephone:	800–474–2737
Specialist:	Susquehanna
Distributor:	SEI Investments
Administrator:	Investors Bank & Trust
Sponsor:	N/A
Exchange:	AMEX

1 Yr	3 Yr	5 Yr	2000	1999	1998	1997
—	—	—	—	—	—	—

Source: AMEX and Morningstar data as of 6/30/2001.

iShares S&P MidCap 400 Index (IJH)

Fund Information

Expense Ratio:	0.20%
Total Net Assets:	$295,430,000
Structure:	Open-Ended
Benchmark:	S&P MidCap 400
Options:	No
Initial Divisor:	1/5
Min. Investment:	1 Share
Date of Inception:	22-May–00
52 Week Range:	86.32–110.17
2000 Total Dist.:	0.77

Fundamentals

Med Mkt Cap:	$2,706,000,000
P/E Ratio:	25.60
P/B Ratio:	4.40
P/C Ratio:	18.50
Standard Dev:	N/A
Sharpe Ratio:	N/A
Alpha:	N/A
Beta:	N/A
3 Yr Earn Gr:	14.90
1 Yr Fwd Gr:	10.80
12 Month Yield:	N/A

Premium/Discount (6/29/2001)

P/D Close:	0.06%
P/D Midpoint:	0.03%

Tickers

Symbol: IJH		ECash:	NJH.EU
NAV:	NJH	TCash:	NJH.TC
Close:	NJH.NV	Div:	NJH.DP
Shares:	NJH.SO	Index:	MID

Top 10 Holdings

1) Concord EFS Inc	1.12%
2) Genzyme Corp	1.10%
3) Electronic Arts Inc	0.92%
4) M & T Bank Corp	0.86%
5) SunGuard Data Syst	0.84%
6) Millennium Pharma	0.83%
7) DST Systems	0.77%
8) Waters Corp	0.77%
9) BJ Services Corp	0.75%
10) IDEC Pharma Corp	0.73%

Sector Breakdown

Utilities:	7.10%
Energy:	7.50%
Financials:	16.20%
Industrial Cyclicals:	10.00%
Consumer Durables:	4.10%
Consumer Staples:	4.00%
Services:	15.10%
Retail:	4.40%
Health:	13.10%
Technology:	18.50%

Fund Management

Manager:	Barclays Global
Web Site:	http://www.ishares.com/
Telephone:	800–474–2737
Specialist:	Hull Trading Co.
Distributor:	SEI Investments
Administrator:	Investors Bank & Trust
Sponsor:	N/A
Exchange:	AMEX

1 Yr	3 Yr	5 Yr	2000	1999	1998	1997
8.07	—	—	—	—	—	—

Source: AMEX and Morningstar data as of 6/30/2001.

iShares S&P MidCap 400/Barra Growth (IJK)

Fund Information

Expense Ratio:	0.25%
Total Net Assets:	$111,120,000
Structure:	Open-Ended
Benchmark:	S&P 400/BARRA Gr
Options:	No
Initial Divisor:	1/2
Min. Investment:	1 Share
Date of Inception:	24-Jul-00
52 Week Range:	93.24–151.50
2000 Total Dist.:	0.47

Top 10 Holdings

1) Concord EFS Inc	2.47%
2) Genzyme Corp	2.42%
3) Electronic Arts Inc	2.04%
4) SunGuard Data Syst	1.85%
5) Millennium Pharma	1.83%
6) Waters Corp	1.70%
7) DST Systems Inc	1.70%
8) BJ Services Corp	1.65%
9) IDEC Pharma Corp	1.62%
10) Fiserv Inc	1.57%

Fundamentals

Med Mkt Cap:	$3,220,000,000
P/E Ratio:	33.50
P/B Ratio:	7.20
P/C Ratio:	24.90
Standard Dev:	N/A
Sharpe Ratio:	N/A
Alpha:	N/A
Beta:	N/A
3 Yr Earn Gr:	19.50
1 Yr Fwd Gr:	16.30
12 Month Yield:	N/A

Sector Breakdown

Utilities:	1.80%
Energy:	4.70%
Financials:	7.80%
Industrial Cyclicals:	7.50%
Consumer Durables:	4.30%
Consumer Staples:	2.70%
Services:	15.20%
Retail:	6.80%
Health:	23.10%
Technology:	26.20%

Premium/Discount (6/29/2001)

P/D Close:	N/A
P/D Midpoint:	N/A

Tickers

Symbol: IJK		ECash:	NNK.EU
NAV:	NNK	TCash:	NNK.TC
Close:	NNK.NV	Div:	NNK.DP
Shares:	NNK.SO	Index:	MDG

Fund Management

Manager:	Barclays Global
Web Site:	http://www.ishares.com/
Telephone:	800-474-2737
Specialist:	Hull Trading Co.
Distributor:	SEI Investments
Administrator:	Investors Bank & Trust
Sponsor:	N/A
Exchange:	AMEX

1 Yr	3 Yr	5 Yr	2000	1999	1998	1997
—	—	—	—	—	—	—

Source: AMEX and Morningstar data as of 6/30/2001.

iShares S&P MidCap 400/BARRA Value (IJJ)

Fund Information

Expense Ratio:	0.25%
Total Net Assets:	$155,110,000
Structure:	Open-Ended
Benchmark:	S&P 400/BARRA Val
Options:	No
Initial Divisor:	1/2
Min. Investment:	1 Share
Date of Inception:	24-Jul-00
52 Week Range:	40.00–95.12
2000 Total Dist.:	0.65

Fundamentals

Med Mkt Cap:	$2,277,000,000
P/E Ratio:	19.30
P/B Ratio:	2.20
P/C Ratio:	12.20
Standard Dev:	N/A
Sharpe Ratio:	N/A
Alpha:	N/A
Beta:	N/A
3 Yr Earn Gr:	12.00
1 Yr Fwd Gr:	6.70
12 Month Yield:	N/A

Premium/Discount (6/29/2001)

P/D Close:	0.24%
P/D Midpoint:	0.12%

Tickers

Symbol: IJJ		ECash:	NJJ.EU
NAV:	NJJ	TCash:	NJJ.TC
Close:	NJJ.NV	Div:	NJJ.DP
Shares:	NJJ.SO	Index:	MUV

Top 10 Holdings

1) M & T Bank Corp	1.58%
2) RJ Reynolds	1.34%
3) Telephone & Data Sys	1.29%
4) Weatherford Intl	1.27%
5) Marshall & Ilsley	1.27%
6) Enso	1.14%
7) Atmel Corp	1.07%
8) Jones Apparel Group	1.06%
9) Zions Bancorp	1.06%
10) North Fork Bancorp Inc	1.00%

Sector Breakdown

Utilities:	11.60%
Energy:	9.90%
Financials:	23.20%
Industrial Cyclicals:	12.20%
Consumer Durables:	3.90%
Consumer Staples:	5.00%
Services:	15.10%
Retail:	2.40%
Health:	4.70%
Technology:	12.00%

Fund Management

Manager:	Barclays Global
Web Site:	http://www.ishares.com/
Telephone:	800–474–2737
Specialist:	Hull Trading Co.
Distributor:	SEI Investments
Administrator:	Investors Bank & Trust
Sponsor:	N/A
Exchange:	AMEX

1 Yr	3 Yr	5 Yr	2000	1999	1998	1997
—	—	—	—	—	—	—

Source: AMEX and Morningstar data as of 6/30/2001.

iShares S&P SmallCap 600 Index (IJR)

Fund Information

Expense Ratio:	0.20%
Total Net Assets:	$437,000,000
Structure:	Open-Ended
Benchmark:	S&P SmallCap 600
Options:	No
Initial Divisor:	1/2
Min. Investment:	1 Share
Date of Inception:	22-May-00
52 Week Range:	93.80–118.29
2000 Total Dist.:	1.34

Fundamentals

Med Mkt Cap:	$836,000,000
P/E Ratio:	23.80
P/B Ratio:	3.40
P/C Ratio:	16.90
Standard Dev:	N/A
Sharpe Ratio:	N/A
Alpha:	N/A
Beta:	N/A
3 Yr Earn Gr:	18.50
1 Yr Fwd Gr:	9.10
12 Month Yield:	N/A

Premium/Discount (6/29/2001)

P/D Close:	N/A
P/D Midpoint:	N/A

Tickers

Symbol:	IJR	ECash:	NIR.EU
NAV:	NIR	TCash:	NIR.TC
Close:	NIR.NV	Div:	NIR.DP
Shares:	NIR.SO	Index:	SML

Top 10 Holdings

1) UniversalHealth Group	0.80%
2) Eaton Vance Corp	0.67%
3) Patterson Dental Co	0.63%
4) Fidelity	0.63%
5) Timberland Co	0.61%
6) Varian Medical Syst	0.61%
7) Barrett Resources	0.60%
8) Cephalon Inc	0.60%
9) Centura Banks Inc	0.59%
10) Shaw Group Inc	0.58%

Sector Breakdown

Utilities:	3.40%
Energy:	7.10%
Financials:	11.00%
Industrial Cyclicals:	19.50%
Consumer Durables:	5.40%
Consumer Staples:	3.40%
Services:	14.00%
Retail:	7.30%
Health:	12.20%
Technology:	16.60%

Fund Management

Manager:	Barclays Global
Web Site:	http://www.ishares.com/
Telephone:	800-474-2737
Specialist:	Hull Trading Co.
Distributor:	SEI Investments
Administrator:	Investors Bank & Trust
Sponsor:	N/A
Exchange:	AMEX

1 Yr	3 Yr	5 Yr	2000	1999	1998	1997
9.83	—	—	—	—	—	—

Source: AMEX and Morningstar data as of 6/30/2001.

iSHARES S&P SMALLCAP 600/BARRA GROWTH (IJT)

FUND INFORMATION

Expense Ratio:	0.25%
Total Net Assets:	$50,280,000
Structure:	Open-Ended
Benchmark:	S&P 600/BARRA Gr
Options:	No
Initial Divisor:	1/2
Min. Investment:	1 Share
Date of Inception:	24-Jul–00
52 Week Range:	63.08–90.00
2000 Total Dist.:	0.62

FUNDAMENTALS

Med Mkt Cap:	$1,073,000,000
P/E Ratio:	28.20
P/B Ratio:	5.10
P/C Ratio:	20.30
Standard Dev:	N/A
Sharpe Ratio:	N/A
Alpha:	N/A
Beta:	N/A
3 Yr Earn Gr:	26.10
1 Yr Fwd Gr:	16.20
12 Month Yield:	N/A

PREMIUM/DISCOUNT (6/29/2001)

P/D Close:	N/A
P/D Midpoint:	N/A

TICKERS

Symbol: IJT	ECash:	NLT.EU
NAV: NLT	TCash:	NLT.TC
Close: NLT.NV	Div:	NLT.DP
Shares: NLT.SO	Index:	CKG

TOP 10 HOLDINGS

1) UniversalHealth Group	1.85%
2) Eaton Vance Corp	1.54%
3) Patterson Dental Co	1.45%
4) Timberland Co	1.41%
5) Varian Medical Syst	1.40%
6) Cephalon Inc	1.40%
7) Barrett Resources	1.39%
8) Shaw Group Inc	1.33%
9) Cross Timbers Oil Co	1.33%
10) National Commerce Bancorp	1.32%

SECTOR BREAKDOWN

Utilities:	0.00%
Energy:	9.70%
Financials:	7.30%
Industrial Cyclicals:	13.10%
Consumer Durables:	4.20%
Consumer Staples:	1.40%
Services:	17.10%
Retail:	6.90%
Health:	21.00%
Technology:	19.30%

FUND MANAGEMENT

Manager:	Barclays Global
Web Site:	http://www.ishares.com/
Telephone:	800–474–2737
Specialist:	Hull Trading Co.
Distributor:	SEI Investments
Administrator:	Investors Bank & Trust
Sponsor:	N/A
Exchange:	AMEX

1 Yr	3 Yr	5 Yr	2000	1999	1998	1997
—	—	—	—	—	—	—

Source: AMEX and Morningstar data as of 6/30/2001.

iSHARES S&P SMALLCAP 600/BARRA VALUE (IJS)

FUND INFORMATION

Expense Ratio:	0.25%
Total Net Assets:	$145,210,000
Structure:	Open-Ended
Benchmark:	S&P 600/BARRA Val
Options:	No
Initial Divisor:	1/2
Min. Investment:	1 Share
Date of Inception:	24-Jul-00
52 Week Range:	35.00–86.58
2000 Total Dist.:	0.60

FUNDAMENTALS

Med Mkt Cap:	$693,000,000
P/E Ratio:	19.90
P/B Ratio:	1.90
P/C Ratio:	13.80
Standard Dev:	N/A
Sharpe Ratio:	N/A
Alpha:	N/A
Beta:	N/A
3 Yr Earn Gr:	12.60
1 Yr Fwd Gr:	2.30
12 Month Yield:	N/A

PREMIUM/DISCOUNT (6/29/2001)

P/D Close:	N/A
P/D Midpoint.	N/A

TICKERS

Symbol: IJS		ECash:	NJS.EU
NAV:	NJS	TCash:	NJS.TC
Close:	NJS.NV	Div:	NJS.DP
Shares:	NJS.SO	Index:	CVK

TOP 10 HOLDINGS

1) Fidelity	1.11%
2) Centura Banks Inc	1.05%
3) Massey Energy Co	0.97%
4) Smithfield Foods Inc	0.95%
5) First American Fin	0.89%
6) Pride International Inc	0.86%
7) Dr Horton Inc	0.86%
8) Constellation Brands	0.78%
9) Washington Federal Inc	0.76%
10) Toll Brothers Inc	0.74%

SECTOR BREAKDOWN

Utilities:	6.20%
Energy:	5.10%
Financials:	14.10%
Industrial Cyclicals:	24.60%
Consumer Durables:	6.40%
Consumer Staples:	5.00%
Services:	11.50%
Retail:	7.70%
Health:	5.00%
Technology:	14.50%

FUND MANAGEMENT

Manager:	Barclays Global
Web Site:	http://www.ishares.com/
Telephone:	800–474–2737
Specialist:	Hull Trading Co.
Distributor:	SEI Investments
Administrator:	Investors Bank & Trust
Sponsor:	N/A
Exchange:	AMEX

1 Yr	3 Yr	5 Yr	2000	1999	1998	1997
—	—	—	—	—	—	—

Source: AMEX and Morningstar data as of 6/30/2001.

streetTRACKS DJ US Large Cap Growth (ELG)

Fund Information

Expense Ratio:	0.20%
Total Net Assets:	$24,340,000
Structure:	Open-Ended
Benchmark:	DJ US Lg Growth
Options:	No
Initial Divisor:	1/20
Min. Investment:	1 Share
Date of Inception:	29-Sep-00
52 Week Range:	40.00–97.31
2000 Total Dist.:	0.02

Top 10 Holdings

1) General Electric Co	13.45%
2) Pfizer Inc	8.38%
3) Microsoft Corp	8.16%
4) Intel Corp	5.44%
5) AOL Time Warner	5.41%
6) Wal-Mart Stores	4.53%
7) Cisco Systems	3.73%
8) Home Depot Inc	3.25%
9) Coca-Cola Co	3.13%
10) Tyco Intl	2.44%

Fundamentals

Med Mkt Cap:	$154,436,000,000
P/E Ratio:	39.60
P/B Ratio:	9.70
P/C Ratio:	26.90
Standard Dev:	N/A
Sharpe Ratio:	N/A
Alpha:	N/A
Beta:	N/A
3 Yr Earn Gr:	25.30
1 Yr Fwd Gr:	9.00
12 Month Yield:	N/A

Sector Breakdown

Utilities:	0.60%
Energy:	0.00%
Financials:	0.60%
Industrial Cyclicals:	17.70%
Consumer Durables:	0.00%
Consumer Staples:	2.90%
Services:	8.80%
Retail:	10.60%
Health:	12.30%
Technology:	46.50%

Premium/Discount (6/29/2001)

P/D Close:	1.82%
P/D Midpoint:	1.25%

Tickers

Symbol:	ELG	ECash:	FLG.EU
NAV:	FLG	TCash:	FLG.TC
Close:	FLG.NV	Div:	FLG.DP
Shares:	FLG.SO	Index:	DJUSGL

Fund Management

Manager:	State Street Global
Web Site:	http://www.streettracks.com/
Telephone:	866–787–2257
Specialist:	N/A
Distributor:	State Street Gl Cap
Administrator:	State Street Gl B&T
Sponsor:	N/A
Exchange:	AMEX

1 Yr	3 Yr	5 Yr	2000	1999	1998	1997
—	—	—	—	—	—	—

Source: AMEX and Morningstar data as of 6/30/2001.

STREETTRACKS DJ US LARGE CAP VALUE (ELV)

FUND INFORMATION

Expense Ratio:	0.20%
Total Net Assets:	$38,830,000
Structure:	Open-Ended
Benchmark:	DJ US Lg Value
Options:	No
Initial Divisor:	1/20
Min. Investment:	1 Share
Date of Inception:	29-Sep–00
52 Week Range:	67.00–138.16
2000 Total Dist.:	0.57

FUNDAMENTALS

Med Mkt Cap:	$74,031,000,000
P/E Ratio:	22.10
P/B Ratio:	5.60
P/C Ratio:	15.80
Standard Dev:	N/A
Sharpe Ratio:	N/A
Alpha:	N/A
Beta:	N/A
3 Yr Earn Gr:	14.60
1 Yr Fwd Gr:	3.00
12 Month Yield:	N/A

PREMIUM/DISCOUNT (6/29/2001)

P/D Close:	0.04%
P/D Midpoint:	N/A

TICKERS

Symbol: ELV	ECash: FLV.EU
NAV: FLV	TCash: FLV.TC
Close: FLV.NV	Div: FLV.DP
Shares: FLV.SO	Index: DJUSVL

TOP 10 HOLDINGS

1) ExxonMobil Corp	6.10%
2) Citigroup Inc	4.95%
3) Merck & Co Inc	3.79%
4) IBM	3.62%
5) AIG Inc	3.49%
6) SBC Communications	3.26%
7) Verizon Comm	2.88%
8) Bristol Myers Squibb	2.52%
9) Johnson & Johnson	2.49%
10) Philip Morris Cos Inc	2.27%

SECTOR BREAKDOWN

Utilities:	1.50%
Energy:	9.00%
Financials:	33.20%
Industrial Cyclicals:	8.30%
Consumer Durables:	2.30%
Consumer Staples:	8.00%
Services:	14.30%
Retail:	2.00%
Health:	16.70%
Technology:	4.80%

FUND MANAGEMENT

Manager:	State Street Global
Web Site:	http://www.streettracks.com/
Telephone:	866-787-2257
Specialist:	KV Executions Services
Distributor:	State Street Gl Cap
Administrator:	State Street Gl B&T
Sponsor:	N/A
Exchange:	AMEX

1 Yr	3 Yr	5 Yr	2000	1999	1998	1997
—	—	—	—	—	—	—

Source: AMEX and Morningstar data as of 6/30/2001.

STREET**TRACKS** DJ US SMALL CAP GROWTH (DSG)

FUND INFORMATION

Expense Ratio:	0.25%
Total Net Assets:	$19,740,000
Structure:	Open-Ended
Benchmark:	DJ US Sm Growth
Options:	No
Initial Divisor:	1/20
Min. Investment:	1 Share
Date of Inception:	29-Sep–00
52 Week Range:	44.50–100.94
2000 Total Dist.:	0.00

FUNDAMENTALS

Med Mkt Cap:	$1,267,000,000
P/E Ratio:	29.90
P/B Ratio:	6.00
P/C Ratio:	23.00
Standard Dev:	N/A
Sharpe Ratio:	N/A
Alpha:	N/A
Beta:	N/A
3 Yr Earn Gr:	29.20
1 Yr Fwd Gr:	9.80
12 Month Yield:	N/A

PREMIUM/DISCOUNT (6/29/2001)

P/D Close:	N/A
P/D Midpoint:	N/A

TICKERS

Symbol:	DSG	ECash:	PSG.EU
NAV:	PSG	TCash:	PSG.TC
Close:	PSG.NV	Div:	PSG.DP
Shares:	PSG.SO	Index:	DJUSGS

TOP 10 HOLDINGS

1) International Game Tech	1.43%
2) Lincare Holdgs Inc	1.11%
3) Expeditors Intl Wash	1.01%
4) AmeriCredit Corp	0.99%
5) Helmerich & Payne Int	0.97%
6) SEI Investments Co	0.95%
7) Rite Aid Corp	0.89%
8) Cephalon Inc	0.81%
9) CSG Sys Intl Inc	0.80%
10) ICOS Corp	0.80%

SECTOR BREAKDOWN

Utilities:	0.00%
Energy:	6.10%
Financials:	6.20%
Industrial Cyclicals:	6.10%
Consumer Durables:	4.30%
Consumer Staples:	2.30%
Services:	20.40%
Retail:	6.90%
Health:	23.10%
Technology:	24.80%

FUND MANAGEMENT

Manager:	State Street Global
Web Site:	http://www.streettracks.com/
Telephone:	866-787-2257
Specialist:	Bear Hunter
Distributor:	State Street Gl Cap
Administrator:	State Street Gl B&T
Sponsor:	N/A
Exchange:	AMEX

1 Yr	3 Yr	5 Yr	2000	1999	1998	1997
—	—	—	—	—	—	—

Source: AMEX and Morningstar data as of 6/30/2001.

STREETTRACKS DJ US SMALL CAP VALUE (DSV)

FUND INFORMATION

Expense Ratio:	0.25%
Total Net Assets:	$25,790,000
Structure:	Open-Ended
Benchmark:	DJ US Sm Value
Options:	No
Initial Divisor:	1/20
Min. Investment:	1 Share
Date of Inception:	29-Sep-00
52 Week Range:	53.50–130.80
2000 Total Dist.:	0.93

FUNDAMENTALS

Med Mkt Cap:	$1,388,000,000
P/E Ratio:	18.00
P/B Ratio:	2.00
P/C Ratio:	9.70
Standard Dev:	N/A
Sharpe Ratio:	N/A
Alpha:	N/A
Beta:	N/A
3 Yr Earn Gr:	5.20
1 Yr Fwd Gr:	13.30
12 Month Yield:	N/A

PREMIUM/DISCOUNT (6/29/2001)

P/D Close:	0.22%
P/D Midpoint:	N/A

TICKERS

Symbol:	DSV	ECash:	PSV.EU
NAV:	PSV	TCash:	PSV.TC
Close:	PSV.NV	Div:	PSV.DP
Shares:	PSV.SO	Index:	DJUSVS

TOP 10 HOLDINGS

1) Old Republic Intl	1.08%
2) Radian Group Inc	1.05%
3) Everest Reinsurance	1.04%
4) Litton Inds Inc	0.97%
5) Ocean Energy Inc	0.96%
6) Astoria Financial	0.91%
7) Equitable Res Inc	0.77%
8) Delhaize Amer Inc	0.75%
9) Valero Energy Corp	0.74%
10) FirstMerit Corp	0.72%

SECTOR BREAKDOWN

Utilities:	7.00%
Energy:	6.00%
Financials:	42.40%
Industrial Cyclicals:	19.90%
Consumer Durables:	4.20%
Consumer Staples:	3.20%
Services:	8.30%
Retail:	4.30%
Health:	2.40%
Technology:	2.20%

FUND MANAGEMENT

Manager:	State Street Global
Web Site:	http://www.streettracks.com/
Telephone:	866-787-2257
Specialist:	Wolverine Trading
Distributor:	State Street Gl Cap
Administrator:	State Street Gl B&T
Sponsor:	N/A
Exchange:	AMEX

1 Yr	3 Yr	5 Yr	2000	1999	1998	1997
—	—	—	—	—	—	—

Source: AMEX and Morningstar data as of 6/30/2001.

SECTOR-BASED DOMESTIC ETFs

FORTUNE E-50 INDEX (FEF)

FUND INFORMATION

Expense Ratio:	0.20%
Total Net Assets:	$16,160,000
Structure:	Open-Ended
Benchmark:	Fortune e-50
Options:	No
Initial Divisor:	1/10
Min. Investment:	1 Share
Date of Inception:	10-Oct-00
52 Week Range:	29.80–83.94
2000 Total Dist.:	—

TOP 10 HOLDINGS

1) Microsoft Corp	8.31%
2) AOL Time Warner	7.95%
3) Intel Corp	7.13%
4) Oracle Corp	6.47%
5) Cisco Systems	6.24%
6) IBM	3.92%
7) SBC Communications	3.69%
8) Dell Computer Corp	3.52%
9) JDS Uniphase Corp	3.11%
10) WorldCom Inc	3.01%

FUNDAMENTALS

Med Mkt Cap:	$62,787,000,000
P/E Ratio:	42.80
P/B Ratio:	9.10
P/C Ratio:	26.40
Standard Dev:	N/A
Sharpe Ratio:	N/A
Alpha:	N/A
Beta:	N/A
3 Yr Earn Gr:	27.90
1 Yr Fwd Gr:	4.60
12 Month Yield:	N/A

SECTOR BREAKDOWN

Utilities:	0.00%
Energy:	0.00%
Financials:	4.10%
Industrial Cyclicals:	2.10%
Consumer Durables:	0.00%
Consumer Staples:	0.00%
Services:	15.40%
Retail:	1.80%
Health:	0.00%
Technology:	76.70%

PREMIUM/DISCOUNT (6/29/2001)

P/D Close:	1.78%
P/D Midpoint:	1.04%

TICKERS

Symbol: FEF		ECash:	FEY.EU
NAV: FEY		TCash:	FEY.TC
Close: FEY.NV		Div:	FEY.DP
Shares: FEY.SO		Index:	FEX

FUND MANAGEMENT

Manager:	State Street Global
Web Site:	http://www.amex.com/
Telephone:	866–787–2257
Specialist:	Bear Hunter
Distributor:	State Street Gl Cap
Administrator:	State Street Gl B&T
Sponsor:	N/A
Exchange:	AMEX

1 Yr	3 Yr	5 Yr	2000	1999	1998	1997
—	—	—	—	—	—	—

Source: AMEX and Morningstar data as of 6/30/2001.

iShares Cohen & Steers Realty Majors (ICF)

Fund Information

Expense Ratio:	0.35%
Total Net Assets:	$42,550,000
Structure:	Open-Ended
Benchmark:	C & S Realty
Options:	No
Initial Divisor:	—
Min. Investment:	1 Share
Date of Inception:	02-Feb-01
52 Week Range:	76.08–84.77
2000 Total Dist.:	—

Fundamentals

Med Mkt Cap:	$3,316,000,000
P/E Ratio:	19.80
P/B Ratio:	1.80
P/C Ratio:	N/A
Standard Dev:	N/A
Sharpe Ratio:	N/A
Alpha:	N/A
Beta:	N/A
3 Yr Earn Gr:	22.50
1 Yr Fwd Gr:	68.20
12 Month Yield:	N/A

Premium/Discount (6/29/2001)

P/D Close:	0.05%
P/D Midpoint:	N/A

Tickers

Symbol:	ICF	ECash:	ICG.EU
NAV:	ICG	TCash:	ICG.TC
Close:	ICG.NV	Div:	ICG.DP
Shares:	ICG.SO	Index:	RMP

Top 10 Holdings

1) Equity Res Prop Trust	8.19%
2) Equity Office REIT	7.58%
3) Simon Property Group	6.39%
4) Spieker Properties	5.17%
5) Public Storage	4.95%
6) Boston Properties	4.77%
7) Prologis Trust	4.76%
8) Apt Inv & Man	4.55%
9) Vornado Realty Trust	4.47%
10) Avalon Bay Comm	4.41%

Sector Breakdown

Utilities:	0.00%
Energy:	0.00%
Financials:	100.00%
Industrial Cyclicals:	0.00%
Consumer Durables:	0.00%
Consumer Staples:	0.00%
Services:	0.00%
Retail:	0.00%
Health:	0.00%
Technology:	0.00%

Fund Management

Manager:	Barclays Global
Web Site:	http://www.ishares.com/
Telephone:	800–474–2737
Specialist:	Bear Hunter
Distributor:	SEI Investments
Administrator:	Investors Bank & Trust
Sponsor:	N/A
Exchange:	AMEX

1 Yr	3 Yr	5 Yr	2000	1999	1998	1997
—	—	—	—	—	—	—

Source: AMEX and Morningstar data as of 6/30/2001.

iSHARES DOW JONES US BASIC MATERIALS (IYM)

FUND INFORMATION

Expense Ratio:	0.60%
Total Net Assets:	$15,650,000
Structure:	Open-Ended
Benchmark:	DJ US Basic Mat.
Options:	No
Initial Divisor:	1/4
Min. Investment:	1 Share
Date of Inception:	12-Jun-00
52 Week Range:	29.56–43.28
2000 Total Dist.:	0.46

FUNDAMENTALS

Med Mkt Cap:	$15,475,000,000
P/E Ratio:	24.40
P/B Ratio:	3.10
P/C Ratio:	12.40
Standard Dev:	N/A
Sharpe Ratio:	N/A
Alpha:	N/A
Beta:	N/A
3 Yr Earn Gr:	4.70
1 Yr Fwd Gr:	−32.30
12 Month Yield:	N/A

PREMIUM/DISCOUNT (6/29/2001)

P/D Close:	0.81%
P/D Midpoint:	0.4%

TICKERS

Symbol:	IYM	ECash:	DXV.EU
NAV:	DXV	TCash:	DXV.TC
Close:	DXV.NV	Div:	DXV.DP
Shares:	DXV.SO	Index:	DJUSBM

TOP 10 HOLDINGS

1) Dupont	17.85%
2) Alcoa Inc	13.10%
3) Dow Chemical Co	11.92%
4) International Paper	7.31%
5) Weyerhaeuser Co	4.58%
6) Air Products & Chem	3.70%
7) Praxair Inc	2.98%
8) Georgia Pacific Group	2.78%
9) Avery Dennison Corp	2.44%
10) Rohm & Haas Co	2.00%

SECTOR BREAKDOWN

Utilities:	0.00%
Energy:	0.70%
Financials:	0.00%
Industrial Cyclicals:	99.30%
Consumer Durables:	0.00%
Consumer Staples:	0.00%
Services:	0.00%
Retail:	0.00%
Health:	0.00%
Technology:	0.00%

FUND MANAGEMENT

Manager:	Barclays Global
Web Site:	http://www.ishares.com/
Telephone.	000 474 2737
Specialist:	Spear, Leeds
Distributor:	SEI Investments
Administrator:	Investors Bank & Trust
Sponsor:	N/A
Exchange:	AMEX

1 Yr	3 Yr	5 Yr 2000	1999 1998	1997	-4.05	9.92
—	—	—	—	—		

Source: AMEX and Morningstar data as of 6/30/2001.

iShares Dow Jones US Chemicals (IYD)

Fund Information

Expense Ratio:	0.60%
Total Net Assets:	$16,970,000
Structure:	Open-Ended
Benchmark:	DJ US Chemicals
Options:	No
Initial Divisor:	1/4
Min. Investment:	1 Share
Date of Inception:	12-Jun-00
52 Week Range:	18.50–46.45
2000 Total Dist.:	0.74

Fundamentals

Med Mkt Cap:	$8,578,000,000
P/E Ratio:	25.20
P/B Ratio:	3.20
P/C Ratio:	15.30
Standard Dev:	N/A
Sharpe Ratio:	N/A
Alpha:	N/A
Beta:	N/A
3 Yr Earn Gr:	3.10
1 Yr Fwd Gr:	−24.00
12 Month Yield:	N/A

Premium/Discount (6/29/2001)

P/D Close:	0.3%
P/D Midpoint:	0.48%

Tickers

Symbol:	IYD	ECash:	NNE.EU
NAV:	NNE	TCash:	NNE.TC
Close:	NNE.NV	Div:	NNE.DP
Shares:	NNE.SO	Index:	DJUSCH

Top 10 Holdings

1) Dupont	20.05%
2) Dow Chemical Co	18.62%
3) Air Products & Chem	6.43%
4) Praxair Inc	5.38%
5) Avery Dennison Corp	4.21%
6) Sigma Aldrich Corp	4.06%
7) Ecolab Inc	4.05%
8) Rohm & Haas Co	3.71%
9) Eastman Chemical	3.66%
10) Engelhard Corp	3.06%

Sector Breakdown

Utilities:	0.00%
Energy:	1.10%
Financials:	0.00%
Industrial Cyclicals:	98.90%
Consumer Durables:	0.00%
Consumer Staples:	0.00%
Services:	0.00%
Retail:	0.00%
Health:	0.00%
Technology:	0.00%

Fund Management

Manager:	Barclays Global
Web Site:	http://www.ishares.com/
Telephone:	800–474–2737
Specialist:	Spear, Leeds
Distributor:	SEI Investments
Administrator:	Investors Bank & Trust
Sponsor:	N/A
Exchange:	AMEX

1 Yr	3 Yr	5 Yr	2000	1999	1998	1997
13.82	—	—	—	—	—	—

Source: AMEX and Morningstar data as of 6/30/2001.

iShares Dow Jones US Cons Non-Cycl (IYK)

Fund Information

Expense Ratio:	0.60%
Total Net Assets:	$16,520,000
Structure:	Open-Ended
Benchmark:	DJ US Non-Con Cyc
Options:	No
Initial Divisor:	1/5
Min. Investment:	1 Share
Date of Inception:	12-Jun–00
52 Week Range:	38.32–44.51
2000 Total Dist.:	0.25

Fundamentals

Med Mkt Cap:	$40,703,000,000
P/E Ratio:	25.90
P/B Ratio:	9.70
P/C Ratio:	18.20
Standard Dev:	N/A
Sharpe Ratio:	N/A
Alpha:	N/A
Beta:	N/A
3 Yr Earn Gr:	5.60
1 Yr Fwd Gr:	8.60
12 Month Yield:	N/A

Premium/Discount (6/29/2001)

P/D Close:	N/A
P/D Midpoint:	N/A

Tickers

Symbol: IYK		ECash:	NMJ.EU
NAV:	NMJ	TCash:	NMJ.TC
Close:	NMJ.NV	Div:	NMJ.DP
Shares:	NMJ.SO	Index:	DJUSNC

Top 10 Holdings

1) Philip Morris Co Inc	12.80%
2) Coca-Cola Co	11.78%
3) Procter & Gamble	9.98%
4) Pepsico Inc	7.76%
5) Anheuser-Busch	5.09%
6) Kimberly-Clark Corp	4.47%
7) Colgate-Palmolive Co	3.88%
8) Gillette Co	3.65%
9) Safeway Inc	3.38%
10) Kroger Co	2.58%

Sector Breakdown

Utilities:	0.00%
Energy:	0.00%
Financials:	0.00%
Industrial Cyclicals:	4.20%
Consumer Durables:	1.20%
Consumer Staples:	80.50%
Services:	4.90%
Retail:	7.90%
Health:	0.00%
Technology:	1.20%

Fund Management

Manager:	Barclays Global
Web Site:	http://www.ishares.com/
Telephone:	800–474–2737
Specialist:	Spear, Leeds
Distributor:	SEI Investments
Administrator:	Investors Bank & Trust
Sponsor:	N/A
Exchange:	AMEX

1 Yr	3 Yr	5 Yr	2000	1999	1998	1997
1.45	—	—	—	—	—	—

Source: AMEX and Morningstar data as of 6/30/2001.

iShares Dow Jones US Consumer Cycl (IYC)

Fund Information

Expense Ratio:	0.60%
Total Net Assets:	$36,290,000
Structure:	Open-Ended
Benchmark:	DJ US Cons Cyc.
Options:	No
Initial Divisor:	1/5
Min. Investment:	1 Share
Date of Inception:	12-Jun–00
52 Week Range:	50.96–64.50
2000 Total Dist.:	0.27

Fundamentals

Med Mkt Cap:	$30,675,000,000
P/E Ratio:	34.30
P/B Ratio:	8.20
P/C Ratio:	23.60
Standard Dev:	N/A
Sharpe Ratio:	N/A
Alpha:	N/A
Beta:	N/A
3 Yr Earn Gr:	19.30
1 Yr Fwd Gr:	13.50
12 Month Yield:	N/A

Premium/Discount (6/29/2001)

P/D Close:	0.89%
P/D Midpoint:	0.16%

Tickers

Symbol: IYC		ECash:	NLL.EU
NAV:	NLL	TCash:	NLL.TC
Close:	NLL.NV	Div:	NLL.DP
Shares:	NLL.SO	Index:	DJUSCY

Top 10 Holdings

1) AOL Time Warner	10.84%
2) Wal-Mart Stores	9.08%
3) Home Depot Inc	6.50%
4) Viacom Inc	4.24%
5) Disney (Walt) Co	3.86%
6) Ford Motor Co	3.33%
7) Walgreen Co	2.69%
8) Comcast Corp	2.47%
9) McDonalds Corp	2.26%
10) AT & T Lib Media Grp	2.16%

Sector Breakdown

Utilities:	0.00%
Energy:	0.00%
Financials:	0.00%
Industrial Cyclicals:	2.40%
Consumer Durables:	10.20%
Consumer Staples:	0.50%
Services:	34.50%
Retail:	36.00%
Health:	3.00%
Technology:	13.30%

Fund Management

Manager:	Barclays Global
Web Site:	http://www.ishares.com/
Telephone:	800–474–2737
Specialist:	Spear, Leeds
Distributor:	SEI Investments
Administrator:	Investors Bank & Trust
Sponsor:	N/A
Exchange:	AMEX

1 Yr	3 Yr	5 Yr	2000	1999	1998	1997
3.30	—	—	—	—	—	—

Source: AMEX and Morningstar data as of 6/30/2001.

iSHARES DOW JONES US ENERGY (IYE)

FUND INFORMATION

Expense Ratio:	0.60%
Total Net Assets:	$45,460,000
Structure:	Open-Ended
Benchmark:	DJ US Energy
Options:	No
Initial Divisor:	1/5
Min. Investment:	1 Share
Date of Inception:	12-Jun–00
52 Week Range:	45.37–59.10
2000 Total Dist.:	0.27

FUNDAMENTALS

Med Mkt Cap:	$25,103,000,000
P/E Ratio:	18.30
P/B Ratio:	3.10
P/C Ratio:	11.80
Standard Dev:	N/A
Sharpe Ratio:	N/A
Alpha:	N/A
Beta:	N/A
3 Yr Earn Gr:	11.80
1 Yr Fwd Gr:	18.40
12 Month Yield:	N/A

PREMIUM/DISCOUNT (6/29/2001)

P/D Close:	0.45%
P/D Midpoint:	0.12%

TICKERS

Symbol:	IYE	ECash:	NLE.EU
NAV:	NLE	TCash:	NLE.TC
Close:	NLE.NV	Div:	NLE.DP
Shares:	NLE.SO	Index:	DJUSEN

TOP 10 HOLDINGS

1) ExxonMobil Corp	21.70%
2) Chevron Corp	10.77%
3) Texaco Inc	7.05%
4) Schlumberger Ltd	5.26%
5) El Paso Corp	5.11%
6) Phillips Petroleum Co	3.57%
7) Williams Co Inc	3.57%
8) Halliburton Co	2.95%
9) Anadarko Petroleum	2.81%
10) Occidental Petroleum	2.63%

SECTOR BREAKDOWN

Utilities:	7.20%
Energy:	90.80%
Financials:	0.00%
Industrial Cyclicals:	1.80%
Consumer Durables:	0.00%
Consumer Staples:	0.00%
Services:	0.20%
Retail:	0.00%
Health:	0.00%
Technology:	0.00%

FUND MANAGEMENT

Manager:	Barclays Global
Web Site:	http://www.ishares.com/
Telephone:	800–474–2737
Specialist:	Spear, Leeds
Distributor:	SEI Investments
Administrator:	Investors Bank & Trust
Sponsor:	N/A
Exchange:	AMEX

1 Yr	3 Yr	5 Yr	2000	1999	1998	1997
4.88	—	—	—	—	—	—

Source: AMEX and Morningstar data as of 6/30/2001.

iShares Dow Jones US Financial Sector (IYF)

Fund Information

Expense Ratio:	0.60%
Total Net Assets:	$59,610,000
Structure:	Open-Ended
Benchmark:	DJ US Fin. Sect.
Options:	No
Initial Divisor:	1/5
Min. Investment:	1 Share
Date of Inception:	22-May–00
52 Week Range:	70.60–90.00
2000 Total Dist.:	1.83

Top 10 Holdings

1) Citigroup Inc	10.87%
2) AIG Inc	7.65%
3) BankAmerica Corp	4.27%
4) JP Morgan Chase & Co	4.06%
5) Wells Fargo & Co	4.00%
6) Fannie Mae	3.85%
7) Morgan Stanley	2.84%
8) American Express	2.31%
9) Freddie Mac	2.15%
10) U.S. Bancorp	2.10%

Fundamentals

Med Mkt Cap:	$38,097,000,000
P/E Ratio:	20.70
P/B Ratio:	3.50
P/C Ratio:	N/A
Standard Dev:	N/A
Sharpe Ratio:	N/A
Alpha:	N/A
Beta:	N/A
3 Yr Earn Gr:	15.70
1 Yr Fwd Gr:	11.00
12 Month Yield:	N/A

Sector Breakdown

Utilities:	0.00%
Energy:	0.00%
Financials:	99.50%
Industrial Cyclicals:	0.10%
Consumer Durables:	0.00%
Consumer Staples:	0.00%
Services:	0.40%
Retail:	0.00%
Health:	0.00%
Technology:	0.10%

Premium/Discount (6/29/2001)

P/D Close:	N/A
P/D Midpoint:	N/A

Tickers

Symbol:	IYF	ECash:	NLF.EU
NAV:	NLF	TCash:	NLF.TC
Close:	NLF.NV	Div:	NLF.DP
Shares:	NLF.SO	Index:	DJUSFN

Fund Management

Manager:	Barclays Global
Web Site:	http://www.ishares.com/
Telephone:	800–474–2737
Specialist:	Susquehanna
Distributor:	SEI Investments
Administrator:	Investors Bank & Trust
Sponsor:	N/A
Exchange:	AMEX

1 Yr	3 Yr	5 Yr	2000	1999	1998	1997
22.01	—	—	—	—	—	—

Source: AMEX and Morningstar data as of 6/30/2001.

iShares Dow Jones US Financial Svcs (IYG)

Fund Information

Expense Ratio:	0.60%
Total Net Assets:	$38,800,000
Structure:	Open-Ended
Benchmark:	DJ US Fin. Serv.
Options:	No
Initial Divisor:	1/5
Min. Investment:	1 Share
Date of Inception:	12-Jun–00
52 Week Range:	80.12–104.22
2000 Total Dist.:	1.06

Fundamentals

Med Mkt Cap:	$43,497,000,000
P/E Ratio:	19.60
P/B Ratio:	3.70
P/C Ratio:	N/A
Standard Dev:	N/A
Sharpe Ratio:	N/A
Alpha:	N/A
Beta:	N/A
3 Yr Earn Gr:	17.50
1 Yr Fwd Gr:	6.60
12 Month Yield:	N/A

Premium/Discount (6/29/2001)

P/D Close:	N/A
P/D Midpoint:	N/A

Tickers

Symbol:	IYG	ECash:	NAG.EU
NAV:	NAG	TCash:	NAG.TC
Close:	NAG.NV	Div:	NAG.DP
Shares:	NAG.SO	Index:	DJUSFV

Top 10 Holdings

1) Citigroup Inc	14.35%
2) BankAmerica Corp	5.64%
3) JP Morgan Chase & Co	5.35%
4) Wells Fargo & Co	5.28%
5) Fannie Mae	5.08%
6) Morgan Stanley	3.74%
7) American Express	3.05%
8) Freddie Mac	2.83%
9) U.S. Bancorp	2.77%
10) Bank One Corp	2.62%

Sector Breakdown

Utilities:	0.00%
Energy:	0.00%
Financials:	99.60%
Industrial Cyclicals:	0.00%
Consumer Durables:	0.00%
Consumer Staples:	0.00%
Services:	0.40%
Retail:	0.00%
Health:	0.00%
Technology:	0.10%

Fund Management

Manager:	Barclays Global
Web Site:	http://www.ishares.com/
Telephone:	800–474–2737
Specialist:	Susquehanna
Distributor:	SEI Investments
Administrator:	Investors Bank & Trust
Sponsor:	N/A
Exchange:	AMEX

1 Yr	3 Yr	5 Yr	2000	1999	1998	1997
22.28	—	—	—	—	—	—

Source: AMEX and Morningstar data as of 6/30/2001.

iSHARES DOW JONES US HEALTHCARE (IYH)

FUND INFORMATION

Expense Ratio:	0.60%
Total Net Assets:	$133,560,000
Structure:	Open-Ended
Benchmark:	DJ US Healthcare
Options:	No
Initial Divisor:	1/5
Min. Investment:	1 Share
Date of Inception:	12-Jun-00
52 Week Range:	52.00–73.00
2000 Total Dist.:	0.16

FUNDAMENTALS

Med Mkt Cap:	$78,932,000,000
P/E Ratio:	36.00
P/B Ratio:	10.70
P/C Ratio:	26.90
Standard Dev:	N/A
Sharpe Ratio:	N/A
Alpha:	N/A
Beta:	N/A
3 Yr Earn Gr:	14.30
1 Yr Fwd Gr:	15.90
12 Month Yield:	N/A

PREMIUM/DISCOUNT (6/29/2001)

P/D Close:	0.26%
P/D Midpoint:	N/A

TICKERS

Symbol: IYH		ECash:	NHG.EU
NAV:	NHG	TCash:	NHG.TC
Close:	NHG.NV	Div:	NHG.DP
Shares:	NHG.SO	Index:	DJUSHC

TOP 10 HOLDINGS

1) Pfizer Inc	16.90%
2) Merck & Co Inc	11.43%
3) Bristol-Myers Squibb Co	7.58%
4) Johnson & Johnson	7.51%
5) American Home Prod	5.03%
6) Lilly (Eli) and Co	4.81%
7) Abbott Laboratories	4.45%
8) Pharmacia Corp	4.24%
9) Amgen Inc	4.09%
10) Medtronic Inc	3.61%

SECTOR BREAKDOWN

Utilities:	0.00%
Energy:	0.00%
Financials:	1.20%
Industrial Cyclicals:	0.50%
Consumer Durables:	0.10%
Consumer Staples:	0.00%
Services:	0.10%
Retail:	0.00%
Health:	98.00%
Technology:	0.20%

FUND MANAGEMENT

Manager:	Barclays Global
Web Site:	http://www.ishares.com/
Telephone:	800–474–2737
Specialist:	Spear, Leeds
Distributor:	SEI Investments
Administrator:	Investors Bank & Trust
Sponsor:	N/A
Exchange:	AMEX

1 Yr	3 Yr	5 Yr	2000	1999	1998	1997
−5.53	—	—	—	—	—	—

Source: AMEX and Morningstar data as of 6/30/2001.

iShares Dow Jones US Industrial (IYJ)

Fund Information

Expense Ratio:	0.60%
Total Net Assets:	$47,210,000
Structure:	Open-Ended
Benchmark:	DJ US Industrial
Options:	No
Initial Divisor:	1/5
Min. Investment:	1 Share
Date of Inception:	12-Jun-00
52 Week Range:	44.85–64.72
2000 Total Dist.:	0.28

Top 10 Holdings

1) General Electric Co	24.19%
2) Tyco International	6.13%
3) Boeing Co	3.97%
4) Minnesota Mining	3.96%
5) Automatic Data Proc	3.07%
6) United Technologies	3.03%
7) Honeywell International	2.72%
8) Emerson Electric	2.62%
9) First Data Corp	2.08%
10) Electronic Data Sys	1.94%

Fundamentals

Med Mkt Cap:	$27,500,000,000
P/E Ratio:	28.20
P/B Ratio:	5.90
P/C Ratio:	17.30
Standard Dev:	N/A
Sharpe Ratio:	N/A
Alpha:	N/A
Beta:	N/A
3 Yr Earn Gr:	13.30
1 Yr Fwd Gr:	9.30
12 Month Yield:	N/A

Sector Breakdown

Utilities:	0.00%
Energy:	0.00%
Financials:	1.20%
Industrial Cyclicals:	62.90%
Consumer Durables:	3.70%
Consumer Staples:	0.00%
Services:	18.00%
Retail:	0.00%
Health:	0.50%
Technology:	13.70%

Premium/Discount (6/29/2001)

P/D Close:	1.48%
P/D Midpoint:	0.24%

Tickers

Symbol: IYJ		ECash:	NIJ.EU
NAV: NIJ		TCash:	NIJ.TC
Close: NIJ.NV		Div:	NIJ.DP
Shares: NIJ.SO		Index:	DJUSIN

Fund Management

Manager:	Barclays Global
Web Site:	http://www.ishares.com/
Telephone:	000 474 2737
Specialist:	Spear, Leeds
Distributor:	SEI Investments
Administrator:	Investors Bank & Trust
Sponsor:	N/A
Exchange:	AMEX

1 Yr	3 Yr	5 Yr	2000	1999	1998	1997
−8.13	—	—	—	—	—	—

Source: AMEX and Morningstar data as of 6/30/2001.

iShares Dow Jones US Internet (IYV)

Fund Information

Expense Ratio:	0.60%
Total Net Assets:	$20,480,000
Structure:	Open-Ended
Benchmark:	DJ US Internet
Options:	No
Initial Divisor:	1/4
Min. Investment:	1 Share
Date of Inception:	15-May–00
52 Week Range:	12.32–82.62
2000 Total Dist.:	1.64

Fundamentals

Med Mkt Cap:	$7,542,000,000
P/E Ratio:	59.20
P/B Ratio:	7.70
P/C Ratio:	32.40
Standard Dev:	N/A
Sharpe Ratio:	N/A
Alpha:	N/A
Beta:	N/A
3 Yr Earn Gr:	N/A
1 Yr Fwd Gr:	50.90
12 Month Yield:	N/A

Premium/Discount (6/29/2001)

P/D Close:	N/A
P/D Midpoint:	N/A

Tickers

Symbol: IYV	ECash:	NNU.EU
NAV: NNU	TCash:	NNU.TC
Close: NNU.NV	Div:	NNU.DP
Shares: NNU.SO	Index:	DJINET

Top 10 Holdings

1) Verisign Inc	9.74%
2) Bea Systems Inc	9.42%
3) eBay Inc	8.32%
4) Yahoo! Inc	7.96%
5) Check Point Software	7.81%
6) Exodus Comm	6.91%
7) I2 Technologies Inc	6.11%
8) Amazon.com	3.65%
9) Ariba Inc	2.77%
10) Commerce One	2.71%

Sector Breakdown

Utilities:	0.00%
Energy:	0.00%
Financials:	3.50%
Industrial Cyclicals:	0.00%
Consumer Durables:	0.00%
Consumer Staples:	0.00%
Services:	18.80%
Retail:	5.10%
Health:	0.00%
Technology:	72.60%

Fund Management

Manager:	Barclays Global
Web Site:	http://www.ishares.com/
Telephone:	800–474–2737
Specialist:	Spear, Leeds
Distributor:	SEI Investments
Administrator:	Investors Bank & Trust
Sponsor:	N/A
Exchange:	AMEX

1 Yr	3 Yr	5 Yr	2000	1999	1998	1997
−71.82	—	—	—	—	—	—

Source: AMEX and Morningstar data as of 6/30/2001.

iSHARES DOW JONES US REAL ESTATE (IYR)

FUND INFORMATION

Expense Ratio:	0.60%
Total Net Assets:	$78,570,000
Structure:	Open-Ended
Benchmark:	DJ US Real Estate
Options:	No
Initial Divisor:	1/2
Min. Investment:	1 Share
Date of Inception:	12-Jun-00
52 Week Range:	69.05–82.46
2000 Total Dist.:	2.56

TOP 10 HOLDINGS

1) Equity Office REIT	8.04%
2) Equity Res Prop Trust	6.44%
3) Spieker Properties	3.38%
4) Simon Property Group	3.32%
5) Prologis Trust	3.10%
6) Apartment Inv & Man	2.86%
7) Archstone Communities	2.79%
8) Avalonbay Comm	2.72%
9) Duke Rty Inv REIT	2.62%
10) Kimco Rlty Corp REIT	2.37%

FUNDAMENTALS

Med Mkt Cap:	$2,475,000,000
P/E Ratio:	18.60
P/B Ratio:	1.80
P/C Ratio:	N/A
Standard Dev:	N/A
Sharpe Ratio:	N/A
Alpha:	N/A
Beta:	N/A
3 Yr Earn Gr:	18.40
1 Yr Fwd Gr:	60.60
12 Month Yield:	N/A

SECTOR BREAKDOWN

Utilities:	0.00%
Energy:	0.00%
Financials:	96.50%
Industrial Cyclicals:	1.90%
Consumer Durables:	0.00%
Consumer Staples:	0.00%
Services:	1.60%
Retail:	0.00%
Health:	0.00%
Technology:	0.00%

PREMIUM/DISCOUNT (6/29/2001)

P/D Close:	N/A
P/D Midpoint:	N/A

TICKERS

Symbol: IYR		ECash:	NLR.EU
NAV:	NLR	TCash:	NLR.TC
Close:	NLR.NV	Div:	NLR.DP
Shares:	NLR.SO	Index:	DJUSRE

FUND MANAGEMENT

Manager:	Barclays Global
Web Site:	http://www.ishares.com/
Telephone:	800–474–2737
Specialist:	Spear, Leeds
Distributor:	SEI Investments
Administrator:	Investors Bank & Trust
Sponsor:	N/A
Exchange:	AMEX

1 Yr	3 Yr	5 Yr	2000	1999	1998	1997
22.09	—	—	—	—	—	—

Source: AMEX and Morningstar data as of 6/30/2001.

iShares Dow Jones US Technology (IYW)

Fund Information

Expense Ratio:	0.60%
Total Net Assets:	$106,960,000
Structure:	Open-Ended
Benchmark:	DJ US Technology
Options:	No
Initial Divisor:	1/10
Min. Investment:	1 Share
Date of Inception:	15-May–00
52 Week Range:	46.20–139.00
2000 Total Dist.:	0.00

Top 10 Holdings

1) Microsoft Corp	13.52%
2) IBM	9.00%
3) Intel Corp	9.00%
4) Cisco Systems	6.18%
5) E M C Corp	3.48%
6) Oracle Corp	3.45%
7) Dell Computer Corp	3.18%
8) Texas Instruments	2.89%
9) Hewlett-Packard	2.72%
10) Sun Microsystems	2.69%

Fundamentals

Med Mkt Cap:	$61,536,000,000
P/E Ratio:	35.90
P/B Ratio:	7.20
P/C Ratio:	24.70
Standard Dev:	N/A
Sharpe Ratio:	N/A
Alpha:	N/A
Beta:	N/A
3 Yr Earn Gr:	32.70
1 Yr Fwd Gr:	−15.80
12 Month Yield:	N/A

Sector Breakdown

Utilities:	0.00%
Energy:	0.00%
Financials:	0.00%
Industrial Cyclicals:	1.40%
Consumer Durables:	0.10%
Consumer Staples:	0.00%
Services:	1.70%
Retail:	0.00%
Health:	0.00%
Technology:	96.80%

Premium/Discount (6/29/2001)

P/D Close:	0.7%
P/D Midpoint:	0.94%

Tickers

Symbol: IYW		ECash:	NJW.EU
NAV: NJW		TCash:	NJW.TC
Close: NJW.NV		Div:	NJW.DP
Shares: NJW.SO		Index:	DJUSTC

Fund Management

Manager:	Barclays Global
Web Site:	http://www.ishares.com/
Telephone:	800–474–2737
Specialist:	Susquehanna
Distributor:	SEI Investments
Administrator:	Investors Bank & Trust
Sponsor:	N/A
Exchange:	AMEX

1 Yr	3 Yr	5 Yr	2000	1999	1998	1997
−51.79	—	—	—	—	—	—

Source: AMEX and Morningstar data as of 6/30/2001.

iSHARES DOW JONES US TELECOM (IYZ)

FUND INFORMATION

Expense Ratio:	0.60%
Total Net Assets:	$52,930,000
Structure:	Open-Ended
Benchmark:	DJ US Telecom.
Options:	No
Initial Divisor:	1/5
Min. Investment:	1 Share
Date of Inception:	22-May-00
52 Week Range:	33.62–63.62
2000 Total Dist.:	0.81

TOP 10 HOLDINGS

1) SBC Communications	17.95%
2) Verizon Comm	15.88%
3) AT&T Corp	8.71%
4) Bellsouth Corp	8.59%
5) WorldCom Inc	4.57%
6) Qwest Communications	4.48%
7) United States Cellular	4.25%
8) Telephone & Data Sys	4.13%
9) Alltel Corp	3.70%
10) Citizens Communications	3.10%

FUNDAMENTALS

Med Mkt Cap:	$55,246,000,000
P/E Ratio:	20.30
P/B Ratio:	3.60
P/C Ratio:	9.40
Standard Dev:	N/A
Sharpe Ratio:	N/A
Alpha:	N/A
Beta:	N/A
3 Yr Earn Gr:	20.20
1 Yr Fwd Gr:	−16.40
12 Month Yield:	N/A

SECTOR BREAKDOWN

Utilities:	0.00%
Energy:	0.00%
Financials:	0.00%
Industrial Cyclicals:	0.00%
Consumer Durables:	0.00%
Consumer Staples:	0.00%
Services:	97.70%
Retail:	0.00%
Health:	0.00%
Technology:	2.30%

PREMIUM/DISCOUNT (6/29/2001)

P/D Close:	0.6%
P/D Midpoint:	0.1%

FUND MANAGEMENT

Manager:	Barclays Global
Web Site:	http://www.ishares.com/
Telephone:	800–474–2737
Specialist:	Spear, Leeds
Distributor:	SEI Investments
Administrator:	Investors Bank & Trust
Sponsor:	N/A
Exchange:	AMEX

TICKERS

Symbol: IYZ		ECash:	NJZ.EU
NAV:	NJZ	TCash:	NJZ.TC
Close:	NJZ.NV	Div:	NJZ.DP
Shares:	NJZ.SO	Index:	DJUSTL

1 Yr	3 Yr	5 Yr	2000	1999	1998	1997
−37.64	—	—	—	—	—	—

Source: AMEX and Morningstar data as of 6/30/2001.

iSHARES DOW JONES US UTILITIES (IDU)

FUND INFORMATION

Expense Ratio:	0.60%
Total Net Assets:	$43,220,000
Structure:	Open-Ended
Benchmark:	DJ US Utilities
Options:	No
Initial Divisor:	1/2
Min. Investment:	1 Share
Date of Inception:	12-Jun–00
52 Week Range:	65.78–89.75
2000 Total Dist.:	1.26

FUNDAMENTALS

Med Mkt Cap:	$10,302,000,000
P/E Ratio:	21.00
P/B Ratio:	3.30
P/C Ratio:	11.40
Standard Dev:	N/A
Sharpe Ratio:	N/A
Alpha:	N/A
Beta:	N/A
3 Yr Earn Gr:	15.80
1 Yr Fwd Gr:	17.50
12 Month Yield:	N/A

PREMIUM/DISCOUNT (6/29/2001)

P/D Close:	N/A
P/D Midpoint:	N/A

TICKERS

Symbol:	IDU	ECash:	NLU.EU
NAV:	NLU	TCash:	NLU.TC
Close:	NLU.NV	Div:	NLU.DP
Shares:	NLU.SO	Index:	DJUSUT

TOP 10 HOLDINGS

1) Enron Corp	10.03%
2) Duke Power Co	7.63%
3) Southern Co	5.32%
4) AES Corp	5.16%
5) Exelon Corporation	4.88%
6) Calpine Corp	3.62%
7) Dominion Resources	3.58%
8) American Electric Pwr	3.53%
9) Reliant Energy Inc	2.65%
10) FPL Group Inc	2.52%

SECTOR BREAKDOWN

Utilities:	85.60%
Energy:	13.90%
Financials:	0.00%
Industrial Cyclicals:	0.10%
Consumer Durables:	0.00%
Consumer Staples:	0.00%
Services:	0.40%
Retail:	0.00%
Health:	0.00%
Technology:	0.00%

FUND MANAGEMENT

Manager:	Barclays Global
Web Site:	http://www.ishares.com/
Telephone:	800–474–2737
Specialist:	Spear, Leeds
Distributor:	SEI Investments
Administrator:	Investors Bank & Trust
Sponsor:	N/A
Exchange:	AMEX

1 Yr	3 Yr	5 Yr	2000	1999	1998	1997
22.26	—	—	—	—	—	—

Source: AMEX and Morningstar data as of 6/30/2001.

ISHARES GOLDMAN SACHS TECHNOLOGY INDEX (IGM)

FUND INFORMATION

Expense Ratio:	0.50%
Total Net Assets:	$126,420,000
Structure:	Open-Ended
Benchmark:	G S Technology
Options:	No
Initial Divisor:	—
Min. Investment:	1 Share
Date of Inception:	19–Mar–01
52 Week Range:	45.46–66.69
2000 Total Dist.:	—

TOP 10 HOLDINGS

1) Microsoft Corp	12.07%
2) Intel Corp	7.33%
3) AOL Time Warner	7.19%
4) IBM	6.98%
5) Cisco Systems	4.71%
6) Oracle Corp	3.47%
7) Dell Computer Corp	2.75%
8) E M C Corp	2.66%
9) Hewlett-Packard	2.56%
10) Texas Instruments	2.22%

FUNDAMENTALS

Med Mkt Cap:	$74,507,000,000
P/E Ratio:	38.70
P/B Ratio:	9.20
P/C Ratio:	26.40
Standard Dev:	N/A
Sharpe Ratio:	N/A
Alpha:	N/A
Beta:	N/A
3 Yr Earn Gr:	32.50
1 Yr Fwd Gr:	−3.50
12 Month Yield:	N/A

SECTOR BREAKDOWN

Utilities:	0.00%
Energy:	0.00%
Financials:	0.50%
Industrial Cyclicals:	0.90%
Consumer Durables:	0.20%
Consumer Staples:	0.00%
Services:	2.50%
Retail:	0.10%
Health:	0.00%
Technology:	95.80%

PREMIUM/DISCOUNT (6/29/2001)

P/D Close:	1.94%
P/D Midpoint:	1.25%

TICKERS

Symbol: IGM		ECash:	IPM.EU
NAV:	IPM	TCash:	IPM.TC
Close:	IPM.NV	Div:	IPM.DP
Shares:	IPM.SO	Index:	GTC

FUND MANAGEMENT

Manager:	Barclays Global
Web Site:	http://www.ishares.com/
Telephone:	800–474–2737
Specialist:	Hull Trading Co.
Distributor:	SEI Investments
Administrator:	Investors Bank & Trust
Sponsor:	N/A
Exchange:	AMEX

1 Yr	3 Yr	5 Yr	2000	1999	1998	1997
—	—	—	—	—	—	—

Source: AMEX and Morningstar data as of 6/30/2001.

iSHARES NASDAQ BIOTECHNOLOGY (IBB)

FUND INFORMATION

Expense Ratio:	0.50%
Total Net Assets:	$131,960,000
Structure:	Open-Ended
Benchmark:	Nasdaq Biotech.
Options:	No
Initial Divisor:	1/10
Min. Investment:	1 Share
Date of Inception:	09-Feb–01
52 Week Range:	61.00–109.30
2000 Total Dist.:[em]	

FUNDAMENTALS

Med Mkt Cap:	$2,950,000,000
P/E Ratio:	55.40
P/B Ratio:	9.40
P/C Ratio:	37.10
Standard Dev:	N/A
Sharpe Ratio:	N/A
Alpha:	N/A
Beta:	N/A
3 Yr Earn Gr:	N/A
1 Yr Fwd Gr:	4.90
12 Month Yield:	N/A

PREMIUM/DISCOUNT (6/29/2001)

P/D Close:	N/A
P/D Midpoint:	N/A

TICKERS

Symbol:	IBB	ECash:	IBF.EU
NAV:	IBF	TCash:	IBF.TC
Close:	IBF.NV	Div:	IBF.DP
Shares:	IBF.SO	Index:	NBI

TOP 10 HOLDINGS

1) Amgen Inc	19.44%
2) Biogen Inc	3.55%
3) Chiron Corp	3.26%
4) Genzyme Corp	3.17%
5) Medimmune Inc	3.01%
6) Immunex Corp	2.73%
7) Millennium Pharma	2.54%
8) Human Genome Sci	2.31%
9) IDEC Pharma Corp	2.27%
10) Aviron	1.68%

SECTOR BREAKDOWN

Utilities:	0.00%
Energy:	0.00%
Financials:	0.00%
Industrial Cyclicals:	0.00%
Consumer Durables:	0.00%
Consumer Staples:	0.00%
Services:	0.00%
Retail:	0.00%
Health:	98.30%
Technology:	1.70%

FUND MANAGEMENT

Manager:	Barclays Global
Web Site:	http://www.ishares.com/
Telephone:	800–474–2737
Specialist:	Hull Trading Co.
Distributor:	SEI Investments
Administrator:	Investors Bank & Trust
Sponsor:	N/A
Exchange:	AMEX

1 Yr	3 Yr	5 Yr	2000	1999	1998	1997
—	—	—	—	—	—	—

Source: AMEX and Morningstar data as of 6/30/2001.

SPDR BASIC INDUSTRIES (XLB)

FUND INFORMATION

Expense Ratio:	0.28%
Total Net Assets:	$106,890,000
Structure:	Open-Ended
Benchmark:	Basic Ind. Select
Options:	No
Initial Divisor:	1/10
Min. Investment:	1 Share
Date of Inception:	22-Dec–98
52 Week Range:	17.00–24.63
2000 Total Dist.:	0.91

FUNDAMENTALS

Med Mkt Cap:	$12,154,000,000
P/E Ratio:	24.40
P/B Ratio:	2.70
P/C Ratio:	11.80
Standard Dev:	N/A
Sharpe Ratio:	N/A
Alpha:	N/A
Beta:	N/A
3 Yr Earn Gr:	4.10
1 Yr Fwd Gr:	−28.10
12 Month Yield:	N/A

PREMIUM/DISCOUNT (6/29/2001)

P/D Close:	0.09%
P/D Midpoint:	0.24%

TICKERS

Symbol:	XLB	ECash:	BXV.EU
NAV:	BXV	TCash:	BXV.TC
Close:	BXV.NV	Div:	BXV.DP
Shares:	BXV.SO	Index:	IXB

TOP 10 HOLDINGS

1) Dupont	16.14%
2) Alcoa Inc	11.82%
3) Dow Chemical Co	10.75%
4) International Paper	6.60%
5) Alcan Inc	4.35%
6) Weyerhaeuser Co	4.19%
7) Air Prods & Chem Inc	3.35%
8) PPG Inds Inc	2.94%
9) Praxair Inc	2.69%
10) Rohm & Haas Co	2.57%

SECTOR BREAKDOWN

Utilities:	0.00%
Energy:	0.00%
Financials:	0.00%
Industrial Cyclicals:	100.00%
Consumer Durables:	0.00%
Consumer Staples:	0.00%
Services:	0.00%
Retail:	0.00%
Health:	0.00%
Technology:	0.00%

FUND MANAGEMENT

Manager:	State Street Global
Web Site:	http://www.spdrindex.com/spdr/
Telephone:	800–843–2639
Specialist:	Bear Hunter
Distributor:	ALPS Mutual Funds
Administrator:	N/A
Sponsor:	PDR Services, LLC
Exchange:	AMEX

1 Yr	3 Yr	5 Yr	2000	1999	1998	1997
17.19	—	—	−15.73	23.23	—	—

Source: AMEX and Morningstar data as of 6/30/2001.

SPDR CONSUMER SERVICES (XLV)

FUND INFORMATION

Expense Ratio:	0.28%
Total Net Assets:	$118,160,000
Structure:	Open-Ended
Benchmark:	Cons Serv Select
Options:	No
Initial Divisor:	1/10
Min. Investment:	1 Share
Date of Inception:	22-Dec-98
52 Week Range:	24.55–30.81
2000 Total Dist.:	0.06

TOP 10 HOLDINGS

1) Viacom Inc	14.47%
2) Disney (Walt) Co	11.22%
3) Clear Channel Comm	6.15%
4) Comcast Corp	6.14%
5) HCA Healthcare Co	4.34%
6) McDonalds Corp	4.31%
7) UnitedHealth Group Inc	3.74%
8) Carnival Corp	3.21%
9) CIGNA Corp	3.11%
10) Gannett Inc	3.08%

FUNDAMENTALS

Med Mkt Cap:	$17,036,000,000
P/E Ratio:	31.90
P/B Ratio:	4.70
P/C Ratio:	19.00
Standard Dev:	N/A
Sharpe Ratio:	N/A
Alpha:	N/A
Beta:	N/A
3 Yr Earn Gr:	17.30
1 Yr Fwd Gr:	6.50
12 Month Yield:	N/A

SECTOR BREAKDOWN

Utilities:	0.00%
Energy:	0.00%
Financials:	3.50%
Industrial Cyclicals:	0.50%
Consumer Durables:	0.00%
Consumer Staples:	0.00%
Services:	79.80%
Retail:	1.40%
Health:	13.30%
Technology:	1.60%

PREMIUM/DISCOUNT (6/29/2001)

P/D Close:	0.4%
P/D Midpoint:	0.3%

TICKERS

Symbol: XLV		ECash:	NXV.EU
NAV:	NXV	TCash:	NXV.TC
Close:	NXV.NV	Div:	NXV.DP
Shares:	NXV.SO	Index:	IXV

FUND MANAGEMENT

Manager:	State Street Global
Web Site:	http://www.spdrindex.com/spdr/
Telephone:	800–843–2639
Specialist:	Spear, Leeds
Distributor:	ALPS Mutual Funds
Administrator:	N/A
Sponsor:	PDR Services, LLC
Exchange:	AMEX

1 Yr	3 Yr	5 Yr	2000	1999	1998	1997
0.21	—	—	−11.60	19.51	—	—

Source: AMEX and Morningstar data as of 6/30/2001.

SPDR Consumer Staples (XLP)

Fund Information

Expense Ratio:	0.28%
Total Net Assets:	$231,900,000
Structure:	Open-Ended
Benchmark:	Cons Stap Select
Options:	No
Initial Divisor:	1/10
Min. Investment:	1 Share
Date of Inception:	22-Dec–98
52 Week Range:	22.52–28.87
2000 Total Dist.:	0.30

Fundamentals

Med Mkt Cap:	$77,296,000,000
P/E Ratio:	31.80
P/B Ratio:	10.80
P/C Ratio:	24.10
Standard Dev:	N/A
Sharpe Ratio:	N/A
Alpha:	N/A
Beta:	N/A
3 Yr Earn Gr:	11.50
1 Yr Fwd Gr:	11.90
12 Month Yield:	N/A

Premium/Discount (6/29/2001)

P/D Close:	N/A
P/D Midpoint:	N/A

Tickers

Symbol:	XLP	ECash:	PXV.EU
NAV:	PXV	TCash:	PXV.TC
Close:	PXV.NV	Div:	PXV.DP
Shares:	PXV.SO	Index:	IXR

Top 10 Holdings

1) Pfizer Inc	11.78%
2) Merck & Co Inc	7.98%
3) Johnson & Johnson	5.54%
4) Bristol Myers Squibb	5.30%
5) Coca-Cola Co	5.12%
6) Philip Morris Cos Inc	4.81%
7) Lilly (Eli) and Co	3.94%
8) Procter & Gamble	3.71%
9) American Home Prod Inc	3.51%
10) Abbott Labs	3.33%

Sector Breakdown

Utilities:	0.00%
Energy:	0.00%
Financials:	0.00%
Industrial Cyclicals:	1.40%
Consumer Durables:	0.00%
Consumer Staples:	31.60%
Services:	0.00%
Retail:	5.60%
Health:	61.40%
Technology:	0.00%

Fund Management

Manager:	State Street Global
Web Site:	http://www.opdrindex.com/spdr/
Telephone:	800–843–2639
Specialist:	Bear Hunter
Distributor:	ALPS Mutual Funds
Administrator:	N/A
Sponsor:	PDR Services, LLC
Exchange:	AMEX

1 Yr	3 Yr	5 Yr	2000	1999	1998	1997
−2.70	—	—	25.57	−14.25	—	—

Source: AMEX and Morningstar data as of 6/30/2001.

SPDR Cyclical/Transportation (XLY)

Fund Information

Expense Ratio:	0.28%
Total Net Assets:	$133,520,000
Structure:	Open-Ended
Benchmark:	Cycl/Trans Select
Options:	No
Initial Divisor:	1/10
Min. Investment:	1 Share
Date of Inception:	22-Dec–98
52 Week Range:	21.56–29.10
2000 Total Dist.:	0.23

Fundamentals

Med Mkt Cap:	$25,029,000,000
P/E Ratio:	29.30
P/B Ratio:	5.00
P/C Ratio:	18.00
Standard Dev:	N/A
Sharpe Ratio:	N/A
Alpha:	N/A
Beta:	N/A
3 Yr Earn Gr:	15.00
1 Yr Fwd Gr:	−1.20
12 Month Yield:	N/A

Premium/Discount (6/29/2001)

P/D Close:	0.47%
P/D Midpoint:	0.1%

Tickers

Symbol:	XLY	ECash:	YXV.EU
NAV:	YXV	TCash:	YXV.TC
Close:	YXV.NV	Div:	YXV.DP
Shares:	YXV.SO	Index:	IXY

Top 10 Holdings

1) Wal-Mart Stores	20.41%
2) Home Depot Inc	12.05%
3) Ford Motor Co Del	6.36%
4) Target Corp	4.00%
5) General Motors Co	3.49%
6) Lowes Cos Inc	2.81%
7) Kohls Corp	2.68%
8) Gap Inc	2.48%
9) Costco Whsl Corp New	2.22%
10) Union Pacific Corp	1.84%

Sector Breakdown

Utilities:	0.00%
Energy:	0.00%
Financials:	0.00%
Industrial Cyclicals:	4.60%
Consumer Durables:	19.80%
Consumer Staples:	1.00%
Services:	11.20%
Retail:	63.50%
Health:	0.00%
Technology:	0.00%

Fund Management

Manager:	State Street Global
Web Site:	http://www.spdrindex.com/spdr/
Telephone:	800–843–2639
Specialist:	Spear, Leeds
Distributor:	ALPS Mutual Funds
Administrator:	N/A
Sponsor:	PDR Services, LLC
Exchange:	AMEX

1 Yr	3 Yr	5 Yr	2000	1999	1998	1997
8.90	—	—	−16.86	19.51	—	—

Source: AMEX and Morningstar data as of 6/30/2001.

SPDR ENERGY (XLE)

FUND INFORMATION

Expense Ratio:	0.28%
Total Net Assets:	$234,230,000
Structure:	Open-Ended
Benchmark:	Energy Select
Options:	No
Initial Divisor:	1/10
Min. Investment:	1 Share
Date of Inception:	22-Dec-98
52 Week Range:	28.28-34.90
2000 Total Dist.:	0.48

FUNDAMENTALS

Med Mkt Cap:	$42,377,000,000
P/E Ratio:	21.50
P/B Ratio:	3.00
P/C Ratio:	12.60
Standard Dev:	N/A
Sharpe Ratio:	N/A
Alpha:	N/A
Beta:	N/A
3 Yr Earn Gr:	12.00
1 Yr Fwd Gr:	16.00
12 Month Yield:	N/A

PREMIUM/DISCOUNT (6/29/2001)

P/D Close:	N/A
P/D Midpoint:	0.14%

TICKERS

Symbol: XLE	ECash:	EXV.EU	
NAV: EXV	TCash:	EXV.TC	
Close: EXV.NV	Div:	EXV.DP	
Shares: EXV.SO	Index:	IXE	

TOP 10 HOLDINGS

1) ExxonMobil Corp	23.35%
2) Royal Dutch Petrol Co	14.87%
3) Chevron Corp	7.27%
4) Texaco Inc	4.62%
5) Enron	4.54%
6) El Paso Corp	4.41%
7) Schlumberger Ltd	4.39%
8) Williams Controls Inc	2.96%
9) Conoco Inc	2.57%
10) Halliburton Co	2.41%

SECTOR BREAKDOWN

Utilities:	6.90%
Energy:	91.80%
Financials:	0.00%
Industrial Cyclicals:	1.20%
Consumer Durables:	0.00%
Consumer Staples:	0.00%
Services:	0.00%
Retail:	0.00%
Health:	0.00%
Technology:	0.00%

FUND MANAGEMENT

Manager:	State Street Global
Web Site:	http://www.spdrindex.com/spdr/
Telephone:	800-843-2639
Specialist:	Susquehanna
Distributor:	ALPS Mutual Funds
Administrator:	N/A
Sponsor:	PDR Services, LLC
Exchange:	AMEX

1 Yr	3 Yr	5 Yr	2000	1999	1998	1997
1.21	—	—	24.38	17.96	—	—

Source: AMEX and Morningstar data as of 6/30/2001.

SPDR FINANCIAL (XLF)

FUND INFORMATION

Expense Ratio:	0.28%
Total Net Assets:	$739,210,000
Structure:	Open-Ended
Benchmark:	Financial Select
Options:	No
Initial Divisor:	1/10
Min. Investment:	1 Share
Date of Inception:	22-Dec-98
52 Week Range:	23.38–30.66
2000 Total Dist.:	0.36

FUNDAMENTALS

Med Mkt Cap:	$50,743,000,000
P/E Ratio:	21.20
P/B Ratio:	3.60
P/C Ratio:	N/A
Standard Dev:	N/A
Sharpe Ratio:	N/A
Alpha:	N/A
Beta:	N/A
3 Yr Earn Gr:	15.80
1 Yr Fwd Gr:	8.30
12 Month Yield:	N/A

PREMIUM/DISCOUNT (6/29/2001)

P/D Close:	N/A
P/D Midpoint:	N/A

TICKERS

Symbol:	XLF	ECash:	FXV.EU
NAV:	FXV	TCash:	FXV.TC
Close:	FXV.NV	Div:	FXV.DP
Shares:	FXV.SO	Index:	IXM

TOP 10 HOLDINGS

1) Citigroup Inc	12.27%
2) AIG Inc	10.18%
3) BankAmerica Corp	4.84%
4) JP Morgan Chase & Co	4.64%
5) Wells Fargo & Co	4.60%
6) Federal Natl Mtg Assn	4.36%
7) Morgan Stanley	3.25%
8) American Express	2.99%
9) Fed Home Loan Mtg	2.45%
10) Merrill Lynch & Co	2.43%

SECTOR BREAKDOWN

Utilities:	0.00%
Energy:	0.00%
Financials:	99.70%
Industrial Cyclicals:	0.00%
Consumer Durables:	0.00%
Consumer Staples:	0.00%
Services:	0.30%
Retail:	0.00%
Health:	0.00%
Technology:	0.00%

FUND MANAGEMENT

Manager:	State Street Global
Web Site:	http://www.spdrindex.com/spdr/
Telephone:	800–843–2639
Specialist:	Spear, Leeds
Distributor:	ALPS Mutual Funds
Administrator:	N/A
Sponsor:	PDR Services, LLC
Exchange:	AMEX

1 Yr	3 Yr	5 Yr	2000	1999	1998	1997
20.84	—	—	25.89	2.66	—	—

Source: AMEX and Morningstar data as of 6/30/2001.

SPDR INDUSTRIAL (XLI)

FUND INFORMATION

Expense Ratio:	0.28%
Total Net Assets:	$74,050,000
Structure:	Open-Ended
Benchmark:	Industrial Select
Options:	No
Initial Divisor:	1/10
Min. Investment:	1 Share
Date of Inception:	22-Dec-98
52 Week Range:	24.50-32.66
2000 Total Dist.:	0.33

TOP 10 HOLDINGS

1) General Electric Co	17.29%
2) Tyco Intl	9.13%
3) Boeing Co	4.98%
4) Minnesota Mining	4.95%
5) Honeywell Intl Inc	4.50%
6) Emerson Elec Co	4.39%
7) Waste Mgmt Inc Del	3.77%
8) United Technologies	3.69%
9) Allied Waste Industries	3.42%
10) Illinois Tool Wks	3.02%

FUNDAMENTALS

Med Mkt Cap:	$24,572,000,000
P/E Ratio:	25.50
P/B Ratio:	4.70
P/C Ratio:	13.60
Standard Dev:	N/A
Sharpe Ratio:	N/A
Alpha:	N/A
Beta:	N/A
3 Yr Earn Gr:	8.30
1 Yr Fwd Gr:	1.10
12 Month Yield:	N/A

SECTOR BREAKDOWN

Utilities:	0.00%
Energy:	0.00%
Financials:	0.00%
Industrial Cyclicals:	84.40%
Consumer Durables:	7.50%
Consumer Staples:	0.00%
Services:	7.70%
Retail:	0.00%
Health:	0.00%
Technology:	0.40%

PREMIUM/DISCOUNT (6/29/2001)

P/D Close:	N/A
P/D Midpoint.	N/A

TICKERS

Symbol:	XLI	ECash:	TXV.EU
NAV:	TXV	TCash:	TXV.TC
Close:	TXV.NV	Div:	TXV.DP
Shares:	TXV.SO	Index:	IXI

FUND MANAGEMENT

Manager:	State Street Global
Web Site:	http://www.opdrindon.oom/opdr/
Telephone:	800-843-2639
Specialist:	AGS/STR/OTA
Distributor:	ALPS Mutual Funds
Administrator:	N/A
Sponsor:	State Street Gl Bank
Exchange:	AMEX

1 Yr	3 Yr	5 Yr	2000	1999	1998	1997
3.13	—	—	6.73	22.22	—	—

Source: AMEX and Morningstar data as of 6/30/2001.

SPDR TECHNOLOGY (XLK)

FUND INFORMATION

Expense Ratio:	0.28%
Total Net Assets:	$1,172,910,000
Structure:	Open-Ended
Benchmark:	Tech. Select
Options:	No
Initial Divisor:	1/10
Min. Investment:	1 Share
Date of Inception:	22-Dec–98
52 Week Range:	21.85–57.75
2000 Total Dist.:	0.00

FUNDAMENTALS

Med Mkt Cap:	$81,236,000,000
P/E Ratio:	37.80
P/B Ratio:	8.70
P/C Ratio:	24.50
Standard Dev:	N/A
Sharpe Ratio:	N/A
Alpha:	N/A
Beta:	N/A
3 Yr Earn Gr:	30.00
1 Yr Fwd Gr:	−7.50
12 Month Yield:	N/A

PREMIUM/DISCOUNT (6/29/2001)

P/D Close:	1.18%
P/D Midpoint:	1.49%

TICKERS

Symbol: XLK		ECash:	KXV.EU
NAV:	KXV	TCash:	KXV.TC
Close:	KXV.NV	Div:	KXV.DP
Shares:	KXV.SO	Index:	IXT

TOP 10 HOLDINGS

1) Microsoft Corp	12.36%
2) Intel Corp	7.50%
3) AOL Time Warner	7.39%
4) IBM	7.15%
5) Cisco Sytems	4.87%
6) Oracle Corp	3.58%
7) AT & T Corp	3.39%
8) Dell Computer Corp	2.83%
9) E M C Corp	2.75%
10) Hewlett-Packard	2.57%

SECTOR BREAKDOWN

Utilities:	0.00%
Energy:	0.00%
Financials:	0.40%
Industrial Cyclicals:	1.20%
Consumer Durables:	0.00%
Consumer Staples:	0.00%
Services:	12.40%
Retail:	0.00%
Health:	0.00%
Technology:	86.00%

FUND MANAGEMENT

Manager:	State Street Global
Web Site:	http://www.spdrindex.com/spdr/
Telephone:	800–843–2639
Specialist:	Susquehanna
Distributor:	ALPS Mutual Funds
Administrator:	N/A
Sponsor:	State Street Gl Bank
Exchange:	AMEX

1 Yr	3 Yr	5 Yr	2000	1999	1998	1997
−48.01	—	—	−41.88	65.14	—	—

Source: AMEX and Morningstar data as of 6/30/2001.

SPDR Utilities (XLU)

Fund Information

Expense Ratio:	0.28%
Total Net Assets:	$76,100,000
Structure:	Open-Ended
Benchmark:	Utilities Select
Options:	No
Initial Divisor:	1/10
Min. Investment:	1 Share
Date of Inception:	22-Dec-98
52 Week Range:	27.16–34.55
2000 Total Dist.:	1.16

Fundamentals

Med Mkt Cap:	$19,656,000,000
P/E Ratio:	17.70
P/B Ratio:	3.80
P/C Ratio:	11.30
Standard Dev:	N/A
Sharpe Ratio:	N/A
Alpha:	N/A
Beta:	N/A
3 Yr Earn Gr:	17.70
1 Yr Fwd Gr:	11.70
12 Month Yield:	N/A

Premium/Discount (6/29/2001)

P/D Close:	0.28%
P/D Midpoint:	N/A

Tickers

Symbol:	XLU	ECash:	UXN.EU
NAV:	UXV	TCash:	UXN.TC
Close:	UXV.NV	Div:	UXN.DP
Shares:	UXN.SO	Index:	IXU

Top 10 Holdings

1) SBC Communications	18.84%
2) Verizon Comm	16.61%
3) Duke Energy Co	4.71%
4) AES Corp	3.93%
5) Exelon Corp	3.69%
6) Southern Co	3.53%
7) BellSouth Corp	3.32%
8) American Elec Pwr Inc	2.83%
9) Dominion Res Inc	2.54%
10) Xcel Energy Inc	2.52%

Sector Breakdown

Utilities:	56.20%
Energy:	2.50%
Financials:	0.00%
Industrial Cyclicals:	0.00%
Consumer Durables:	0.00%
Consumer Staples:	0.00%
Services:	41.20%
Retail:	0.00%
Health:	0.00%
Technology:	0.00%

Fund Management

Manager:	State Street Global
Web Site:	http://www.spdrindex.com/spdr/
Telephone:	800–843–2639
Specialist:	AGS/STR/OTA
Distributor:	ALPS Mutual Funds
Administrator:	N/A
Sponsor:	State Street Gl Bank
Exchange:	AMEX

1 Yr	3 Yr	5 Yr	2000	1999	1998	1997
17.78	—	—	22.47	−3.80	—	—

Source: AMEX and Morningstar data as of 6/30/2001.

streetTRACKS MORGAN STANLEY HIGHTECH (MTK)

FUND INFORMATION

Expense Ratio:	0.50%
Total Net Assets:	$72,790,000
Structure:	Open-Ended
Benchmark:	MS High Tech 35
Options:	No
Initial Divisor:	1/10
Min. Investment:	1 Share
Date of Inception:	29-Sep–00
52 Week Range:	46.00–98.25
2000 Total Dist.:	0.00

FUNDAMENTALS

Med Mkt Cap:	$29,402,000,000
P/E Ratio:	39.80
P/B Ratio:	7.20
P/C Ratio:	25.90
Standard Dev:	N/A
Sharpe Ratio:	N/A
Alpha:	N/A
Beta:	N/A
3 Yr Earn Gr:	30.00
1 Yr Fwd Gr:	−15.50
12 Month Yield:	N/A

PREMIUM/DISCOUNT (6/29/2001)

P/D Close:	0.56%
P/D Midpoint:	0.3%

TICKERS

Symbol: MTK		ECash:	JMT.EU
NAV:	JMT	TCash:	JMT.TC
Close:	JMT.NV	Div:	JMT.DP
Shares:	JMT.SO	Index:	MSH

TOP 10 HOLDINGS

1) Electronic Arts Inc	5.72%
2) Dell Computer Corp	5.15%
3) Micron Technology	4.62%
4) Computer Assoc Intl	4.46%
5) Microsoft Corp	4.44%
6) Applied Materials Inc	4.39%
7) IBM	4.38%
8) Compaq Computer	4.18%
9) Electronic Data Sys	4.11%
10) Hewlett-Packard	3.94%

SECTOR BREAKDOWN

Utilities:	0.00%
Energy:	0.00%
Financials:	0.00%
Industrial Cyclicals:	0.00%
Consumer Durables:	0.00%
Consumer Staples:	0.00%
Services:	3.30%
Retail:	2.70%
Health:	0.00%
Technology:	94.00%

FUND MANAGEMENT

Manager:	State Street Global
Web Site:	http://www.streettracks.com/
Telephone:	866–787–2257
Specialist:	KV Executions Services
Distributor:	State Street Gl Cap
Administrator:	State Street Gl B&T
Sponsor:	N/A
Exchange:	AMEX

1 Yr	3 Yr	5 Yr	2000	1999	1998	1997
—	—	—	—	—	—	—

Source: AMEX and Morningstar data as of 6/30/2001.

streetTRACKS Morgan Stanley Internet (MII)

Fund Information

Expense Ratio:	0.50%
Total Net Assets:	$6,770,000
Structure:	Open-Ended
Benchmark:	MS Internet
Options:	No
Initial Divisor:	1
Min. Investment:	1 Share
Date of Inception:	29-Sep-00
52 Week Range:	13.57–66.50
2000 Total Dist.:	0.00

Fundamentals

Med Mkt Cap:	$7,303,000,000
P/E Ratio:	47.30
P/B Ratio:	5.80
P/C Ratio:	28.10
Standard Dev:	N/A
Sharpe Ratio:	N/A
Alpha:	N/A
Beta:	N/A
3 Yr Earn Gr:	N/A
1 Yr Fwd Gr:	24.20
12 Month Yield:	N/A

Premium/Discount (6/29/2001)

P/D Close:	N/A
P/D Midpoint:	N/A

Tickers

Symbol:	MII	ECash:	MMI.EU
NAV:	MMI	TCash:	MMI.TC
Close:	MMI.NV	Div:	MMI.DP
Shares:	MMI.SO	Index:	MOX

Top 10 Holdings

1) AOL Time Warner	3.52%
2) Amazon.com	3.21%
3) Ariba Inc	2.68%
4) At Home Corp	3.22%
5) CNET Networks Inc	4.93%
6) Ciena Corp	2.74%
7) Cisco Sytems	2.74%
8) Doubleclick Inc	3.85%
9) E M C Corp	3.08%
10) e.piphany Inc	2.99%

Sector Breakdown

Utilities:	0.00%
Energy:	0.00%
Financials:	3.30%
Industrial Cyclicals:	0.00%
Consumer Durables:	0.00%
Consumer Staples:	0.00%
Services:	23.40%
Retail:	4.40%
Health:	0.00%
Technology:	69.00%

Fund Management

Manager:	State Street Global
Web Site:	http://www.streettracks.com/
Telephone:	866–787–2257
Specialist:	Wolverine Trading
Distributor:	State Street Gl Cap
Administrator:	State Street Gl B&T
Sponsor:	N/A
Exchange:	AMEX

1 Yr	3 Yr	5 Yr	2000	1999	1998	1997
—	—	—	—	—	—	—

Source: AMEX and Morningstar data as of 6/30/2001.

streetTRACKS Wilshire REIT (RWR)

Fund Information

Expense Ratio:	0.25%
Total Net Assets:	$18,110,000
Structure:	Open-Ended
Benchmark:	Wilshire REIT
Options:	No
Initial Divisor:	—
Min. Investment:	1 Share
Date of Inception:	27-Apr-01
52 Week Range:	110.55–120.00
2000 Total Dist.:	—

Fundamentals

Med Mkt Cap:	N/A
P/E Ratio:	N/A
P/B Ratio:	N/A
P/C Ratio:	N/A
Standard Dev:	N/A
Sharpe Ratio:	N/A
Alpha:	N/A
Beta:	N/A
3 Yr Earn Gr:	N/A
1 Yr Fwd Gr:	N/A
12 Month Yield:	N/A

Premium/Discount (6/29/2001)

P/D Close:	N/A
P/D Midpoint:	N/A

Tickers

Symbol: RWR	ECash:	EWR.EU
NAV: EWR	TCash:	EWR.TC
Close: EWR.NV	Div:	EWR.DP
Shares: EWR.SO	Index:	N/A

Top 10 Holdings

1) Equity Office REIT	7.36%
2) Equity Res Prop Trust	5.88%
3) Simon Property Group	3.75%
4) Spieker Properties	3.08%
5) Prologis Trust	2.97%
6) Boston Properties, Inc.	2.84%
7) Apt Inv & Man	2.70%
8) Pub Storage Prop	2.69%
9) Vornado Realty Trust	2.65%
10) Avalon Bay Comm	2.62%

Sector Breakdown

Utilities:	0.00%
Energy:	0.00%
Financials:	0.00%
Industrial Cyclicals:	0.00%
Consumer Durables:	0.00%
Consumer Staples:	0.00%
Services:	0.00%
Retail:	0.00%
Health:	0.00%
Technology:	0.00%

Fund Management

Manager:	State Street Global
Web Site:	http://www.streettracks.com/
Telephone:	866-787-2257
Specialist:	N/A
Distributor:	State Street Gl Cap
Administrator:	State Street Gl B&T
Sponsor:	N/A
Exchange:	AMEX

1 Yr	3 Yr	5 Yr	2000	1999	1998	1997
—	—	—	—	—	—	—

Source: AMEX and Morningstar data as of 6/30/2001.

INTERNATIONAL ETFS TRADING ON U.S. MARKETS

iSHARES S&P GLOBAL 100 INDEX (IOO)

FUND INFORMATION

Expense Ratio:	0.40%
Total Net Assets:	$119,810,000
Structure:	Open-Ended
Benchmark:	S&P Global 100
Options:	No
Initial Divisor:	—
Min. Investment:	1 Share
Date of Inception:	08-Dec-00
52 Week Range:	57.60–73.70
2000 Total Dist.:	0.02

FUNDAMENTALS

Med Mkt Cap:	$126,114,000,000
P/E Ratio:	28.70
P/B Ratio:	7.00
P/C Ratio:	18.80
Standard Dev:	N/A
Sharpe Ratio:	N/A
Alpha:	N/A
Beta:	N/A
3 Yr Earn Gr:	16.40
1 Yr Fwd Gr:	3.40
12 Month Yield:	N/A

PREMIUM/DISCOUNT (6/29/2001)

P/D Close:	N/A
P/D Midpoint:	N/A

TICKERS

Symbol: IOO		ECash:	OOE
NAV:	OON	TCash:	OOU
Close:	OOV	Div:	OOU
Shares:	OOS	Index:	OOI

TOP 10 HOLDINGS

1) General Electric Co	6.19%
2) ExxonMobil Corp	3.99%
3) Pfizer Inc	3.83%
4) Citigroup Inc	3.23%
5) Vodafone Group	2.97%
6) American Intl Grp	2.83%
7) Merck & Co Inc	2.69%
8) Intel Corp	2.50%
9) Nokia Corp Cl A Adr	2.50%
10) Bp Amoco Corp	2.39%

SECTOR BREAKDOWN

Utilities:	1.10%
Energy:	11.30%
Financials:	15.20%
Industrial Cyclicals:	13.10%
Consumer Durables:	6.40%
Consumer Staples:	8.00%
Services:	7.10%
Retail:	2.70%
Health:	12.80%
Technology:	22.40%

FUND MANAGEMENT

Manager:	Barclays Global
Web Site:	http://www.ishares.com/
Telephone:	800–474–2737
Specialist:	Susquehanna
Distributor:	SEI Investments
Administrator:	Investors Bank & Trust
Sponsor:	N/A
Exchange:	NYSE

1 Yr	3 Yr	5 Yr	2000	1999	1998	1997
—	—	—	—	—	—	—

Source: AMEX and Morningstar data as of 6/30/2001.

STREETTRACKS DJ GLOBAL TITANS (DGT)

FUND INFORMATION

Expense Ratio:	0.50%
Total Net Assets:	$21,180,000
Structure:	Open-Ended
Benchmark:	DJ Global Titans
Options:	No
Initial Divisor:	1/4
Min. Investment:	1 Share
Date of Inception:	29-Sep-00
52 Week Range:	64.37-85.50
2000 Total Dist.:	0.13

TOP 10 HOLDINGS

1) General Electric Co	7.79%
2) ExxonMobil Corp	5.26%
3) Microsoft Corp	4.72%
4) Citigroup Inc	4.29%
5) Bp Amoco Corp	3.50%
6) Vodafone Group	3.28%
7) Merck & Co Inc	3.27%
8) IBM	3.16%
9) Intel Corp	3.15%
10) AIG Inc	3.01%

FUNDAMENTALS

Med Mkt Cap:	$141,298,000,000
P/E Ratio:	26.50
P/B Ratio:	5.20
P/C Ratio:	17.40
Standard Dev:	N/A
Sharpe Ratio:	N/A
Alpha:	N/A
Beta:	N/A
3 Yr Earn Gr:	16.70
1 Yr Fwd Gr:	−1.70
12 Month Yield:	N/A

SECTOR BREAKDOWN

Utilities:	0.00%
Energy:	13.40%
Financials:	20.60%
Industrial Cyclicals:	9.80%
Consumer Durables:	5.50%
Consumer Staples:	6.90%
Services:	14.60%
Retail:	2.60%
Health:	8.10%
Technology:	18.60%

PREMIUM/DISCOUNT (6/29/2001)

P/D Close:	0.49%
P/D Midpoint:	0.21%

TICKERS

Symbol: DGT		ECash:	UGT.EU
NAV:	UGT	TCash:	UGT.TC
Close:	UGT.NV	Div:	UGT.DP
Shares:	UGT.SO	Index:	DJGT

FUND MANAGEMENT

Manager:	State Street Global
Web Site:	http://www.streettracks.com/
Telephone:	866-787-2257
Specialist:	KV Executions Services
Distributor:	State Street Gl Cap
Administrator:	State Street Gl B&T
Sponsor:	N/A
Exchange:	AMEX

1 Yr	3 Yr	5 Yr	2000	1999	1998	1997
—	—	—	—	—	—	—

Source: AMEX and Morningstar data as of 6/30/2001.

iShares S&P Europe 350 Index (IEV)

Fund Information

Expense Ratio:	0.60%
Total Net Assets:	$171,490,000
Structure:	Open-Ended
Benchmark:	S&P Europe 350
Options:	No
Initial Divisor:	—
Min. Investment:	1 Share
Date of Inception:	25-Jul–00
52 Week Range:	59.02–80.75
2000 Total Dist.:	0.19

Top 10 Holdings

1) Bp Amoco Corp	3.91%
2) Vodafone Group	3.70%
3) GlaxoSmithKline	3.41%
4) Novartis	2.47%
5) HSBC Holdings	2.32%
6) Nokia Corp	2.20%
7) Royal Dutch Petrol Co	2.17%
8) Total SA - Series B	2.09%
9) Zeneca Group Plc	1.77%
10) Nestle SA	1.65%

Fundamentals

Med Mkt Cap:	$39,188,000,000
P/E Ratio:	22.70
P/B Ratio:	5.00
P/C Ratio:	14.50
Standard Dev:	N/A
Sharpe Ratio:	N/A
Alpha:	N/A
Beta:	N/A
3 Yr Earn Gr:	N/A
1 Yr Fwd Gr:	15.00
12 Month Yield:	N/A

Sector Breakdown

Utilities:	3.30%
Energy:	14.30%
Financials:	31.30%
Industrial Cyclicals:	8.60%
Consumer Durables:	4.20%
Consumer Staples:	7.40%
Services:	13.20%
Retail:	4.70%
Health:	5.60%
Technology:	7.50%

Premium/Discount (6/29/2001)

P/D Close:	1.83%
P/D Midpoint:	1.35%

Tickers

Symbol: IEV		ECash:	NLG.EU
NAV:	NLG	TCash:	NLG.TC
Close:	NLG.NV	Div:	NLG.DP
Shares:	NLG.SO	Index:	N/A

Fund Management

Manager:	Barclays Global
Web Site:	http://www.ishares.com/
Telephone:	800–474–2737
Specialist:	Susquehanna
Distributor:	SEI Investments
Administrator:	Investors Bank & Trust
Sponsor:	N/A
Exchange:	AMEX

1 Yr	3 Yr	5 Yr	2000	1999	1998	1997
—	—	—	—	—	—	—

Source: AMEX and Morningstar data as of 6/30/2001.

iSHARES MSCI EMU INDEX (EZU)

FUND INFORMATION

Expense Ratio:	0.84%
Total Net Assets:	$80,690,000
Structure:	Open-Ended
Benchmark:	MSCI-EMU
Options:	No
Initial Divisor:	—
Min. Investment:	1 Share
Date of Inception:	14-Jul–00
52 Week Range:	56.84–79.19
2000 Total Dist.:	0.01

FUNDAMENTALS

Med Mkt Cap:	$38,721,000,000
P/E Ratio:	24.80
P/B Ratio:	4.40
P/C Ratio:	13.80
Standard Dev:	N/A
Sharpe Ratio:	N/A
Alpha:	N/A
Beta:	N/A
3 Yr Earn Gr:	N/A
1 Yr Fwd Gr:	N/A
12 Month Yield:	N/A

PREMIUM/DISCOUNT (6/29/2001)

P/D Close:	1.02%
P/D Midpoint:	1.14%

TICKERS

Symbol: EZU		ECash:	N/A
NAV: WWE		TCash:	N/A
Close: N/A		Div:	N/A
Shares: SJE		Index: MSDEUMU	

TOP 10 HOLDINGS

1) Nokia Corp	5.08%
2) Royal Dutch/Shell Group	4.03%
3) TotalFinaElf	3.47%
4) Vivendi Universal	2.89%
5) Deutsche Telekom	2.57%
6) France Telecom	2.43%
7) Telefonica SA	2.41%
8) Siemens	2.17%
9) Allianz	2.17%
10) ING Groep	2.15%

SECTOR BREAKDOWN

Utilities:	5.60%
Energy:	11.40%
Financials:	26.00%
Industrial Cyclicals:	10.50%
Consumer Durables:	6.10%
Consumer Staples:	6.00%
Services:	15.20%
Retail:	4.10%
Health:	6.20%
Technology:	8.90%

FUND MANAGEMENT

Manager:	Barclays Global
Web Site:	http://www.ishares.com/
Telephone:	800–474–2737
Specialist:	Susquehanna
Distributor:	SEI Investments
Administrator:	N/A
Sponsor:	N/A
Exchange:	AMEX

1 Yr	3 Yr	5 Yr	2000	1999	1998	1997
—	—	—	—	—	—	—

Source: AMEX and Morningstar data as of 6/30/2001.

iSHARES MSCI AUSTRALIA INDEX (EWA)

FUND INFORMATION

Expense Ratio:	0.84%
Total Net Assets:	$52,970,000
Structure:	Open-Ended
Benchmark:	MSCI-Australia
Options:	No
Initial Divisor:	—
Min. Investment:	1 Share
Date of Inception:	18-Mar–96
52 Week Range:	8.25–10.81
2000 Total Dist.:	0.27

FUNDAMENTALS

Med Mkt Cap:	$11,853,000,000
P/E Ratio:	24.00
P/B Ratio:	3.50
P/C Ratio:	17.10
Standard Dev:	22.99
Sharpe Ratio:	−0.07
Alpha:	0.64
Beta:	0.78
3 Yr Earn Gr:	N/A
1 Yr Fwd Gr:	N/A
12 Month Yield:	2.73

PREMIUM/DISCOUNT (6/29/2001)

P/D Close:	N/A
P/D Midpoint:	0.2%

TICKERS

Symbol: EWA	ECash:	N/A
NAV: WBJ	TCash:	N/A
Close: N/A	Div:	N/A
Shares: QAW	Index:	MSDUAS

TOP 10 HOLDINGS

1) Telstra Corp	10.43%
2) National Australia Bk	9.25%
3) Commonwealth Bk of Aust Or	8.24%
4) News Corp Ords	7.04%
5) News Corp Pre	6.24%
6) BHP Limited	5.87%
7) AMP Limited	5.08%
8) Westpac Banking	4.39%
9) Rio Tinto Ltd	3.00%
10) WMC Ltd	2.54%

SECTOR BREAKDOWN

Utilities:	0.70%
Energy:	3.80%
Financials:	36.70%
Industrial Cyclicals:	23.20%
Consumer Durables:	0.30%
Consumer Staples:	5.80%
Services:	21.10%
Retail:	4.60%
Health:	2.50%
Technology:	1.40%

FUND MANAGEMENT

Manager:	Barclays Global
Web Site:	http://www.ishares.com/
Telephone:	800–474–2737
Specialist:	AIM Securities
Distributor:	SEI Investments
Administrator:	N/A
Sponsor:	N/A
Exchange:	AMEX

1 Yr	3 Yr	5 Yr	2000	1999	1998	1997
−8.02	3.33	0.91	−11.86	19.31	4.23	−12.15

Source: AMEX and Morningstar data as of 6/30/2001.

IShares MSCI Austria Index (EWO)

Fund Information

Expense Ratio:	0.84%
Total Net Assets:	$10,890,000
Structure:	Open-Ended
Benchmark:	MSCI-Austria
Options:	No
Initial Divisor:	—
Min. Investment:	1 Share
Date of Inception:	18-Mar–96
52 Week Range:	6.75–8.70
2000 Total Dist.:	0.04

Fundamentals

Med Mkt Cap:	$1,661,000,000
P/E Ratio:	18.00
P/B Ratio:	2.10
P/C Ratio:	6.50
Standard Dev:	18.18
Sharpe Ratio:	−1.21
Alpha:	−15.74
Beta:	0.39
3 Yr Earn Gr:	N/A
1 Yr Fwd Gr:	N/A
12 Month Yield:	0.57

Premium/Discount (6/29/2001)

P/D Close:	1.15%
P/D Midpoint:	0.51%

Tickers

Symbol: EWO		ECash:	N/A
NAV: INY		TCash:	N/A
Close: N/A		Div:	N/A
Shares: QAU		Index:	MSDUAT

Top 10 Holdings

1) Osterr Elek A	20.61%
2) OMV AG	14.10%
3) Austria Tabakwerke	8.44%
4) Telekom Austria	6.39%
5) Erste Bk Spark	5.20%
6) VA Technologie	5.05%
7) Generali Holding Vienna	4.63%
8) Flughafen Wien	4.61%
9) Lenzing Gruppe	4.53%
10) Mayr-Melnhof Karton	4.52%

Sector Breakdown

Utilities:	22.10%
Energy:	15.10%
Financials:	10.50%
Industrial Cyclicals:	26.10%
Consumer Durables:	0.00%
Consumer Staples:	12.70%
Services:	13.50%
Retail:	0.00%
Health:	0.00%
Technology:	0.00%

Fund Management

Manager:	Barclays Global
Web Site:	http://www.ishares.com/
Telephone:	800–474–2737
Specialist:	AIM Securities
Distributor:	SEI Investments
Administrator:	N/A
Sponsor:	N/A
Exchange:	AMEX

1 Yr	3 Yr	5 Yr	2000	1999	1998	1997
−0.55	−12.43	−4.86	−8.51	−14.34	−3.05	2.38

Source: AMEX and Morningstar data as of 6/30/2001.

iSHARES MSCI BELGIUM INDEX (EWK)

FUND INFORMATION

Expense Ratio:	0.84%
Total Net Assets:	$9,430,000
Structure:	Open-Ended
Benchmark:	MSCI-Belgium
Options:	No
Initial Divisor:	—
Min. Investment:	1 Share
Date of Inception:	18-Mar–96
52 Week Range:	10.20–14.31
2000 Total Dist.:	0.40

FUNDAMENTALS

Med Mkt Cap:	$10,130,000,000
P/E Ratio:	16.10
P/B Ratio:	2.30
P/C Ratio:	10.80
Standard Dev:	17.40
Sharpe Ratio:	−1.19
Alpha:	−14.97
Beta:	0.43
3 Yr Earn Gr:	N/A
1 Yr Fwd Gr:	N/A
12 Month Yield:	3.58

PREMIUM/DISCOUNT (6/29/2001)

P/D Close:	N/A
P/D Midpoint:	N/A

TICKERS

Symbol: EWK	ECash:	N/A
NAV: INK	TCash:	N/A
Close: N/A	Div:	N/A
Shares: BES	Index:	MSDUBE

TOP 10 HOLDINGS

1) Fortis AG 'B'	23.33%
2) Electrabel Bef Ords	13.36%
3) Kbc Bankverz	11.91%
4) Groupe Bruxelles	7.02%
5) Almanij	4.70%
6) Colruyt	4.69%
7) Interbrew	4.61%
8) Delhaize-Le Lion	4.60%
9) UCB	4.60%
10) Solvay	4.24%

SECTOR BREAKDOWN

Utilities:	13.80%
Energy:	0.00%
Financials:	51.70%
Industrial Cyclicals:	13.00%
Consumer Durables:	5.80%
Consumer Staples:	4.60%
Services:	1.20%
Retail:	9.90%
Health:	0.00%
Technology:	0.00%

FUND MANAGEMENT

Manager:	Barclays Global
Web Site:	http://www.ishares.com/
Telephone:	800–474–2737
Specialist:	Spear, Leeds
Distributor:	SEI Investments
Administrator:	N/A
Sponsor:	N/A
Exchange:	AMEX

1 Yr	3 Yr	5 Yr	2000	1999	1998	1997
−15.75	−11.86	0.64	−18.61	−13.98	52.05	10.92

Source: AMEX and Morningstar data as of 6/30/2001.

iSHARES MSCI BRAZIL (FREE) INDEX (EWZ)

FUND INFORMATION

Expense Ratio:	0.99%
Total Net Assets:	$18,000,000
Structure:	Open-Ended
Benchmark:	MSCI-Brazil
Options:	No
Initial Divisor:	—
Min. Investment:	1 Share
Date of Inception:	14-Jul-00
52 Week Range:	13.00–20.37
2000 Total Dist.:	0.36

FUNDAMENTALS

Med Mkt Cap:	$6,042,000,000
P/E Ratio:	18.60
P/B Ratio:	2.50
P/C Ratio:	29.30
Standard Dev:	N/A
Sharpe Ratio:	N/A
Alpha:	N/A
Beta:	N/A
3 Yr Earn Gr:	N/A
1 Yr Fwd Gr:	N/A
12 Month Yield:	N/A

PREMIUM/DISCOUNT (6/29/2001)

P/D Close:	N/A
P/D Midpoint:	0.2%

TICKERS

Symbol: EWZ		ECash:	N/A
NAV: WWC		TCash:	N/A
Close: N/A		Div:	N/A
Shares: SKH		Index:	MSEUSBR

TOP 10 HOLDINGS

1) Petroleo Brasileiro Pfd	11.77%
2) Petroleo Brasileiro SA	10.46%
3) Vale do Rio Doce Pn	9.66%
4) Cia de Bebid	7.35%
5) Centrais Electricas	5.21%
6) Tele Norte Leste	4.87%
7) Banco Itau Pfd	4.42%
8) Banco Bradesco	3.98%
9) Centrais Electricas	3.87%
10) Brasilera Distrib Pao	3.18%

SECTOR BREAKDOWN

Utilities:	15.50%
Energy:	25.10%
Financials:	11.60%
Industrial Cyclicals:	22.20%
Consumer Durables:	0.00%
Consumer Staples:	3.60%
Services:	18.40%
Retail:	3.60%
Health:	0.00%
Technology:	0.00%

FUND MANAGEMENT

Manager:	Barclays Global
Web Site:	http://www.ishares.com/
Telephone:	800–474–2737
Specialist:	Susquehanna
Distributor:	SEI Investments
Administrator:	N/A
Sponsor:	N/A
Exchange:	AMEX

1 Yr	3 Yr	5 Yr	2000	1999	1998	1997
—	—	—	—	—	—	—

Source: AMEX and Morningstar data as of 6/30/2001.

iShares MSCI Canada Index (EWC)

Fund Information

Expense Ratio:	0.84%
Total Net Assets:	$30,890,000
Structure:	Open-Ended
Benchmark:	MSCI-Canada
Options:	No
Initial Divisor:	—
Min. Investment:	1 Share
Date of Inception:	18-Mar–96
52 Week Range:	10.55–21.81
2000 Total Dist.:	5.36

Fundamentals

Med Mkt Cap:	$11,383,000,000
P/E Ratio:	23.10
P/B Ratio:	2.90
P/C Ratio:	11.80
Standard Dev:	27.70
Sharpe Ratio:	N/A
Alpha:	2.89
Beta:	1.16
3 Yr Earn Gr:	10.20
1 Yr Fwd Gr:	9.10
12 Month Yield:	46.51

Premium/Discount (6/29/2001)

P/D Close:	0.7%
P/D Midpoint:	0.48%

Tickers

Symbol:	EWC	ECash:	N/A
NAV:	WPB	TCash:	N/A
Close:	N/A	Div:	N/A
Shares:	QCN	Index:	MSDUCA

Top 10 Holdings

1) Nortel Networks Corp	11.66%
2) Thomson Corp	5.63%
3) Canadian Imperial Bank	5.38%
4) BCE Inc	5.11%
5) Bombardier Inc B	4.74%
6) Bank of Nova Scotia	4.45%
7) Canadian Pacific Ltd	3.68%
8) Manulife Financial	3.37%
9) Royal Bank of Canada	3.19%
10) Alcan Inc	2.97%

Sector Breakdown

Utilities:	2.90%
Energy:	14.60%
Financials:	24.90%
Industrial Cyclicals:	18.70%
Consumer Durables:	1.20%
Consumer Staples:	2.10%
Services:	17.40%
Retail:	0.60%
Health:	2.80%
Technology:	14.90%

Fund Management

Manager:	Barclays Global
Web Site:	http://www.ishares.com/
Telephone:	800–474–2737
Specialist:	AIM Securities
Distributor:	SEI Investments
Administrator:	N/A
Sponsor:	N/A
Exchange:	AMEX

1 Yr	3 Yr	5 Yr	2000	1999	1998	1997
−23.02	4.94	10.38	8.19	48.62	−7.78	10.60

Source: AMEX and Morningstar data as of 6/30/2001.

iSHARES S&P/TSE 60 (CANADA) INDEX (IKC)

FUND INFORMATION

Expense Ratio:	0.50%
Total Net Assets:	$7,010,000
Structure:	Open-Ended
Benchmark:	S&P/TSE 60
Options:	No
Initial Divisor:	1/10
Min. Investment:	1 Share
Date of Inception:	12-Jun–00
52 Week Range:	43.75–67.56
2000 Total Dist.:	0.72

FUNDAMENTALS

Med Mkt Cap:	$13,249,000,000
P/E Ratio:	19.40
P/B Ratio:	2.50
P/C Ratio:	11.80
Standard Dev:	N/A
Sharpe Ratio:	N/A
Alpha:	N/A
Beta:	N/A
3 Yr Earn Gr:	17.50
1 Yr Fwd Gr:	1.70
12 Month Yield:	N/A

PREMIUM/DISCOUNT (6/29/2001)

P/D Close:	0.72%
P/D Midpoint:	0.08%

TICKERS

Symbol:	IKC	ECash:	NLJv.EU
NAV:	NLJ	TCash:	NLJ.TC
Close:	NLJ.NV	Div:	NLJ.DP
Shares:	NLJ.SO	Index:	SPTSE

TOP 10 HOLDINGS

1) Nortel Networks Corp	11.77%
2) Toronto-Dominion Bk	6.88%
3) BCE Inc	5.57%
4) Canadian Natl Railway	4.81%
5) Canadian Pacific Ltd	4.75%
6) Bank of Nova Scotia	4.62%
7) Canadian Imp Bank	4.12%
8) Bombardier Inc	4.11%
9) Manulife Financial	4.03%
10) Magna International Inc	3.11%

SECTOR BREAKDOWN

Utilities:	2.30%
Energy:	10.60%
Financials:	29.40%
Industrial Cyclicals:	16.20%
Consumer Durables:	2.90%
Consumer Staples:	0.00%
Services:	21.90%
Retail:	0.80%
Health:	0.70%
Technology:	15.20%

FUND MANAGEMENT

Manager:	Barclays Global
Web Site:	http://www.ishares.com/
Telephone:	800-474-2737
Specialist:	Susquehanna
Distributor:	SEI Investments
Administrator:	Investors Bank & Trust
Sponsor:	N/A
Exchange:	AMEX

1 Yr	3 Yr	5 Yr	2000	1999	1998	1997
−22.55	—	—	—	—	—	—

Source: AMEX and Morningstar data as of 6/30/2001.

iSHARES MSCI FRANCE INDEX (EWQ)

FUND INFORMATION

Expense Ratio:	0.84%
Total Net Assets:	$64,310,000
Structure:	Open-Ended
Benchmark:	MSCI-France
Options:	No
Initial Divisor:	—
Min. Investment:	1 Share
Date of Inception:	18-Mar-96
52 Week Range:	18.90–29.31
2000 Total Dist.:	1.23

FUNDAMENTALS

Med Mkt Cap:	$40,833,000,000
P/E Ratio:	27.90
P/B Ratio:	4.20
P/C Ratio:	17.70
Standard Dev:	20.77
Sharpe Ratio:	−0.27
Alpha:	−3.00
Beta:	0.74
3 Yr Earn Gr:	N/A
1 Yr Fwd Gr:	N/A
12 Month Yield:	6.17

PREMIUM/DISCOUNT (6/29/2001)

P/D Close:	N/A
P/D Midpoint:	N/A

TICKERS

Symbol: EWQ	ECash:	N/A
NAV: WBF	TCash:	N/A
Close: N/A	Div:	N/A
Shares: SXF	Index:	MSDUFR

TOP 10 HOLDINGS

1) Total - Class B	11.91%
2) France Telecom	8.01%
3) Vivendi Universal	7.82%
4) Aventis	6.38%
5) L'Oreal	5.26%
6) AXA Financial Inc	5.01%
7) Sanofi-Synthelabo	4.65%
8) Banque Nationale	4.40%
9) Carrefour	4.22%
10) Alcatel A Shares	4.10%

SECTOR BREAKDOWN

Utilities:	7.80%
Energy:	12.20%
Financials:	14.00%
Industrial Cyclicals:	12.70%
Consumer Durables:	6.50%
Consumer Staples:	11.10%
Services:	10.30%
Retail:	7.30%
Health:	11.40%
Technology:	6.80%

FUND MANAGEMENT

Manager:	Barclays Global
Web Site:	http://www.ishares.com/
Telephone:	800–474–2737
Specialist:	AIM Securities
Distributor:	SEI Investments
Administrator:	N/A
Sponsor:	N/A
Exchange:	AMEX

1 Yr	3 Yr	5 Yr	2000	1999	1998	1997
−27.31	0.01	10.64	−6.42	32.01	39.46	11.15

Source: AMEX and Morningstar data as of 6/30/2001.

iSHARES MSCI GERMANY INDEX (EWG)

FUND INFORMATION

Expense Ratio:	0.84%
Total Net Assets:	$129,260,000
Structure:	Open-Ended
Benchmark:	MSCI-Germany
Options:	No
Initial Divisor:	—
Min. Investment:	1 Share
Date of Inception:	18-Mar–96
52 Week Range:	15.20–25.44
2000 Total Dist.:	2.52

FUNDAMENTALS

Med Mkt Cap:	$37,970,000,000
P/E Ratio:	26.50
P/B Ratio:	3.70
P/C Ratio:	10.50
Standard Dev:	21.45
Sharpe Ratio:	−0.68
Alpha:	−9.78
Beta:	0.77
3 Yr Earn Gr:	N/A
1 Yr Fwd Gr:	N/A
12 Month Yield:	15.25

PREMIUM/DISCOUNT (6/29/2001)

P/D Close:	0.18%
P/D Midpoint:	N/A

TICKERS

Symbol: EWG	ECash:	N/A
NAV: WDG	TCash:	N/A
Close: N/A	Div:	N/A
Shares: QGE	Index:	MSDUGR

TOP 10 HOLDINGS

1) Deutsche Telekom	11.65%
2) Allianz	11.35%
3) Siemans Ord	10.60%
4) E.ON	5.04%
5) Dresdner Bank	4.96%
6) DaimlerChrysler	4.84%
7) Muenchener Ruck	4.81%
8) Deutsche Bank	4.75%
9) Bayer	4.07%
10) BASF Ord	3.87%

SECTOR BREAKDOWN

Utilities:	0.00%
Energy:	3.70%
Financials:	30.50%
Industrial Cyclicals:	19.70%
Consumer Durables:	9.50%
Consumer Staples:	1.50%
Services:	16.30%
Retail:	2.90%
Health:	9.20%
Technology:	6.70%

FUND MANAGEMENT

Manager:	Barclays Global
Web Site:	http://www.ishares.com/
Telephone:	800–474–2737
Specialist:	AIM Securities
Distributor:	SEI Investments
Administrator:	N/A
Sponsor:	N/A
Exchange:	AMEX

1 Yr	3 Yr	5 Yr	2000	1999	1998	1997
−23.19	−6.92	7.39	−18.02	22.59	28.04	23.57

Source: AMEX and Morningstar data as of 6/30/2001.

iShares MSCI Hong Kong Index (EWH)

Fund Information

Expense Ratio:	0.84%
Total Net Assets:	$59,200,000
Structure:	Open-Ended
Benchmark:	MSCI-Hong Kong
Options:	No
Initial Divisor:	—
Min. Investment:	1 Share
Date of Inception:	18-Mar–96
52 Week Range:	9.88–14.06
2000 Total Dist.:	0.28

Fundamentals

Med Mkt Cap:	$13,133,000,000
P/E Ratio:	14.00
P/B Ratio:	2.50
P/C Ratio:	19.90
Standard Dev:	38.06
Sharpe Ratio:	0.21
Alpha:	11.28
Beta:	0.99
3 Yr Earn Gr:	N/A
1 Yr Fwd Gr:	N/A
12 Month Yield:	2.68

Premium/Discount (6/29/2001)

P/D Close:	0.9%
P/D Midpoint:	0.7%

Tickers

Symbol: EWH	ECash:	N/A
NAV: INH	TCash:	N/A
Close: N/A	Div:	N/A
Shares: SHK	Index:	MSDUHK

Top 10 Holdings

1) Hutchison Whampoa	24.33%
2) Hang Seng Bank	12.39%
3) Sun Hung Kai Properties	11.63%
4) CLP Holdings	5.24%
5) Henderson Land	4.59%
6) Swire Pacific A	4.48%
7) Johnson Electric Hldgs	4.34%
8) Hong Kong and China Gas Co	4.02%
9) Wharf Holdings	3.81%
10) Li & Fung	3.79%

Sector Breakdown

Utilities:	5.60%
Energy:	4.80%
Financials:	64.20%
Industrial Cyclicals:	0.00%
Consumer Durables:	4.20%
Consumer Staples:	0.00%
Services:	13.20%
Retail:	4.10%
Health:	0.00%
Technology:	4.10%

Fund Management

Manager:	Barclays Global
Web Site:	http://www.ishares.com/
Telephone:	800–474–2737
Specialist:	Spear, Leeds
Distributor:	SEI Investments
Administrator:	N/A
Sponsor:	N/A
Exchange:	AMEX

1 Yr	3 Yr	5 Yr	2000	1999	1998	1997
−17.26	12.99	−3.37	−17.61	56.67	−9.15	−28.62

Source: AMEX and Morningstar data as of 6/30/2001.

iSHARES MSCI ITALY INDEX (EWI)

FUND INFORMATION

Expense Ratio:	0.84%
Total Net Assets:	$35,060,000
Structure:	Open-Ended
Benchmark:	MSCI-Italy
Options:	No
Initial Divisor:	—
Min. Investment:	1 Share
Date of Inception:	18-Mar–96
52 Week Range:	17.35–27.00
2000 Total Dist.:	2.24

FUNDAMENTALS

Med Mkt Cap:	$36,817,000,000
P/E Ratio:	23.50
P/B Ratio:	5.10
P/C Ratio:	11.80
Standard Dev:	22.87
Sharpe Ratio:	−0.45
Alpha:	−6.08
Beta:	0.51
3 Yr Earn Gr:	N/A
1 Yr Fwd Gr:	N/A
12 Month Yield:	12.44

PREMIUM/DISCOUNT (6/29/2001)

P/D Close:	N/A
P/D Midpoint:	0.25%

TICKERS

Symbol:	EWI	ECash:	N/A
NAV:	INE	TCash:	N/A
Close:	N/A	Div:	N/A
Shares:	SIT	Index:	MSDUIT

TOP 10 HOLDINGS

1) ENI	14.10%
2) TIM Ord	13.94%
3) Telecom Italia Ord	10.66%
4) Assicurazioni Gen	10.52%
5) Unicredito Italiano	4.60%
6) ENEL	4.39%
7) San Paolo - Imi Ord	4.25%
8) Banca Intesa Ord	4.15%
9) Mediaset	3.45%
10) Ras Ord	2.72%

SECTOR BREAKDOWN

Utilities:	6.60%
Energy:	14.80%
Financials:	32.70%
Industrial Cyclicals:	2.30%
Consumer Durables:	6.20%
Consumer Staples:	0.70%
Services:	35.60%
Retail:	1.10%
Health:	0.00%
Technology:	0.00%

FUND MANAGEMENT

Manager:	Barclays Global
Web Site:	http://www.ishares.com/
Telephone:	800-474-2737
Specialist:	AIM Securities
Distributor:	SEI Investments
Administrator:	N/A
Sponsor:	N/A
Exchange:	AMEX

1 Yr	3 Yr	5 Yr	2000	1999	1998	1997
−24.31	−3.40	10.01	−0.51	0.82	47.92	36.79

Source: AMEX and Morningstar data as of 6/30/2001.

iSHARES MSCI JAPAN INDEX (EWJ)

FUND INFORMATION

Expense Ratio:	0.84%
Total Net Assets:	$584,260,000
Structure:	Open-Ended
Benchmark:	MSCI-Japan
Options:	No
Initial Divisor:	—
Min. Investment:	1 Share
Date of Inception:	18-Mar–96
52 Week Range:	9.05–16.19
2000 Total Dist.:	0.45

FUNDAMENTALS

Med Mkt Cap:	$15,129,000,000
P/E Ratio:	35.50
P/B Ratio:	2.40
P/C Ratio:	13.70
Standard Dev:	24.57
Sharpe Ratio:	−0.09
Alpha:	0.49
Beta:	0.85
3 Yr Earn Gr:	N/A
1 Yr Fwd Gr:	N/A
12 Month Yield:	4.42

PREMIUM/DISCOUNT (6/29/2001)

P/D Close:	N/A
P/D Midpoint:	N/A

TICKERS

Symbol: EWJ		ECash:	N/A
NAV: INJ		TCash:	N/A
Close: N/A		Div:	N/A
Shares: SJA		Index:	MSDUJN

TOP 10 HOLDINGS

1) Toyota Motor Corp	6.32%
2) Nippon T&T Corp	4.09%
3) Sony Corp	3.32%
4) Mitsubishi Tokyo Fin	3.12%
5) Sumitomo Mitsui Bk	2.72%
6) Mizuho Holding	2.64%
7) Nomura Securities	2.26%
8) Takeda Chemical	2.21%
9) Honda Motor Co	1.85%
10) Canon Inc	1.80%

SECTOR BREAKDOWN

Utilities:	4.30%
Energy:	1.00%
Financials:	12.30%
Industrial Cyclicals:	20.20%
Consumer Durables:	24.20%
Consumer Staples:	3.80%
Services:	11.50%
Retail:	3.50%
Health:	6.30%
Technology:	12.90%

FUND MANAGEMENT

Manager:	Barclays Global
Web Site:	http://www.ishares.com/
Telephone:	800–474–2737
Specialist:	AIM Securities
Distributor:	SEI Investments
Administrator:	N/A
Sponsor:	N/A
Exchange:	AMEX

1 Yr	3 Yr	5 Yr	2000	1999	1998	1997
−30.43	2.91	−7.58	−29.96	60.89	3.93	−24.37

Source: AMEX and Morningstar data as of 6/30/2001.

iShares MSCI Malaysia (Free) Index (EWM)

Fund Information

Expense Ratio:	0.84%
Total Net Assets:	$69,980,000
Structure:	Open-Ended
Benchmark:	MSCI-Malaysia
Options:	No
Initial Divisor:	—
Min. Investment:	1 Share
Date of Inception:	18-Mar–96
52 Week Range:	3.85–6.75
2000 Total Dist.:	0.07

Fundamentals

Med Mkt Cap:	$2,591,000,000
P/E Ratio:	18.30
P/B Ratio:	3.30
P/C Ratio:	10.30
Standard Dev:	82.00
Sharpe Ratio:	0.11
Alpha:	23.15
Beta:	1.15
3 Yr Earn Gr:	N/A
1 Yr Fwd Gr:	N/A
12 Month Yield:	1.59

Premium/Discount (6/29/2001)

P/D Close:	N/A
P/D Midpoint:	N/A

Tickers

Symbol: EWM		ECash:	N/A
NAV: INM		TCash:	N/A
Close: N/A		Div:	N/A
Shares: SMY		Index: MSDUMAF	

Top 10 Holdings

1) Tenaga Nasional	14.13%
2) Telekom Malaysia	13.84%
3) Malayan Banking	11.10%
4) Malaysia Intl Ship	5.83%
5) British American Tob	5.06%
6) Sime Darby	4.32%
7) Public Bank (Fgn)	3.39%
8) Resorts World	2.94%
9) Commerce Asset-Hldg	2.91%
10) YTL Corp	2.88%

Sector Breakdown

Utilities:	14.60%
Energy:	0.30%
Financials:	25.10%
Industrial Cyclicals:	12.30%
Consumer Durables:	6.60%
Consumer Staples:	11.60%
Services:	28.70%
Retail:	0.00%
Health:	0.20%
Technology:	0.70%

Fund Management

Manager:	Barclays Global
Web Site:	http://www.ishares.com/
Telephone:	800-474-2737
Specialist:	AIM Securities
Distributor:	SEI Investments
Administrator:	N/A
Sponsor:	N/A
Exchange:	AMEX

1 Yr	3 Yr	5 Yr	2000	1999	1998	1997
−30.39	11.81	−19.43	−27.47	106.08	−24.28	−66.71

Source: AMEX and Morningstar data as of 6/30/2001.

iSHARES MSCI MEXICO (FREE) INDEX (EWW)

FUND INFORMATION

Expense Ratio:	0.84%
Total Net Assets:	$41,500,000
Structure:	Open-Ended
Benchmark:	MSCI-Mexico
Options:	No
Initial Divisor:	—
Min. Investment:	1 Share
Date of Inception:	18-Mar–96
52 Week Range:	12.37–19.19
2000 Total Dist.:	0.44

TOP 10 HOLDINGS

1) Telefonos de Mexico	21.53%
2) America Movil SA	12.41%
3) Wal-Mart Mex V	7.18%
4) Grupo Fin Banacci O	7.17%
5) Grupo Fin Bbva	5.91%
6) Grupo Modelo C	5.34%
7) FEMSA Ubd	5.32%
8) Cemex Cpo	5.16%
9) Kimberly-Clark Corp	4.25%
10) Grupo Televisa	3.81%

FUNDAMENTALS

Med Mkt Cap:	$11,858,000,000
P/E Ratio:	15.70
P/B Ratio:	3.40
P/C Ratio:	16.00
Standard Dev:	43.85
Sharpe Ratio:	0.18
Alpha:	13.41
Beta:	1.39
3 Yr Earn Gr:	N/A
1 Yr Fwd Gr:	N/A
12 Month Yield:	2.95

SECTOR BREAKDOWN

Utilities:	0.00%
Energy:	0.00%
Financials:	15.00%
Industrial Cyclicals:	18.20%
Consumer Durables:	1.60%
Consumer Staples:	23.20%
Services:	29.00%
Retail:	13.00%
Health:	0.00%
Technology:	0.00%

PREMIUM/DISCOUNT (6/29/2001)

P/D Close:	1.93%
P/D Midpoint:	1.17%

TICKERS

Symbol: EWW	ECash:	N/A
NAV: INW	TCash:	N/A
Close: N/A	Div:	N/A
Shares: QMX	Index: MSEUTMXF	

FUND MANAGEMENT

Manager:	Barclays Global
Web Site:	http://www.ishares.com/
Telephone:	800–474–2737
Specialist:	Spear, Leeds
Distributor:	SEI Investments
Administrator:	N/A
Sponsor:	N/A
Exchange:	AMEX

1 Yr	3 Yr	5 Yr	2000	1999	1998	1997
5.84	13.89	10.19	−23.90	77.33	−35.38	46.97

Source: AMEX and Morningstar data as of 6/30/2001.

iSHARES MSCI NETHERLANDS INDEX (EWN)

FUND INFORMATION

Expense Ratio:	0.84%
Total Net Assets:	$25,270,000
Structure:	Open-Ended
Benchmark:	MSCI-Netherlands
Options:	No
Initial Divisor:	—
Min. Investment:	1 Share
Date of Inception:	18-Mar–96
52 Week Range:	18.10–25.06
2000 Total Dist.:	0.23

FUNDAMENTALS

Med Mkt Cap:	$43,784,000,000
P/E Ratio:	17.70
P/B Ratio:	4.50
P/C Ratio:	9.60
Standard Dev:	17.59
Sharpe Ratio:	−0.81
Alpha:	−10.11
Beta:	0.61
3 Yr Earn Gr:	N/A
1 Yr Fwd Gr:	N/A
12 Month Yield:	1.17

PREMIUM/DISCOUNT (6/29/2001)

P/D Close:	N/A
P/D Midpoint:	0%

TICKERS

Symbol: EWN		ECash:	N/A
NAV: INN		TCash:	N/A
Close: N/A		Div:	N/A
Shares: NTS		Index:	MSDUNE

TOP 10 HOLDINGS

1) Royal Dutch Petrol Co	24.83%
2) ING Groep	11.33%
3) AEGON	7.85%
4) Philips Electronics	5.90%
5) Ahold (Kon)	4.92%
6) Unilever NV Cert	4.88%
7) Heineken NV	4.80%
8) ABN Amro Holding	4.78%
9) Akzo Nobel	3.81%
10) Tnt Post Groep	3.57%

SECTOR BREAKDOWN

Utilities:	0.00%
Energy:	24.90%
Financials:	26.00%
Industrial Cyclicals:	7.80%
Consumer Durables:	7.30%
Consumer Staples:	10.10%
Services:	14.90%
Retail:	5.70%
Health:	0.00%
Technology:	3.30%

FUND MANAGEMENT

Manager:	Barclays Global
Web Site:	http://www.ishares.com/
Telephone:	800–474–2737
Specialist:	Spear, Leeds
Distributor:	SEI Investments
Administrator:	N/A
Sponsor:	N/A
Exchange:	AMEX

1 Yr	3 Yr	5 Yr	2000	1999	1998	1997
−22.09	−6.97	6.25	−9.53	5.74	23.72	19.99

Source: AMEX and Morningstar data as of 6/30/2001.

iSHARES MSCI SINGAPORE (FREE) INDEX (EWS)

FUND INFORMATION

Expense Ratio:	0.84%
Total Net Assets:	$53,560,000
Structure:	Open-Ended
Benchmark:	MSCI-Singapore
Options:	No
Initial Divisor:	—
Min. Investment:	1 Share
Date of Inception:	18-Mar–96
52 Week Range:	5.01–8.31
2000 Total Dist.:	0.29

FUNDAMENTALS

Med Mkt Cap:	$6,780,000,000
P/E Ratio:	15.40
P/B Ratio:	2.20
P/C Ratio:	12.90
Standard Dev:	47.55
Sharpe Ratio:	0.13
Alpha:	12.50
Beta:	1.42
3 Yr Earn Gr:	N/A
1 Yr Fwd Gr:	N/A
12 Month Yield:	5.30

PREMIUM/DISCOUNT (6/29/2001)

P/D Close:	0.36%
P/D Midpoint:	0.18%

TICKERS

Symbol: EWS	ECash:	N/A
NAV: INR	TCash:	N/A
Close: N/A	Div:	N/A
Shares: QSG	Index:	MSDUSGF

TOP 10 HOLDINGS

1) DBS Group Holdings	15.73%
2) Singapore Airlines	12.91%
3) Oversea-Chinese Banking Corp	11.48%
4) Singapore Telecomm	7.56%
5) Sing Tech Engineer	5.40%
6) Chartered Semicon	4.98%
7) Capital Land	4.55%
8) City Developments	4.43%
9) Singapore Press Hldg	4.13%
10) United Overseas Bank	3.92%

SECTOR BREAKDOWN

Utilities:	0.00%
Energy:	0.00%
Financials:	41.80%
Industrial Cyclicals:	13.30%
Consumer Durables:	2.30%
Consumer Staples:	2.30%
Services:	31.00%
Retail:	0.00%
Health:	0.00%
Technology:	9.40%

FUND MANAGEMENT

Manager:	Barclays Global
Web Site:	http://www.ishares.com/
Telephone:	800–474–2737
Specialist:	Spear, Leeds
Distributor:	SEI Investments
Administrator:	N/A
Sponsor:	N/A
Exchange:	AMEX

1 Yr	3 Yr	5 Yr	2000	1999	1998	1997
−24.09	9.95	−13.26	−26.44	52.70	−5.11	−44.45

Source: AMEX and Morningstar data as of 6/30/2001.

iSHARES MSCI SOUTH KOREA INDEX (EWY)

FUND INFORMATION

Expense Ratio:	0.99%
Total Net Assets:	$25,430,000
Structure:	Open-Ended
Benchmark:	MSCI-South Korea
Options:	No
Initial Divisor:	—
Min. Investment:	1 Share
Date of Inception:	12–May–00
52 Week Range:	11.01–22.00
2000 Total Dist.:	0.00

FUNDAMENTALS

Med Mkt Cap:	$10,760,000,000
P/E Ratio:	19.10
P/B Ratio:	1.90
P/C Ratio:	7.50
Standard Dev:	N/A
Sharpe Ratio:	N/A
Alpha:	N/A
Beta:	N/A
3 Yr Earn Gr:	N/A
1 Yr Fwd Gr:	N/A
12 Month Yield:	N/A

PREMIUM/DISCOUNT (6/29/2001)

P/D Close:	0.91%
P/D Midpoint:	0.49%

TICKERS

Symbol: EWY		ECash:	N/A
NAV:	WWK	TCash:	N/A
Close:	N/A	Div:	N/A
Shares:	SXK	Index:	MSEUSKO

TOP 10 HOLDINGS

1) Samsung Electronics	27.04%
2) SK Telecom Co Ltd	13.62%
3) Korea Electric Power Corp	9.80%
4) Pohang Iron Steel Co	5.35%
5) Hyundai Motor Co	4.52%
6) Kookmin Bank	3.65%
7) Korea Telecom Corp	3.30%
8) Samsung Elect Mech	2.77%
9) Housing & Comm Bank	2.32%
10) Samsung SDI Co Ltd	2.15%

SECTOR BREAKDOWN

Utilities:	10.00%
Energy:	0.40%
Financials:	15.30%
Industrial Cyclicals:	12.20%
Consumer Durables:	4.50%
Consumer Staples:	2.10%
Services:	16.80%
Retail:	1.20%
Health:	0.10%
Technology:	37.60%

FUND MANAGEMENT

Manager:	Barclays Global
Web Site:	http://www.ishares.com/
Telephone:	800–474–2737
Specialist:	Susquehanna
Distributor:	SEI Investments
Administrator:	N/A
Sponsor:	N/A
Exchange:	AMEX

1 Yr	3 Yr	5 Yr	2000	1999	1998	1997
−32.67	—	—	—	—	—	—

Source: AMEX and Morningstar data as of 6/30/2001.

iShares MSCI Spain Index (EWP)

Fund Information

Expense Ratio:	0.84%
Total Net Assets:	$27,260,000
Structure:	Open-Ended
Benchmark:	MSCI-Spain
Options:	No
Initial Divisor:	—
Min. Investment:	1 Share
Date of Inception:	18-Mar–96
52 Week Range:	20.75–27.12
2000 Total Dist.:	0.95

Fundamentals

Med Mkt Cap:	$23,278,000,000
P/E Ratio:	18.60
P/B Ratio:	3.10
P/C Ratio:	9.30
Standard Dev:	21.16
Sharpe Ratio:	−0.66
Alpha:	−9.27
Beta:	0.75
3 Yr Earn Gr:	N/A
1 Yr Fwd Gr:	N/A
12 Month Yield:	4.47

Premium/Discount (6/29/2001)

P/D Close:	N/A
P/D Midpoint:	0.23%

Tickers

Symbol: EWP	ECash:	N/A
NAV: INP	TCash:	N/A
Close: N/A	Div:	N/A
Shares: QSN	Index:	MSDUSP

Top 10 Holdings

1) Telefonica SA	25.14%
2) Banco Bilbao Viz	12.39%
3) Banco Santander Central	12.22%
4) Repsol Yps	5.11%
5) Iberdrola	4.67%
6) Union Electrica-Fen	4.60%
7) Endesa	4.59%
8) Gas Natural Sdg	4.47%
9) Acerinox	3.10%
10) Acesa-Autopistas	2.47%

Sector Breakdown

Utilities:	20.10%
Energy:	5.20%
Financials:	27.70%
Industrial Cyclicals:	11.70%
Consumer Durables:	0.00%
Consumer Staples:	2.70%
Services:	31.00%
Retail:	0.60%
Health:	1.20%
Technology:	0.00%

Fund Management

Manager:	Barclays Global
Web Site:	http://www.ishares.com/
Telephone:	800–474-2737
Specialist:	Spear, Leeds
Distributor:	SEI Investments
Administrator:	N/A
Sponsor:	N/A
Exchange:	AMEX

1 Yr	3 Yr	5 Yr	2000	1999	1998	1997
−15.11	−6.71	10.82	−15.66	−1.43	50.34	17.57

Source: AMEX and Morningstar data as of 6/30/2001.

iShares MSCI Sweden Index (EWD)

Fund Information

Expense Ratio:	0.84%
Total Net Assets:	$11,280,000
Structure:	Open-Ended
Benchmark:	MSCI-Sweden
Options:	No
Initial Divisor:	—
Min. Investment:	1 Share
Date of Inception:	18-Mar–96
52 Week Range:	12.50–33.31
2000 Total Dist.:	5.40

Fundamentals

Med Mkt Cap:	$12,031,000,000
P/E Ratio:	27.10
P/B Ratio:	4.80
P/C Ratio:	25.50
Standard Dev:	30.80
Sharpe Ratio:	−0.46
Alpha:	−7.48
Beta:	1.02
3 Yr Earn Gr:	N/A
1 Yr Fwd Gr:	N/A
12 Month Yield:	39.79

Premium/Discount (6/29/2001)

P/D Close:	N/A
P/D Midpoint:	N/A

Tickers

Symbol:	EWD	ECash:	N/A
NAV:	WBQ	TCash:	N/A
Close:	N/A	Div:	N/A
Shares:	SWE	Index:	MSDUSW

Top 10 Holdings

1) LM Ericsson Telephone Co-B Shs	23.61%
2) Nordea	10.69%
3) Hennes & Mauritz AB-B Shs	6.76%
4) Svenska Handelsb	5.47%
5) Telia AB	4.85%
6) Skandia Forsakring	4.57%
7) Svenska Cellulosa	4.11%
8) Assa Abloy Ser B	4.07%
9) Tele2 AB	3.88%
10) Securitas AB-B Shs	3.86%

Sector Breakdown

Utilities:	0.00%
Energy:	0.00%
Financials:	27.50%
Industrial Cyclicals:	13.40%
Consumer Durables:	13.10%
Consumer Staples:	0.80%
Services:	10.30%
Retail:	7.50%
Health:	1.80%
Technology:	25.70%

Fund Management

Manager:	Barclays Global
Web Site:	http://www.ishares.com/
Telephone:	800–474–2737
Specialist:	Spear, Leeds
Distributor:	SEI Investments
Administrator:	N/A
Sponsor:	N/A
Exchange:	AMEX

1 Yr	3 Yr	5 Yr	2000	1999	1998	1997
−46.65	−7.23	6.41	−25.75	63.20	12.08	10.40

Source: AMEX and Morningstar data as of 6/30/2001.

iSHARES MSCI SWITZERLAND INDEX (EWL)

FUND INFORMATION

Expense Ratio:	0.84%
Total Net Assets:	$33,610,000
Structure:	Open-Ended
Benchmark:	MSCI-Switzerland
Options:	No
Initial Divisor:	—
Min. Investment:	1 Share
Date of Inception:	18-Mar–96
52 Week Range:	12.81–17.75
2000 Total Dist.:	0.16

FUNDAMENTALS

Med Mkt Cap:	$52,251,000,000
P/E Ratio:	17.90
P/B Ratio:	3.90
P/C Ratio:	16.60
Standard Dev:	20.02
Sharpe Ratio:	−0.76
Alpha:	−10.48
Beta:	0.59
3 Yr Earn Gr:	N/A
1 Yr Fwd Gr:	N/A
12 Month Yield:	1.17

PREMIUM/DISCOUNT (6/29/2001)

P/D Close:	0.29%
P/D Midpoint:	N/A

TICKERS

Symbol: EWL	ECash:	N/A
NAV: INL	TCash:	N/A
Close: N/A	Div:	N/A
Shares: QSW	Index:	MSDUSZ

TOP 10 HOLDINGS

1) Novartis Namen	20.39%
2) Nestle	10.49%
3) UBS	10.11%
4) Roche Holding Genuss	8.49%
5) Credit Suisse Group	5.28%
6) Swiss Re N	4.65%
7) Zurich Financial	4.18%
8) ABB Ltd	3.96%
9) Swisscom AG-Reg	3.17%
10) Julius Baer Holding	2.92%

SECTOR BREAKDOWN

Utilities:	0.00%
Energy:	0.00%
Financials:	31.90%
Industrial Cyclicals:	15.70%
Consumer Durables:	1.70%
Consumer Staples:	10.80%
Services:	7.70%
Retail:	1.20%
Health:	29.70%
Technology:	1.40%

FUND MANAGEMENT

Manager:	Barclays Global
Web Site:	http://www.ishares.com/
Telephone:	800–474–2737
Specialist:	Spear, Leeds
Distributor:	SEI Investments
Administrator:	N/A
Sponsor:	N/A
Exchange:	AMEX

1 Yr	3 Yr	5 Yr	2000	1999	1998	1997
−14.79	−7.43	4.89	6.11	−3.49	18.40	33.96

Source: AMEX and Morningstar data as of 6/30/2001.

iShares MSCI Taiwan Index (EWT)

Fund Information

Expense Ratio:	0.99%
Total Net Assets:	$99,800,000
Structure:	Open-Ended
Benchmark:	MSCI-Taiwan
Options:	No
Initial Divisor:	—
Min. Investment:	1 Share
Date of Inception:	23-Jun–00
52 Week Range:	9.29–19.44
2000 Total Dist.:	0.86

Fundamentals

Med Mkt Cap:	$5,452,000,000
P/E Ratio:	23.00
P/B Ratio:	3.20
P/C Ratio:	13.10
Standard Dev:	N/A
Sharpe Ratio:	N/A
Alpha:	N/A
Beta:	N/A
3 Yr Earn Gr:	N/A
1 Yr Fwd Gr:	N/A
12 Month Yield:	N/A

Premium/Discount (6/29/2001)

P/D Close:	5.92%
P/D Midpoint:	5.52%

Tickers

Symbol: EWT	ECash:	N/A
NAV: WWM	TCash:	N/A
Close: N/A	Div:	N/A
Shares: SJF	Index: MSEUSTW

Top 10 Holdings

1) Taiwan Semiconductor	19.79%
2) United Microelec	11.13%
3) Hon Hai Precision Industry	5.24%
4) Cathay Life Insurance	5.01%
5) Asustek Computer	4.06%
6) China Development Ind	3.66%
7) Quanta Computer Inc	3.58%
8) Nan Ya Plastic	3.53%
9) China Steel Ords	3.11%
10) Formosa Plastics Corp	2.90%

Sector Breakdown

Utilities:	0.00%
Energy:	0.00%
Financials:	17.70%
Industrial Cyclicals:	16.30%
Consumer Durables:	4.40%
Consumer Staples:	1.20%
Services:	1.00%
Retail:	0.20%
Health:	0.00%
Technology:	59.40%

Fund Management

Manager:	Barclays Global
Web Site:	http://www.ishares.com/
Telephone:	800–474–2737
Specialist:	Susquehanna
Distributor:	SEI Investments
Administrator:	N/A
Sponsor:	N/A
Exchange:	AMEX

1 Yr	3 Yr	5 Yr	2000	1999	1998	1997
–41.01	—	—	—	—	—	—

Source: AMEX and Morningstar data as of 6/30/2001.

iShares MSCI United Kingdom Index (EWU)

Fund Information

Expense Ratio:	0.84%
Total Net Assets:	$122,400,000
Structure:	Open-Ended
Benchmark:	MSCI-U.K.
Options:	No
Initial Divisor:	—
Min. Investment:	1 Share
Date of Inception:	18-Mar–96
52 Week Range:	14.55–19.94
2000 Total Dist.:	0.95

Top 10 Holdings

1) Vodafone Group	9.16%
2) Bp Amoco Corp	7.59%
3) GlaxoSmithKline	6.93%
4) HSBC Hldgs	5.02%
5) Astrazeneca	4.72%
6) Royal Bank of Scot	3.64%
7) Lloyds Tsb Group	3.54%
8) British Telecom	3.45%
9) Barclays	3.09%
10) CGNU Plc	2.58%

Fundamentals

Med Mkt Cap:	$32,009,000,000
P/E Ratio:	23.90
P/B Ratio:	3.80
P/C Ratio:	15.70
Standard Dev:	14.05
Sharpe Ratio:	−0.82
Alpha:	−8.61
Beta:	0.60
3 Yr Earn Gr:	N/A
1 Yr Fwd Gr:	−15.20
12 Month Yield:	5.99

Sector Breakdown

Utilities:	4.90%
Energy:	8.20%
Financials:	31.30%
Industrial Cyclicals:	7.40%
Consumer Durables:	0.90%
Consumer Staples:	6.90%
Services:	25.60%
Retail:	4.10%
Health:	6.30%
Technology:	4.40%

Premium/Discount (6/29/2001)

P/D Close:	1.09%
P/D Midpoint:	1.57%

Tickers

Symbol: EWU	ECash:	N/A
NAV: INU	TCash:	N/A
Close: N/A	Div:	N/A
Shares: UKS	Index:	MSDUUK

Fund Management

Manager:	Barclays Global
Web Site:	http://www.ishares.com/
Telephone:	800–474–2737
Specialist:	Spear, Leeds
Distributor:	SEI Investments
Administrator:	N/A
Sponsor:	N/A
Exchange:	AMEX

1 Yr	3 Yr	5 Yr	2000	1999	1998	1997
−13.71	−4.62	8.79	−13.57	12.06	19.47	18.22

Source: AMEX and Morningstar data as of 6/30/2001.

HOLDRs

HOLDRs B2B Internet (BHH)

Fund Information

Expense Ratio:	*
Total Net Assets:	$109,200,000
Structure:	Grantor Trust
Benchmark:	(Basket)
Options:	No
Initial Divisor:	—
Min. Investment:	100 Shares
Date of Inception:	01-Feb-00
52 Week Range:	4.18–58.78
2000 Total Dist.:	2.65

Top 10 Holdings

1) Ariba	37.78%
2) Internet Cap Grp	11.81%
3) Commerce One	11.75%
4) Verticalnet	6.67%
5) CheckFree Corp	5.66%
6) Scient Corp	5.43%
7) Agile Software	5.15%
8) Proxicom	3.85%
9) FreeMarkets Inc	3.36%
10) Careinsite	2.30%

Fundamentals

Med Mkt Cap:	$4,945,000,000
P/E Ratio:	N/A
P/B Ratio:	2.60
P/C Ratio:	36.60
Standard Dev:	N/A
Sharpe Ratio:	N/A
Alpha:	N/A
Beta:	N/A
3 Yr Earn Gr:	N/A
1 Yr Fwd Gr:	N/A
12 Month Yield:	N/A

Sector Breakdown

Utilities:	0.00%
Energy:	0.00%
Financials:	0.00%
Industrial Cyclicals:	0.00%
Consumer Durables:	0.00%
Consumer Staples:	0.00%
Services:	24.70%
Retail:	3.40%
Health:	0.00%
Technology:	71.90%

Premium/Discount (6/29/2001)

P/D Close:	N/A
P/D Midpoint:	0%

Tickers

Symbol:	BHH	ECash:	N/A
NAV:	BUX	TCash:	N/A
Close:	N/A	Div:	N/A
Shares:	N/A	Index:	N/A

Fund Management

Manager:	Bank of New York
Web Site:	http://www.holdrs.com
Telephone:	N/A
Specialist:	N/A
Distributor:	N/A
Administrator:	Merrill Lynch
Sponsor:	N/A
Exchange:	AMEX

1 Yr	3 Yr	5 Yr	2000	1999	1998	1997
−84.74	—	—	—	—	—	—

*Expense ratio is $8 per 100 shares per year.
Source: AMEX and Morningstar data as of 6/30/2001.

HOLDRs Biotech (BBH)

Fund Information

Expense Ratio:	*
Total Net Assets:	$1,045,600,000
Structure:	Grantor Trust
Benchmark:	(Basket)
Options:	No
Initial Divisor:	—
Min. Investment:	100 Shares
Date of Inception:	01-Nov–99
52 Week Range:	92.51–206.00
2000 Total Dist.	—

Top 10 Holdings

1) Genentech Inc	19.86%
2) Amgen Inc	17.72%
3) Immunex Corp	12.63%
4) PE Corp - PE Biosys	9.31%
5) Medimmune	5.30%
6) Biogen Inc	4.09%
7) Chiron Corp	3.98%
8) Sepracor Inc	3.76%
9) Millennium Pharma	3.43%
10) IDEC Pharma Corp	2.91%

Fundamentals

Med Mkt Cap:	$9,585,000,000
P/E Ratio:	52.70
P/B Ratio:	8.00
P/C Ratio:	37.40
Standard Dev:	N/A
Sharpe Ratio:	N/A
Alpha:	N/A
Beta:	N/A
3 Yr Earn Gr:	N/A
1 Yr Fwd Gr:	15.20
12 Month Yield:	N/A

Sector Breakdown

Utilities:	0.00%
Energy:	0.00%
Financials:	0.00%
Industrial Cyclicals:	9.30%
Consumer Durables:	0.00%
Consumer Staples:	0.00%
Services:	0.00%
Retail:	0.00%
Health:	90.70%
Technology:	0.00%

Premium/Discount (6/29/2001)

P/D Close:	0.11%
P/D Midpoint:	N/A

Tickers

Symbol:	BBH	ECash:	N/A
NAV:	IBH	TCash:	N/A
Close:	N/A	Div:	N/A
Shares:	N/A	Index:	N/A

Fund Management

Manager:	Bank of New York
Web Site:	http://www.holdrs.com
Telephone:	N/A
Specialist:	N/A
Distributor:	N/A
Administrator:	Merrill Lynch
Sponsor:	N/A
Exchange:	AMEX

1 Yr	3 Yr	5 Yr	2000	1999	1998	1997
−25.46	—	—	18.69	—	—	—

*Expense ratio is $8 per 100 shares per year.

Source: AMEX and Morningstar data as of 6/30/2001.

HOLDRs Broadband (BDH)

Fund Information

Expense Ratio:	*
Total Net Assets:	$241,600,000
Structure:	Grantor Trust
Benchmark:	(Basket)
Options:	No
Initial Divisor:	—
Min. Investment:	100 Shares
Date of Inception:	01-Apr–00
52 Week Range:	19.67–103.56
2000 Total Dist.:	0.01

Top 10 Holdings

1) Nortel Networks	23.77%
2) Lucent Tech	14.48%
3) JDS Uniphase	10.78%
4) Corning Inc	8.01%
5) Motorola Inc	6.79%
6) QUALCOMM Inc	5.93%
7) Broadcom Cl A	5.12%
8) Sycamore Networks	4.22%
9) SDL Corp	3.96%
10) Tellabs Inc	2.97%

Fundamentals

Med Mkt Cap:	$19,810,000,000
P/E Ratio:	44.50
P/B Ratio:	2.20
P/C Ratio:	30.80
Standard Dev:	N/A
Sharpe Ratio:	N/A
Alpha:	N/A
Beta:	N/A
3 Yr Earn Gr:	22.80
1 Yr Fwd Gr:	−40.90
12 Month Yield:	N/A

Sector Breakdown

Utilities:	0.00%
Energy:	0.00%
Financials:	0.00%
Industrial Cyclicals:	8.00%
Consumer Durables:	0.00%
Consumer Staples:	0.00%
Services:	0.00%
Retail:	0.00%
Health:	0.00%
Technology:	92.00%

Premium/Discount (6/29/2001)

P/D Close:	0.05%
P/D Midpoint:	N/A

Tickers

Symbol: BDH	ECash:	N/A
NAV: XDH	TCash:	N/A
Close: N/A	Div:	N/A
Shares: N/A	Index:	N/A

Fund Management

Manager:	Bank of New York
Web Site:	http://www.holdrs.com
Telephone:	N/A
Specialist:	N/A
Distributor:	N/A
Administrator:	Merrill Lynch
Sponsor:	N/A
Exchange:	AMEX

1 Yr	3 Yr	5 Yr	2000	1999	1998	1997
−76.34	—	—	—	—	—	—

*Expense ratio is $8 per 100 shares per year.
Source: AMEX and Morningstar data as of 6/30/2001.

HOLDRs Internet (HHH)

Fund Information

Expense Ratio:	*
Total Net Assets:	$182,000,000
Structure:	Grantor Trust
Benchmark:	(Basket)
Options:	No
Initial Divisor:	—
Min. Investment:	100 Shares
Date of Inception:	01-Oct-99
52 Week Range:	27.91–124.94
2000 Total Dist.:	0.00

Top 10 Holdings

1) Yahoo! Inc	32.24%
2) AOL Time Warner	21.57%
3) Exodus Comms	6.85%
4) Inktomi Corp	6.19%
5) eBay Inc	5.78%
6) Amazon.com	5.22%
7) CMGI	3.65%
8) Realnetworks	3.27%
9) Lycos	2.34%
10) At Home Corp Cl A	2.29%

Fundamentals

Med Mkt Cap:	$10,975,000,000
P/E Ratio:	59.20
P/B Ratio:	11.20
P/C Ratio:	27.60
Standard Dev:	N/A
Sharpe Ratio:	N/A
Alpha:	N/A
Beta:	N/A
3 Yr Earn Gr:	N/A
1 Yr Fwd Gr:	75.00
12 Month Yield:	N/A

Sector Breakdown

Utilities:	0.00%
Energy:	0.00%
Financials:	2.90%
Industrial Cyclicals:	0.00%
Consumer Durables:	0.00%
Consumer Staples:	0.00%
Services:	7.40%
Retail:	5.20%
Health:	0.00%
Technology:	84.60%

Premium/Discount (6/29/2001)

P/D Close:	N/A
P/D Midpoint:	N/A

Tickers

Symbol: HHH	ECash:	N/A
NAV: HHI	TCash:	N/A
Close: N/A	Div:	N/A
Shares: N/A	Index:	N/A

Fund Management

Manager:	Bank of New York
Web Site:	http://www.holdrs.com
Telephone:	N/A
Specialist:	N/A
Distributor:	N/A
Administrator:	Merrill Lynch
Sponsor:	N/A
Exchange:	AMEX

1 Yr	3 Yr	5 Yr	2000	1999	1998	1997
−56.70	—	—	−76.34	—	—	—

*Expense ratio is $8 per 100 shares per year.
Source: AMEX and Morningstar data as of 6/30/2001.

HOLDRs Internet Architecture (IAH)

Fund Information

Expense Ratio:	*
Total Net Assets:	$166,900,000
Structure:	Grantor Trust
Benchmark:	(Basket)
Options:	No
Initial Divisor:	—
Min. Investment:	100 Shares
Date of Inception:	01-Feb–00
52 Week Range:	36.25–108.50
2000 Total Dist.:	0.03

Fundamentals

Med Mkt Cap:	$64,316,000,000
P/E Ratio:	33.90
P/B Ratio:	7.00
P/C Ratio:	23.50
Standard Dev:	N/A
Sharpe Ratio:	N/A
Alpha:	N/A
Beta:	N/A
3 Yr Earn Gr:	23.30
1 Yr Fwd Gr:	−11.50
12 Month Yield:	N/A

Premium/Discount (6/29/2001)

P/D Close:	0.39%
P/D Midpoint:	0.03%

Tickers

Symbol: IAH	ECash:	N/A	
NAV: XAH	TCash:	N/A	
Close: N/A	Div:	N/A	
Shares: N/A	Index:	N/A	

Top 10 Holdings

1) Cisco Systems	18.36%
2) IBM	15.78%
3) E M C Corp	14.70%
4) Sun Microsystems	13.66%
5) Dell Computer Corp	9.01%
6) Hewlett-Packard	8.25%
7) Compaq Computer	3.94%
8) Juniper Networks	3.07%
9) Sycamore Networks	2.66%
10) Network Appliance	1.86%

Sector Breakdown

Utilities:	0.00%
Energy:	0.00%
Financials:	0.00%
Industrial Cyclicals:	0.00%
Consumer Durables:	0.00%
Consumer Staples:	0.00%
Services:	0.00%
Retail:	0.00%
Health:	0.00%
Technology:	100.00%

Fund Management

Manager:	Bank of New York
Web Site:	http://www.holdrs.com
Telephone:	N/A
Specialist:	N/A
Distributor:	N/A
Administrator:	Merrill Lynch
Sponsor:	N/A
Exchange:	AMEX

1 Yr	3 Yr	5 Yr	2000	1999	1998	1997
−50.23	—	—	—	—	—	—

*Expense ratio is $8 per 100 shares per year.

Source: AMEX and Morningstar data as of 6/30/2001.

HOLDRs INTERNET INFRASTRUCTURE (IIH)

FUND INFORMATION

Expense Ratio:	*
Total Net Assets:	$207,900,000
Structure:	Grantor Trust
Benchmark:	(Basket)
Options:	No
Initial Divisor:	—
Min. Investment:	100 Shares
Date of Inception:	01-Feb-00
52 Week Range:	6.85–67.56
2000 Total Dist.:	0.00

TOP 10 HOLDINGS

1) Verisign Inc	18.99%
2) Exodus Comms	10.38%
3) BEA Sys	8.38%
4) Inktomi Corp	8.33%
5) Broadvision Inc	6.34%
6) Portal Software	5.88%
7) Infospace	5.26%
8) Alteon Websystems	5.14%
9) Realnetworks	4.96%
10) Akamai Tech	4.60%

FUNDAMENTALS

Med Mkt Cap:	$1,229,000,000
P/E Ratio:	N/A
P/B Ratio:	3.10
P/C Ratio:	28.50
Standard Dev:	N/A
Sharpe Ratio:	N/A
Alpha:	N/A
Beta:	N/A
3 Yr Earn Gr:	N/A
1 Yr Fwd Gr:	68.00
12 Month Yield:	N/A

SECTOR BREAKDOWN

Utilities:	0.00%
Energy:	0.00%
Financials:	0.00%
Industrial Cyclicals:	0.00%
Consumer Durables:	0.00%
Consumer Staples:	0.00%
Services:	0.00%
Retail:	0.00%
Health:	0.00%
Technology:	100.00%

PREMIUM/DISCOUNT (6/29/2001)

P/D Close:	N/A
P/D Midpoint:	N/A

TICKERS

Symbol: IIH		ECash:	N/A
NAV:	YIH	TCash:	N/A
Close:	N/A	Div:	N/A
Shares:	N/A	Index:	N/A

FUND MANAGEMENT

Manager:	Bank of New York
Web Site:	http://www.holdrs.com
Telephone:	N/A
Specialist:	N/A
Distributor:	N/A
Administrator:	Merrill Lynch
Sponsor:	N/A
Exchange:	AMEX

1 Yr	3 Yr	5 Yr	2000	1999	1998	1997
−79.75	—	—	—	—	—	—

*Expense ratio is $8 per 100 shares per year.

Source: AMEX and Morningstar data as of 6/30/2001.

HOLDRs Regional Bank (RKH)

Fund Information

Expense Ratio:	*
Total Net Assets:	$70,800,000
Structure:	Grantor Trust
Benchmark:	(Basket)
Options:	No
Initial Divisor:	—
Min. Investment:	100 Shares
Date of Inception:	01-Jun–00
52 Week Range:	90.56–127.00
2000 Total Dist.:	1.22

Fundamentals

Med Mkt Cap:	$25,550,000,000
P/E Ratio:	20.10
P/B Ratio:	3.30
P/C Ratio:	N/A
Standard Dev:	N/A
Sharpe Ratio:	N/A
Alpha:	N/A
Beta:	N/A
3 Yr Earn Gr:	12.50
1 Yr Fwd Gr:	7.70
12 Month Yield:	N/A

Premium/Discount (6/29/2001)

P/D Close:	N/A
P/D Midpoint:	N/A

Tickers

Symbol: RKH	ECash:	N/A	
NAV: XRH	TCash:	N/A	
Close: N/A	Div:	N/A	
Shares: N/A	Index:	N/A	

Top 10 Holdings

1) Bank One Corp	11.00%
2) Wells Fargo & Co	10.39%
3) FleetBoston Finl	9.38%
4) First Union Corp	7.84%
5) First Star Bancorp	6.00%
6) Fifth Third Bancorp	5.84%
7) Mellon Finl	5.53%
8) Northern Trust	5.49%
9) State Street Global	5.26%
10) PNC Finl Svcs Grp	4.80%

Sector Breakdown

Utilities:	0.00%
Energy:	0.00%
Financials:	100.00%
Industrial Cyclicals:	0.00%
Consumer Durables:	0.00%
Consumer Staples:	0.00%
Services:	0.00%
Retail:	0.00%
Health:	0.00%
Technology:	0.00%

Fund Management

Manager:	Bank of New York
Web Site:	http://www.holdrs.com
Telephone:	N/A
Specialist:	N/A
Distributor:	N/A
Administrator:	Merrill Lynch
Sponsor:	N/A
Exchange:	AMEX

1 Yr	3 Yr	5 Yr	2000	1999	1998	1997
30.02	—	—	—	—	—	—

*Expense ratio is $8 per 100 shares per year.
Source: AMEX and Morningstar data as of 6/30/2001.

HOLDRs Semiconductor (SMH)

Fund Information

Expense Ratio:	*
Total Net Assets:	$661,200,000
Structure:	Grantor Trust
Benchmark:	(Basket)
Options:	No
Initial Divisor:	—
Min. Investment:	100 Shares
Date of Inception:	01-May–00
52 Week Range:	34.81–105.75
2000 Total Dist.:	0.00

Fundamentals

Med Mkt Cap:	$33,390,000,000
P/E Ratio:	28.40
P/B Ratio:	5.10
P/C Ratio:	21.50
Standard Dev:	N/A
Sharpe Ratio:	N/A
Alpha:	N/A
Beta:	N/A
3 Yr Earn Gr:	42.50
1 Yr Fwd Gr:	−54.60
12 Month Yield:	N/A

Premium/Discount (6/29/2001)

P/D Close:	0.09%
P/D Midpoint:	N/A

Tickers

Symbol: SMH	ECash:	N/A	
NAV: XSH	TCash:	N/A	
Close: N/A	Div:	N/A	
Shares: N/A	Index:	N/A	

Top 10 Holdings

1) Intel Corp	19.84%
2) Texas Instruments	18.37%
3) Applied Materials	13.65%
4) Micron Technology	6.24%
5) Analog Devices	4.55%
6) Broadcom Corp	3.91%
7) Xilinx	3.71%
8) Maxim Integrated	3.56%
9) Teradyne	3.34%
10) Altera Corp	3.22%

Sector Breakdown

Utilities:	0.00%
Energy:	0.00%
Financials:	0.00%
Industrial Cyclicals:	0.00%
Consumer Durables:	0.00%
Consumer Staples:	0.00%
Services:	0.00%
Retail:	0.00%
Health:	0.00%
Technology:	100.00%

Fund Management

Manager:	Bank of New York
Web Site:	http://www.holdrs.com
Telephone:	N/A
Specialist:	N/A
Distributor:	N/A
Administrator:	Merrill Lynch
Sponsor:	N/A
Exchange:	AMEX

1 Yr	3 Yr	5 Yr	2000	1999	1998	1997
−48.72	—	—	—	—	—	—

*Expense ratio is $8 per 100 shares per year.

Source: AMEX and Morningstar data as of 6/30/2001.

HOLDRs Europe 2001 (EKH)

Fund Information

Expense Ratio:	*
Total Net Assets:	N/A
Structure:	Grantor Trust
Benchmark:	(Basket)
Options:	No
Initial Divisor:	—
Min. Investment:	100 Shares
Date of Inception:	30-Aug–00
52 Week Range:	66.30–98.25
2000 Total Dist.:	—

Fundamentals

Med Mkt Cap:	N/A
P/E Ratio:	N/A
P/B Ratio:	N/A
P/C Ratio:	N/A
Standard Dev:	N/A
Sharpe Ratio:	N/A
Alpha:	N/A
Beta:	N/A
3 Yr Earn Gr:	N/A
1 Yr Fwd Gr:	N/A
12 Month Yield:	N/A

Premium/Discount (6/29/2001)

P/D Close:	N/A
P/D Midpoint:	0.06%

Tickers

Symbol:	EKH	ECash:	N/A
NAV:	EKI	TCash:	N/A
Close:	N/A	Div:	N/A
Shares:	N/A	Index:	N/A

Top 10 Holdings

1) GlaxoSmithKline	3.45%
2) Amdocs	2.41%
3) TotalFinaElf	2.35%
4) Vivendi Universal	2.25%
5) Shire Pharma	2.25%
6) Novartis	2.22%
7) AXA Financial Inc	2.20%
8) Infineon	2.18%
9) Diageo	2.16%
10) Ryanair Holdings	2.16%

Sector Breakdown

Utilities:	0.00%
Energy:	0.00%
Financials:	0.00%
Industrial Cyclicals:	0.00%
Consumer Durables:	0.00%
Consumer Staples:	0.00%
Services:	0.00%
Retail:	0.00%
Health:	0.00%
Technology:	0.00%

Fund Management

Manager:	Bank of New York
Web Site:	http://www.holdrs.com
Telephone:	N/A
Specialist:	Wolverine Trading
Distributor:	N/A
Administrator:	Merrill Lynch
Sponsor:	N/A
Exchange:	AMEX

1 Yr	3 Yr	5 Yr	2000	1999	1998	1997
—	—	—	—	—	—	—

*Expense ratio is $8 per 100 shares per year.

Source: AMEX and Morningstar data as of 6/30/2001.

HOLDRs Market2000+ (MKH)

FUND INFORMATION

Expense Ratio:	*
Total Net Assets:	N/A
Structure:	Grantor Trust
Benchmark:	(Basket)
Options:	No
Initial Divisor:	—
Min. Investment:	100 Shares
Date of Inception:	18-Jan–01
52 Week Range:	61.15–97.25
2000 Total Dist.:	—

FUNDAMENTALS

Med Mkt Cap:	N/A
P/E Ratio:	N/A
P/B Ratio:	N/A
P/C Ratio:	N/A
Standard Dev:	N/A
Sharpe Ratio:	N/A
Alpha:	N/A
Beta:	N/A
3 Yr Earn Gr:	N/A
1 Yr Fwd Gr:	N/A
12 Month Yield:	N/A

PREMIUM/DISCOUNT (6/29/2001)

P/D Close:	N/A
P/D Midpoint:	0.41%

TICKERS

Symbol: MKH		ECash:	N/A
NAV: XKH		TCash:	N/A
Close: N/A		Div:	N/A
Shares: N/A		Index:	N/A

TOP 10 HOLDINGS

1) IBM	2.73%
2) Sun Microsystems	2.68%
3) JDS Uniphase Corp	2.59%
4) British Telecomm	2.56%
5) Hewlett-Packard	2.53%
6) France Telecom	2.52%
7) Sony Corp	2.36%
8) Merck & Co Inc	2.28%
9) Microsoft Corp	2.24%
10) Morgan Stanley	2.15%

SECTOR BREAKDOWN

Utilities:	0.00%
Energy:	0.00%
Financials:	0.00%
Industrial Cyclicals:	0.00%
Consumer Durables:	0.00%
Consumer Staples:	0.00%
Services:	0.00%
Retail:	0.00%
Health:	0.00%
Technology:	0.00%

FUND MANAGEMENT

Manager:	Bank of New York
Web Site:	http://www.holdrs.com
Telephone:	N/A
Specialist:	N/A
Distributor:	N/A
Administrator:	Merrill Lynch
Sponsor:	N/A
Exchange:	AMEX

1 Yr	3 Yr	5 Yr	2000	1999	1998	1997
—	—	—	—	—	—	—

*Expense ratio is $8 per 100 shares per year.

Source: AMEX and Morningstar data as of 6/30/2001.

HOLDRs Oil Service (OIH)

FUND INFORMATION

Expense Ratio:	*
Total Net Assets:	N/A
Structure:	Grantor Trust
Benchmark:	(Basket)
Options:	No
Initial Divisor:	—
Min. Investment:	100 Shares
Date of Inception:	01-Mar-01
52 Week Range:	73.30–98.85
2000 Total Dist.:	—

TOP 10 HOLDINGS

1) Halliburton Company	9.88%
2) Baker Hughes Inc	9.87%
3) Transocean Sedco	9.41%
4) Schlumberger	9.38%
5) Nabors Industries	7.84%
6) BJ Services Co	6.12%
7) Noble Drilling Corp	5.71%
8) Diamond Offshore Drilling	5.02%
9) Weatherford Intl	4.97%
10) Global Marine	4.93%

FUNDAMENTALS

Med Mkt Cap:	N/A
P/E Ratio:	N/A
P/B Ratio:	N/A
P/C Ratio:	N/A
Standard Dev:	N/A
Sharpe Ratio:	N/A
Alpha:	N/A
Beta:	N/A
3 Yr Earn Gr:	N/A
1 Yr Fwd Gr:	N/A
12 Month Yield:	N/A

SECTOR BREAKDOWN

Utilities:	0.00%
Energy:	0.00%
Financials:	0.00%
Industrial Cyclicals:	0.00%
Consumer Durables:	0.00%
Consumer Staples:	0.00%
Services:	0.00%
Retail:	0.00%
Health:	0.00%
Technology:	0.00%

PREMIUM/DISCOUNT (6/29/2001)

P/D Close:	0.08%
P/D Midpoint:	0.12%

TICKERS

Symbol: OIH	ECash:	N/A
NAV: OXH	TCash:	N/A
Close: N/A	Div:	N/A
Shares: N/A	Index:	N/A

FUND MANAGEMENT

Manager:	Bank of New York
Web Site:	http://www.holdrs.com
Telephone:	N/A
Specialist:	N/A
Distributor:	N/A
Administrator:	Merrill Lynch
Sponsor:	N/A
Exchange:	AMEX

1 Yr	3 Yr	5 Yr	2000	1999	1998	1997
—	—	—	—	—	—	—

*Expense ratio is $8 per 100 shares per year.

Source: AMEX and Morningstar data as of 6/30/2001.

HOLDRS PHARM (PPH)

FUND INFORMATION

Expense Ratio:	*
Total Net Assets:	N/A
Structure:	Grantor Trust
Benchmark:	(Basket)
Options:	No
Initial Divisor:	—
Min. Investment:	100 Shares
Date of Inception:	01-Mar–00
52 Week Range:	84.32–115.87
2000 Total Dist.:	0.05

FUNDAMENTALS

Med Mkt Cap:	N/A
P/E Ratio:	N/A
P/B Ratio:	N/A
P/C Ratio:	N/A
Standard Dev:	N/A
Sharpe Ratio:	N/A
Alpha:	N/A
Beta:	N/A
3 Yr Earn Gr:	N/A
1 Yr Fwd Gr:	N/A
12 Month Yield:	N/A

PREMIUM/DISCOUNT (6/29/2001)

P/D Close:	N/A
P/D Midpoint:	0%

TICKERS

Symbol: PPH	ECash:	N/A
NAV: IPH	TCash:	N/A
Close: N/A	Div:	N/A
Shares: N/A	Index:	N/A

TOP 10 HOLDINGS

1) Merck & Co Inc	17.50%
2) Pfizer Inc	13.75%
3) Johnson & Johnson	13.72%
4) Bristol Myers Squibb	13.37%
5) Lilly (Eli) and Co	7.63%
6) Warner-Lambert	7.56%
7) Schering-Plough	7.04%
8) American Home Prod	6.38%
9) Abbott Labs	5.45%
10) Pharmacia & Upjohn	3.02%

SECTOR BREAKDOWN

Utilities:	0.00%
Energy:	0.00%
Financials:	0.00%
Industrial Cyclicals:	0.00%
Consumer Durables:	0.00%
Consumer Staples:	0.00%
Services:	0.00%
Retail:	0.00%
Health:	0.00%
Technology:	0.00%

FUND MANAGEMENT

Manager:	Bank of New York
Web Site:	http://www.holdrs.com
Telephone:	N/A
Specialist:	N/A
Distributor:	N/A
Administrator:	Merrill Lynch
Sponsor:	N/A
Exchange:	AMEX

1 Yr	3 Yr	5 Yr	2000	1999	1998	1997
—	—	—	—	—	—	—

*Expense ratio is $8 per 100 shares per year.
Source: AMEX and Morningstar data as of 6/30/2001.

HOLDRS RETAIL (RTH)

FUND INFORMATION

Expense Ratio:	*
Total Net Assets:	$70,800,000
Structure:	Grantor Trust
Benchmark:	(Basket)
Options:	No
Initial Divisor:	—
Min. Investment:	100 Shares
Date of Inception:	01-Jun-00
52 Week Range:	88.70-100.90
2000 Total Dist.:	0.00

TOP 10 HOLDINGS

1) Home Depot Inc	20.73%
2) Wal-Mart Stores	19.01%
3) Walgreen Co	7.94%
4) Target Corp	6.20%
5) Gap Inc	5.21%
6) Lowes Cos Inc	5.13%
7) Safeway Inc	4.78%
8) CVS Corp	3.94%
9) Kroger Co	3.83%
10) Kohls Corp	3.72%

FUNDAMENTALS

Med Mkt Cap:	N/A
P/E Ratio:	N/A
P/B Ratio:	N/A
P/C Ratio:	N/A
Standard Dev:	N/A
Sharpe Ratio:	N/A
Alpha:	N/A
Beta:	N/A
3 Yr Earn Gr:	N/A
1 Yr Fwd Gr:	N/A
12 Month Yield:	N/A

SECTOR BREAKDOWN

Utilities:	0.00%
Energy:	0.00%
Financials:	0.00%
Industrial Cyclicals:	0.00%
Consumer Durables:	0.00%
Consumer Staples:	0.00%
Services:	0.00%
Retail:	0.00%
Health:	0.00%
Technology:	0.00%

PREMIUM/DISCOUNT (6/29/2001)

P/D Close:	N/A
P/D Midpoint:	N/A

TICKERS

Symbol: RTH	ECash:	N/A	
NAV: XRH	TCash:	N/A	
Close: N/A	Div:	N/A	
Shares: N/A	Index:	N/A	

FUND MANAGEMENT

Manager:	Bank of New York
Web Site:	http://www.holdrs.com
Telephone:	N/A
Specialist:	N/A
Distributor:	N/A
Administrator:	Merrill Lynch
Sponsor:	N/A
Exchange:	AMEX

1 Yr	3 Yr	5 Yr	2000	1999	1998	1997
—	—	—	—	—	—	—

*Expense ratio is $8 per 100 shares per year.
Source: AMEX and Morningstar data as of 6/30/2001.

HOLDRs Software (SWH)

Fund Information

Expense Ratio:	*
Total Net Assets:	N/A
Structure:	Grantor Trust
Benchmark:	(Basket)
Options:	No
Initial Divisor:	—
Min. Investment:	100 Shares
Date of Inception:	01-Nov–00
52 Week Range:	36.80–99.84
2000 Total Dist.:	0.00

Top 10 Holdings

1) Veritas	9.99%
2) Oracle Corp	9.95%
3) SAP-AG	9.77%
4) Microsoft Corp	9.67%
5) I2 Technologies	9.61%
6) Siebel Sys Inc	9.07%
7) Check Point Software	6.42%
8) Computer Assoc Intl	4.69%
9) Adobe	4.66%
10) TIBCO	4.40%

Fundamentals

Med Mkt Cap:	N/A
P/E Ratio:	N/A
P/B Ratio:	N/A
P/C Ratio:	N/A
Standard Dev:	N/A
Sharpe Ratio:	N/A
Alpha:	N/A
Beta:	N/A
3 Yr Earn Gr:	N/A
1 Yr Fwd Gr:	N/A
12 Month Yield:	N/A

Sector Breakdown

Utilities:	0.00%
Energy:	0.00%
Financials:	0.00%
Industrial Cyclicals:	0.00%
Consumer Durables:	0.00%
Consumer Staples:	0.00%
Services:	0.00%
Retail:	0.00%
Health:	0.00%
Technology:	0.00%

Premium/Discount (6/29/2001)

P/D Close:	0.3%
P/D Midpoint:	N/A

Tickers

Symbol: SWH	ECash:	N/A
NAV: XWH	TCash:	N/A
Close: N/A	Div:	N/A
Shares: N/A	Index:	N/A

Fund Management

Manager:	Bank of New York
Web Site:	http://www.holdrs.com
Telephone:	N/A
Specialist:	N/A
Distributor:	N/A
Administrator:	Merrill Lynch
Sponsor:	N/A
Exchange:	AMEX

1 Yr	3 Yr	5 Yr	2000	1999	1998	1997
—	—	—	—	—	—	—

*Expense ratio is $8 per 100 shares per year.

Source: AMEX and Morningstar data as of 6/30/2001.

HOLDRs Telebras (TBH)

Fund Information

Expense Ratio:	*
Total Net Assets:	$2,116,100,000
Structure:	Grantor Trust
Benchmark:	(Basket)
Options:	No
Initial Divisor:	—
Min. Investment:	100 Shares
Date of Inception:	01-Jun–00
52 Week Range:	41.25–104.88
2000 Total Dist.:	—

Fundamentals

Med Mkt Cap:	N/A
P/E Ratio:	N/A
P/B Ratio:	N/A
P/C Ratio:	N/A
Standard Dev:	N/A
Sharpe Ratio:	N/A
Alpha:	N/A
Beta:	N/A
3 Yr Earn Gr:	N/A
1 Yr Fwd Gr:	N/A
12 Month Yield:	N/A

Premium/Discount (6/29/2001)

P/D Close:	N/A
P/D Midpoint:	N/A

Tickers

Symbol: TBH	ECash:	N/A
NAV: N/A	TCash:	N/A
Close: N/A	Div:	N/A
Shares: N/A	Index:	N/A

Top 10 Holdings

1) N/A	0.00%
2) N/A	0.00%
3) N/A	0.00%
4) N/A	0.00%
5) N/A	0.00%
6) N/A	0.00%
7) N/A	0.00%
8) N/A	0.00%
9) N/A	0.00%
10) N/A	0.00%

Sector Breakdown

Utilities:	0.00%
Energy:	0.00%
Financials:	0.00%
Industrial Cyclicals:	0.00%
Consumer Durables:	0.00%
Consumer Staples:	0.00%
Services:	0.00%
Retail:	0.00%
Health:	0.00%
Technology:	0.00%

Fund Management

Manager:	Bank of New York
Web Site:	http://www.holdrs.com
Telephone:	N/A
Specialist:	N/A
Distributor:	N/A
Administrator:	Merrill Lynch
Sponsor:	N/A
Exchange:	AMEX

1 Yr	3 Yr	5 Yr	2000	1999	1998	1997
—	—	—	—	—	—	—

*Expense ratio is $8 per 100 shares per year.
Source: AMEX and Morningstar data as of 6/30/2001.

HOLDRs Telecom (TTH)

Fund Information

Expense Ratio:	*
Total Net Assets:	$330,800,000
Structure:	Grantor Trust
Benchmark:	(Basket)
Options:	No
Initial Divisor:	—
Min. Investment:	100 Shares
Date of Inception:	01-Mar–00
52 Week Range:	47.20–81.19
2000 Total Dist.:	—

Top 10 Holdings

1) SBC Comms	16.95%
2) Verizon Comms	15.09%
3) WorldCom	12.68%
4) AT & T Corp	11.41%
5) Qwest Comms Intl	8.95%
6) BellSouth	8.81%
7) Nextel Comms	.95%
8) Sprint (PCS Group)	4.89%
9) Sprint	3.15%
10) Level 3 Comms	3.03%

Fundamentals

Med Mkt Cap:	$68,096,000,000
P/E Ratio:	21.40
P/B Ratio:	3.40
P/C Ratio:	9.00
Standard Dev:	N/A
Sharpe Ratio:	N/A
Alpha:	N/A
Beta:	N/A
3 Yr Earn Gr:	18.30
1 Yr Fwd Gr:	−18.70
12 Month Yield:	N/A

Sector Breakdown

Utilities:	0.00%
Energy:	0.00%
Financials:	0.00%
Industrial Cyclicals:	0.00%
Consumer Durables:	0.00%
Consumer Staples:	0.00%
Services:	100.00%
Retail:	0.00%
Health:	0.00%
Technology:	0.00%

Premium/Discount (6/29/2001)

P/D Close:	0.18%
P/D Midpoint:	0.31%

Tickers

Symbol: TTH	ECash:	N/A
NAV: ITH	TCash:	N/A
Close: N/A	Div:	N/A
Shares: N/A	Index:	N/A

Fund Management

Manager:	Bank of New York
Web Site:	http://www.holdrs.com
Telephone:	N/A
Specialist:	N/A
Distributor:	N/A
Administrator:	Merrill Lynch
Sponsor:	N/A
Exchange:	AMEX

1 Yr	3 Yr	5 Yr	2000	1999	1998	1997
−31.51	—	—	—	—	—	—

*Expense ratio is $8 per 100 shares per year.

Source: AMEX and Morningstar data as of 6/30/2001.

HOLDRs UTILITIES (UTH)

FUND INFORMATION

Expense Ratio:	*
Total Net Assets:	$63,500,000
Structure:	Grantor Trust
Benchmark:	(Basket)
Options:	No
Initial Divisor:	—
Min. Investment:	100 Shares
Date of Inception:	01-Jun-00
52 Week Range:	86.67–120.83
2000 Total Dist.:	1.62

FUNDAMENTALS

Med Mkt Cap:	$15,232,000,000
P/E Ratio:	21.80
P/B Ratio:	3.60
P/C Ratio:	13.10
Standard Dev:	N/A
Sharpe Ratio:	N/A
Alpha:	N/A
Beta:	N/A
3 Yr Earn Gr:	15.50
1 Yr Fwd Gr:	16.10
12 Month Yield:	N/A

PREMIUM/DISCOUNT (6/29/2001)

P/D Close:	0.17%
P/D Midpoint:	N/A

TICKERS

Symbol: UTH	ECash:	N/A
NAV: XUH	TCash:	N/A
Close: N/A	Div:	N/A
Shares: N/A	Index:	N/A

TOP 10 HOLDINGS

1) Duke Energy	10.07%
2) Enron	9.62%
3) Williams Controls Inc	9.09%
4) Southern Co	7.71%
5) Dominion Resources	5.44%
6) El Paso Energy	5.26%
7) American Elec Pwr	5.00%
8) PG & E	4.79%
9) Reliant Energy	4.74%
10) Dynegy	4.60%

SECTOR BREAKDOWN

Utilities:	85.80%
Energy:	14.20%
Financials:	0.00%
Industrial Cyclicals:	0.00%
Consumer Durables:	0.00%
Consumer Staples:	0.00%
Services:	0.00%
Retail:	0.00%
Health:	0.00%
Technology:	0.00%

FUND MANAGEMENT

Manager:	Bank of New York
Web Site:	http://www.holdrs.com
Telephone:	N/A
Specialist:	N/A
Distributor:	N/A
Administrator:	Merrill Lynch
Sponsor:	N/A
Exchange:	AMEX

1 Yr	3 Yr	5 Yr	2000	1999	1998	1997
20.62	—	—	—	—	—	—

*Expense ratio is $8 per 100 shares per year.
Source: AMEX and Morningstar data as of 6/30/2001.

HOLDRs Wireless (WMH)

FUND INFORMATION

Expense Ratio:	*
Total Net Assets:	N/A
Structure:	Grantor Trust
Benchmark:	(Basket)
Options:	No
Initial Divisor:	—
Min. Investment:	100 Shares
Date of Inception:	01–Dec–00
52 Week Range:	56.40–103.12
2000 Total Dist.:	—

FUNDAMENTALS

Med Mkt Cap:	N/A
P/E Ratio:	N/A
P/B Ratio:	N/A
P/C Ratio:	N/A
Standard Dev:	N/A
Sharpe Ratio:	N/A
Alpha:	N/A
Beta:	N/A
3 Yr Earn Gr:	N/A
1 Yr Fwd Gr:	N/A
12 Month Yield:	N/A

PREMIUM/DISCOUNT (6/29/2001)

P/D Close:	0.41%
P/D Midpoint:	0.72%

TICKERS

Symbol: WMH		ECash:	N/A
NAV: IWH		TCash:	N/A
Close: N/A		Div:	N/A
Shares: N/A		Index:	N/A

TOP 10 HOLDINGS

1) Verizon Comms	9.96%
2) AT & T Wireless Group	9.76%
3) Motorola Co	9.76%
4) Lm Ericsson Telephone Co	9.74%
5) Nokia Corp	9.66%
6) QUALCOMM Inc	9.37%
7) Vodafone Group	9.29%
8) Sprint (PCS Group)	7.81%
9) Voicestream Wireless	6.75%
10) Nextel	5.83%

SECTOR BREAKDOWN

Utilities:	0.00%
Energy:	0.00%
Financials:	0.00%
Industrial Cyclicals:	0.00%
Consumer Durables:	0.00%
Consumer Staples:	0.00%
Services:	0.00%
Retail:	0.00%
Health:	0.00%
Technology:	0.00%

FUND MANAGEMENT

Manager:	Bank of New York
Web Site:	http://www.holdrs.com
Telephone:	N/A
Specialist:	N/A
Distributor:	N/A
Administrator:	Merrill Lynch
Sponsor:	N/A
Exchange:	AMEX

1 Yr	3 Yr	5 Yr	2000	1999	1998	1997
—	—	—	—	—	—	—

*Expense ratio is $8 per 100 shares per year.

Source: AMEX and Morningstar data as of 6/30/2001.

ETFs Trading on International Markets

DAX Ex Anteile (DAXEX GY)

Expense Ratio:	0.50%
Total Net Assets:	N/A
Category:	Country
Benchmark:	DAX Index
Init Divisor:	—
Exchange:	Deutsche Börse
Manager:	IndexChange AG
Inception:	27-Dec–00

Top 10 Holdings

1) Allianz AG Vink.NA O.N.	9.55%
2) Deutsche Telekom AG NA O.N.	8.96%
3) Siemens AG NA O.N.	8.81%
4) Münch.Rück. Vink. NA O.N.	6.86%
5) SAP AG Vz O.N.	6.10%
6) E.On AG O.N.	5.40%
7) Deutsche Bank AG NA	6.64%
8) Daimlerchrysler AG O.N.	6.73%
9) Bayer AG O.N.	4.14%
10) BASF AG O.N.	3.53%

DJ Euro STOXX 50 LDRS

Expense Ratio:	0.50%
Total Net Assets:	N/A
Category:	Regional
Benchmark:	DJ Euro STOXX 50 Index
Init Divisor:	—
Exchange:	Deutsche Börse
Manager:	EETFC
Inception:	11-Apr–00

Top 10 Holdings

1) Nokia Corp	8.02%
2) Royal Dutch Petrol Co	7.67%
3) TotalFinaElf	6.35%
4) Vivendi Universal	3.77%
5) Telefonica	3.54%
6) Siemens	3.52%
7) ING Groep	3.16%
8) Aventis	2.92%
9) Deutsche Bank R	2.79%
10) Bco Bilbao Vizcaya Argentaria	2.57%

DJ Euro STOXX Banks Ex (SX7EEX GY)

Expense Ratio:	0.50%
Total Net Assets:	N/A
Category:	Sector
Benchmark:	DJ Euro STOXX Banks Index
Init Divisor:	—
Exchange:	Deutsche Börse
Manager:	IndexChange AG
Inception:	4-May–01

Top 10 Holdings

1) Deutsche Bank AG NA	10.00%
2) Banque Nat.de Paris SA	8.55%
3) Societe Generale SA	5.33%
4) Bayer. Hypo- U.Vereinsbank AG Inhst O.N.	4.11%
5) Unicredito Italiano SPA	3.72%
6) Intesabci NA Li 1000	3.72%
7) Dresdner Bank AG NA O.N.	3.45%
8) San Paolo-Imi SPA	3.21%
9) Commerzbank AG O.N.	2.39%
10) Dexia SA O.N.	2.21%

Source: AMEX and Morningstar data as of 6/30/2001.

DJ Euro STOXX Healthcare Ex (SXDEEX GY)

Expense Ratio:	0.50%
Total Net Assets:	N/A
Category:	Sector
Benchmark:	DJ Euro STOXX Healthcare Index
Init Divisor:	—
Exchange:	Deutsche Börse
Manager:	IndexChange AG
Inception:	4-May–01

Top 10 Holdings

1) Aventis SA	10.00%
2) Sanofi-Synthelabo Eo 2	10.00%
3) Elan Corp.Plc NA Eo-.05	10.00%
4) Schering AG O.N.	8.14%
5) UCB SA Cap. O.N.	2.43%
6) Quiagen NV	2.24%
7) Essilor Intl. Eo 3.50	2.13%
8) Fresenius Medical Care AG O.N.	2.12%
9) Altana AG O.N.	2.07%
10) Luxottica Group Li 100	1.87%

DJ Euro STOXX Technology Ex (SX8EEX GY)

Expense Ratio:	0.50%
Total Net Assets:	N/A
Category:	Sector
Benchmark:	DJ Euro STOXX Technology Index
Init Divisor:	—
Exchange:	Deutsche Börse
Manager:	IndexChange AG
Inception:	4-May–01

Top 10 Holdings

1) Nokia Corp	10.00%
2) Siemens AG NA O.N.	10.00%
3) Alcatel SA	10.00%
4) STMicroelectronics NV Eo 1.04	5.92%
5) SAP AG Vz O.N.	5.85%
6) Asm Lithogr.Hldg NA Eo–02	3.39%
7) Olivetti Ord. NA Eo 1	3.28%
8) Infineon AG NA O.N. 1.	89%
9) Tietoenator OYJ NA O.N.	0.61%
10) Business Obj. Nom. NA Eo 0.1	0.57%

DJ Euro STOXX Telecommunications Ex (SXKEEX GY)

Expense Ratio:	0.50%
Total Net Assets:	N/A
Category:	Sector
Benchmark:	DJ Euro STOXX Telecommunications Index
Init Divisor:	—
Exchange:	Deutsche Börse
Manager:	IndexChange AG
Inception:	4-May–01

Top 10 Holdings

1) Telefonica de Espana SA	10.00%
2) Deutsche Telekom AG NA O.N.	10.00%
3) Telecom Italia Mob. NA Eo0.06	10.00%
4) Telecom Italia SPA	10.00%
5) France Telecom	10.00%
6) Port.Tel.Sg. NA Eo 1	4.52%
7) Kon. Ptt Nederland NV	3.42%
8) Equant NV Fl -.02	1.82%
9) Hellenic Telec. Org.Nam.	1.77%
10) Sonera OYJ O.N.	1.58%

Source: AMEX and Morningstar data as of 6/30/2001.

DJ STOXX 50 LDRS

Expense Ratio:	0.50%
Total Net Assets:	N/A
Category:	Country
Benchmark:	DJ STOXX 50 Index
Init Divisor:	—
Exchange:	Deutsche Börse
Manager:	EETFC
Inception:	11-Apr–01

TOP 10 HOLDINGS

1) British Petroleum Plc	7.03%
2) GlaxoSmithKline	5.93%
3) Vodafone Corp	5.84%
4) Nokia Corp	4.78%
5) Royal Dutch Petrol Co	4.57%
6) HSBC Holdings Plc	3.83%
7) TotalFinaElf	3.78%
8) Novartis R	3.51%
9) Shell Transport & Tradng	3.03%
10) Nestle R	2.83%

DJ STOXX 600 BANKS EX (SX7PEX GY)

Expense Ratio:	0.50%
Total Net Assets:	N/A
Category:	Sector
Benchmark:	DJ STOXX 600 Banks Index
Init Divisor:	—
Exchange:	Deutsche Börse
Manager:	IndexChange AG
Inception:	4-May–01

TOP 10 HOLDINGS

1) HSBC Holdings Plc	10.00%
2) UBS NA	7.29%
3) Royal Bank of Scotland Plc	6.37%
4) Lloyds Tsb Group	6.27%
5) Societe Generale SA	2.53%
6) Intesabci NA Li 1000	1.77%
7) Unicredito Italiano SPA	1.77%
8) San Paolo-Imi SPA	1.53%
9) Stand. Chart. Plc NA Dl-,50	1.49%
10) Nordea AB NA Eo–40	1.42%

DJ STOXX 600 HEALTHCARE EX (SXDPEX GY)

Expense Ratio:	0.50%
Total Net Assets:	N/A
Category:	Sector
Benchmark:	DJ STOXX 600 Healthcare Index
Init Divisor:	—
Exchange:	Deutsche Börse
Manager:	IndexChange AG
Inception:	4-May–01

TOP 10 HOLDINGS

1) GlaxoSmithKline	10.00%
2) Novartis NA	10.00%
3) Astrazeneca Plc	10.00%
4) Roche Holding Genußschein	9.48%
5) Aventis SA	8.82%
6) Sanofi-Synthelabo Eo 2	3.66%
7) Elan Corp.Plc NA Eo-.05	2.60%
8) Novo-Nordisk B NA Dk 2	1.92%
9) Schering AG O.N.	1.64%
10) Shire Pharma. Grp NA Ls-.05	1.40%

Source: AMEX and Morningstar data as of 6/30/2001.

DJ STOXX 600 TECHNOLOGY EX (SX8PEX GY)

Expense Ratio:	0.50%
Total Net Assets:	N/A
Category:	Sector
Benchmark:	DJ STOXX 600 Technology Index
Init Divisor:	—
Exchange:	Deutsche Börse
Manager:	IndexChange AG
Inception:	4-May–01

TOP 10 HOLDINGS

1) Nokia Corp	10.00%
2) Siemens AG NA O.N.	10.00%
3) Ericsson B	10.00%
4) Alcatel SA	7.91%
5) Stmicroelectronics NV Eo 1.04	4.61%
6) SAP AG Vz O.N.	4.55%
7) Marconi Electr. Sys Ls-.05	3.64%
8) Asm Lithogr.Hldg NA Eo–02	2.64%
9) Olivetti Ord. NA Eo 1	2.55%
10) Logica Plc NA Ls-.10	1.48%

DJ STOXX 600 TELECOMMUNICATIONS EX (SXKPEX GY)

Expense Ratio:	0.50%
Total Net Assets:	N/A
Category:	Sector
Benchmark:	DJ STOXX 600 Telecommunications Index
Init Divisor:	—
Exchange:	Deutsche Börse
Manager:	IndexChange AG
Inception:	4-May–01

TOP 10 HOLDINGS

1) Vodafone Group Plc	10.00%
2) Telefonica de Espana SA	10.00%
3) British Telecommunications Plc	10.00%
4) Deutsche Telekom AG NA O.N.	5.76%
5) Telecom Italia Mob. NA Eo0.06	5.49%
6) Telecom Italia SPA	4.89%
7) France Telecom	4.70%
8) Cable Wireless NA Ls-.25	3.93%
9) Port.Tel.Sg. NA Eo 1	1.90%
10) Kon. Ptt Nederland NV	1.43%

DOW JONES CANADA 40 INDEX FUND (DJF CN)

Expense Ratio:	0.08%
Total Net Assets:	N/A
Category:	Country
Benchmark:	DJ Canada 40 Index
Init Divisor:	—
Exchange:	Toronto
Manager:	State Street Global Advisors
Inception:	3-Oct–00

TOP 10 HOLDINGS

1) N/A	0.00%
2) N/A	0.00%
3) N/A	0.00%
4) N/A	0.00%
5) N/A	0.00%
6) N/A	0.00%
7) N/A	0.00%
8) N/A	0.00%
9) N/A	0.00%
10) N/A	0.00%

Source: AMEX and Morningstar data as of 6/30/2001.

DOW JONES EURO STOXX 50 EX

Expense Ratio:	0.50%	
Total Net Assets:	N/A	
Category:	Country	
Benchmark:	Dow Jones Euro STOXX 50 Index	
Init Divisor:	—	
Exchange:	Deutsche Börse	
Manager:	IndexChange AG	
Inception:	27-Dec–00	

TOP 10 HOLDINGS

1) Nokia Corp	8.02%
2) Royal Dutch Petrol Co	7.70%
3) TotalFina SA Ser.B	6.44%
4) Vivendi Universal	3.77%
5) Telefonica de Espana SA	3.54%
6) Siemens AG NA O.N.	3.50%
7) ING Groep NV	3.13%
8) Aventis SA	2.89%
9) Deutsche Bank AG NA	2.78%
10) Banco Bilbao Viz. Arg	2.57%

DOW JONES STOXX 50 EX

Expense Ratio:	0.50%	
Total Net Assets:	N/A	
Category:	Country	
Benchmark:	Dow Jones STOXX 50 Index	
Init Divisor:	—	
Exchange:	Deutsche Börse	
Manager:	IndexChange AG	
Inception:	27-Dec–00	

TOP 10 HOLDINGS

1) British Petroleum Plc	7.08%
2) GlaxoSmithKline	5.94%
3) Vodafone Group	5.80%
4) Nokia Corp	4.77%
5) Royal Dutch Petrol Co	4.58%
6) TotalFina SA Ser.B	3.83%
7) HSBC Holdings Plc	3.80%
8) Novartis NA	3.56%
9) Shell Transport and Trading Co Plc	3.06%
10) Nestle SA NA	2.81%

EASYETF EURO STOXX 50 (ETE FP)

Expense Ratio:	1.00%	
Total Net Assets:	N/A	
Category:	Regional	
Benchmark:	DJ EuroSTOXX 50 Index	
Init Divisor:	1/1000	
Exchange:	Euronext Paris	
Manager:	AXA Investment Manager	
Inception:	25-Apr–01	

TOP 10 HOLDINGS

1) Nokia Corp	8.12%
2) Royal Dutch Petrol Co	7.03%
3) TotalFinaElf	6.05%
4) Telefonica	3.89%
5) Vivendi Universal	3.77%
6) Siemens	3.51%
7) ING Groep	3.10%
8) Aventis	2.86%
9) Deutsche Bank R	2.74%
10) Bco Bilbao Vizcaya Argentaria	2.44%

Source: AMEX and Morningstar data as of 6/30/2001.

EASYETF GLOBAL TITANS 50 (ETT FP)

Expense Ratio:	1.00%	
Total Net Assets:	N/A	
Category:	Global	
Benchmark:	DJ Global Titans 50 Index	
Init Divisor:	36901	
Exchange:	Euronext Paris	
Manager:	AXA Investment Manager	
Inception:	25-Apr–01	

TOP 10 HOLDINGS

1) General Electric Co	8.82%
2) Microsoft Corp	5.71%
3) ExxonMobil Corp	5.29%
4) Citigroup Inc	4.63%
5) IBM	3.61%
6) British Petroleum Plc	3.47%
7) Intel Corp	3.22%
8) Vodafone Group Plc	3.04%
9) Cisco Sys	2.89%
10) Merck & Co Inc	2.89%

EASYETF STOXX 50 (ETN FP)

Expense Ratio:	1.00%
Total Net Assets:	N/A
Category:	Country
Benchmark:	DJ STOXX 50 Index
Init Divisor:	1/1000
Exchange:	Euronext Paris
Manager:	AXA Investment Manager
Inception:	25-Apr–01

TOP 10 HOLDINGS

1) British Petroleum Plc	7.00%
2) Vodafone Group	5.94%
3) GlaxoSmithKline	5.74%
4) Nokia Corp	4.97%
5) Royal Dutch Petrol Co	4.50%
6) TotalFinaElf	3.84%
7) HSBC Holdings Plc	3.80%
8) Novartis R	3.64%
9) Shell Transport & Tradng	3.00%
10) Nestle SA R	2.70%

EUROSTOXX 50 EX ANTEILE (SX5EEX GY)

Expense Ratio:	0.50%
Total Net Assets:	N/A
Category:	Regional
Benchmark:	DJ EuroSTOXX 50 Index
Init Divisor:	—
Exchange:	Deutsche Borse
Manager:	IndexChange AG
Inception:	27-Dec–00

TOP 10 HOLDINGS

1) Nokia Corp	8.02%
2) Royal Dutch Petrol Co	7.70%
3) TotalFina SA Ser.B	6.44%
4) Vivendi Universal	3.77%
5) Telefonica de Espana SA	3.54%
6) Siemens AG NA O.N.	3.50%
7) ING Groep NV	3.13%
8) Aventis SA	2.89%
9) Deutsche Bank AG NA	2.78%
10) Banco Bilbao Viz. Arg	2.57%

Source: AMEX and Morningstar data as of 6/30/2001.

EuroSTOXX 50 LDRs - Amsterdam (EUN2)

Expense Ratio:	0.50%
Total Net Assets:	N/A
Category:	Regional
Benchmark:	DJ EuroSTOXX 50 Index
Init Divisor:	1/100
Exchange:	Euronext Amsterdam
Manager:	LDRs (Merrill Lynch)
Inception:	11-Apr–01

Top 10 Holdings

1) Royal Dutch Petrol Co	7.92%
2) TotalFinaElf	6.58%
3) Nokia Corp	6.11%
4) Vivendi Universal	3.70%
5) Telefonica	3.25%
6) Siemens	3.24%
7) Aventis	3.19%
8) ING Groep	3.12%
9) Deutsche Bank R	2.78%
10) Deutsche Telekom	2.72%

EuroSTOXX 50 LDRs - Paris (EUN2)

Expense Ratio:	0.50%
Total Net Assets:	N/A
Category:	Regional
Benchmark:	DJ EuroSTOXX 50 Index
Init Divisor:	1/100
Exchange:	Euronext Paris
Manager:	LDRs (Merrill Lynch)
Inception:	11 Apr–01

Top 10 Holdings

1) Royal Dutch Petrol Co	7.92%
2) TotalFinaElf	6.58%
3) Nokia Corp	6.11%
4) Vivendi Universal	3.70%
5) Telefonica	3.25%
6) Siemens	3.24%
7) Aventis	3.19%
8) ING Groep	3.12%
9) Deutsche Bank R	2.78%
10) Deutsche Telekom	2.72%

iBloomberg European Financials (IBEF)

Expense Ratio:	0.50%
Total Net Assets:	N/A
Category:	Sector
Benchmark:	Bloomberg European Investable Financials Index
Init Divisor:	1/100
Exchange:	Euronext Amsterdam
Manager:	Barclays Global Investors
Inception:	12-Feb–01

Top 10 Holdings

1) Royal Bank of Scotland 25P	4.92%
2) Lloyds Tsb Group 25P	4.61%
3) CS Holdings Szf20 (Reg)	4.60%
4) BNP Paribas SA Eur4	4.48%
5) UBS (United Bank of Switzerland	4.44%
6) Banco Bilbao Vizcaya Argentari	4.26%
7) Barclays Plc Gbp 1	4.26%
8) Bco Santander Central Hisp Eur	4.13%
9) Allianz AG No Par Value	4.12%
10) Deutsche Bank AG Npv	4.10%

Source: AMEX and Morningstar data as of 6/30/2001.

iBLOOMBERG EUROPEAN PHARMACEUTICALS (IBEP)

Expense Ratio:	0.50%
Total Net Assets:	N/A
Category:	Sector
Benchmark:	Bloomberg European Investable Pharmaceuticals Index
Init Divisor:	1/100
Exchange:	Euronext Amsterdam
Manager:	Barclays Global Investors
Inception:	12-Feb–01

TOP 10 HOLDINGS

1) Novo-Nordisk As 'B' Dkk2	5.77%
2) Serono SA-B Par Chf25	4.73%
3) Schering Npv	4.61%
4) H. Lundbeck A/S	4.61%
5) Shire Pharmaceuticals Grp Plc	4.59%
6) GlaxoSmithKline Ord Gbp0.25	4.45%
7) Sanofi-Synthelabo Eur 2	4.43%
8) Astrazeneca Group 25P Ord	4.40%
9) Aventis SA	4.26%
10) Celltech Group Plc Ord 50P	4.22%

iBLOOMBERG EUROPEAN TECHNOLOGY (IBQQ)

Expense Ratio:	0.50%
Total Net Assets:	N/A
Category:	Sector
Benchmark:	Bloomberg European Investable Technology Index
Init Divisor:	1/100
Exchange:	Euronext Amsterdam
Manager:	Barclays Global Investors
Inception:	12-Feb–01

TOP 10 HOLDINGS

1) SAP AG	7.34%
2) Asml Holding NV Eur0.02	6.98%
3) Wanadoo Eur 0.3	6.35%
4) Equant NV	5.69%
5) Infineon Technologies AG	5.58%
6) STMicroelectronic Eur1.04	5.24%
7) T-Online International Ordinar	4.64%
8) Sage Group Plc Ord 1P	4.31%
9) Cap Gemini SA Eur 8	4.16%
10) Aixtron AG Npv	4.12%

iBLOOMBERG EUROPEAN TELECOMS (IBET)

Expense Ratio:	0.50%
Total Net Assets:	N/A
Category:	Sector
Benchmark:	Bloomberg European Investable Telecoms Index
Init Divisor:	1/100
Exchange:	Euronext Amsterdam
Manager:	Barclays Global Investors
Inception:	12-Feb–01

TOP 10 HOLDINGS

1) British Telecom 25P	6.16%
2) Telia AB Sek1000	6.10%
3) Swisscom AG - Reg	5.82%
4) Telefonica SA Eur 1	5.67%
5) Telecom Italia SPA Eur0.55	5.61%
6) TDC A/S Dkk5	5.60%
7) Deutsche Telecom AG Npv	4.88%
8) Olivetti & C SPA Ord Eur1	4.76%
9) TIM SPA	4.56%
10) Vodafone Group Plc Usd0.10	4.20%

Source: AMEX and Morningstar data as of 6/30/2001.

iShares FTSE ExUK 100 Index Fund (IEUR LN)

		Top 10 Holdings	
Expense Ratio:	0.50%		
Total Net Assets:	N/A	1) N/A	0.00%
Category:	Global	2) N/A	0.00%
Benchmark:	FTSE ExUK 100 Index	3) N/A	0.00%
Init Divisor:	—	4) N/A	0.00%
Exchange:	London	5) N/A	0.00%
Manager:	Barclays Global Investors	6) N/A	0.00%
Inception:	18-Dec–00	7) N/A	0.00%
		8) N/A	0.00%
		9) N/A	0.00%
		10) N/A	0.00%

iShares FTSE TMT Index Fund (ITMT LN)

		Top 10 Holdings	
Expense Ratio:	0.50%		
Total Net Assets:	N/A	1) N/A	0.00%
Category:	Country	2) N/A	0.00%
Benchmark:	FTSE TMT Index	3) N/A	0.00%
Init Divisor:	—	4) N/A	0.00%
Exchange:	London	5) N/A	0.00%
Manager:	Barclays Global Investors	6) N/A	0.00%
Inception:	17-Oct–00	7) N/A	0.00%
		8) N/A	0.00%
		9) N/A	0.00%
		10) N/A	0.00%

iShares FTSE 100 Index Fund (ISF LN)

		Top 10 Holdings	
Expense Ratio:	0.35%		
Total Net Assets:	N/A	1) N/A	0.00%
Category:	Global	2) N/A	0.00%
Benchmark:	FTSE 100 Index	3) N/A	0.00%
Init Divisor:	—	4) N/A	0.00%
Exchange:	London	5) N/A	0.00%
Manager:	Barclays Global Investors	6) N/A	0.00%
Inception:	27-Apr–00	7) N/A	0.00%
		8) N/A	0.00%
		9) N/A	0.00%
		10) N/A	0.00%

Source: AMEX and Morningstar data as of 6/30/2001.

IUNITS GOVERNMENT OF CANADA 10 YEAR BOND FUND (XGX CN)

		TOP 10 HOLDINGS	
Expense Ratio:	0.25%		
Total Net Assets:	N/A	1) N/A	0.00%
Category:	Fixed	2) N/A	0.00%
Benchmark:	Government of	3) N/A	0.00%
	Canada 10 year Bond	4) N/A	0.00%
Init Divisor:	—	5) N/A	0.00%
Exchange:	Toronto	6) N/A	0.00%
Manager:	Barclays Global Investors	7) N/A	0.00%
Inception:	23-Nov–00	8) N/A	0.00%
		9) N/A	0.00%
		10) N/A	0.00%

IUNITS GOVERNMENT OF CANADA 5 YEAR BOND FUND (XGV CN)

		TOP 10 HOLDINGS	
Expense Ratio:	0.25%		
Total Net Assets:	N/A	1) N/A	0.00%
Category:	Fixed	2) N/A	0.00%
Benchmark:	Government of	3) N/A	0.00%
	Canada 5 year Bond	4) N/A	0.00%
Init Divisor:	—	5) N/A	0.00%
Exchange:	Toronto	6) N/A	0.00%
Manager:	Barclays Global Investors	7) N/A	0.00%
Inception:	23-Nov–00	8) N/A	0.00%
		9) N/A	0.00%
		10) N/A	0.00%

IUNITS S&P 500 INDEX RSP FUND (XSP CN)

		TOP 10 HOLDINGS	
Expense Ratio:	0.30%		
Total Net Assets:	N/A	1) S&P 500	10.00%
Category:	Country	2) N/A	0.00%
Benchmark:	S&P 500 Index	3) N/A	0.00%
Init Divisor:	—	4) N/A	0.00%
Exchange:	Toronto	5) N/A	0.00%
Manager:	BGI	6) N/A	0.00%
Inception:	29-May–01	7) N/A	0.00%
		8) N/A	0.00%
		9) N/A	0.00%
		10) N/A	0.00%

Source: AMEX and Morningstar data as of 6/30/2001.

iUNITS S&P/TSE 60 INDEX FUND (XIU CN)

Expense Ratio:	0.17%
Total Net Assets:	N/A
Category:	Country
Benchmark:	S&P/TSE 60 Index
Init Divisor:	36901
Exchange:	Toronto
Manager:	Barclays Global Investors
Inception:	4-Oct–99

TOP 10 HOLDINGS

1) Nortel Networks Corp	7.03%
2) Royal Bk Cda Montreal	6.56%
3) BCE Inc	6.12%
4) Bombardier Inc B	4.63%
5) Toronto Dominion Bk On	4.63%
6) Bank of Nova Scotia	4.42%
7) Bank of Montreal	3.91%
8) Manulife Financial	3.90%
9) Canada Imperial Bk of Com	3.78%
10) Alcan Inc	3.53%

iUNITS S&P/TSE CANADIAN ENERGY INDEX FUND (XEG CN)

Expense Ratio:	0.55%
Total Net Assets:	N/A
Category:	Sector
Benchmark:	S&P/TSE Canadian Energy Index
Init Divisor:	36895
Exchange:	Toronto
Manager:	Barclays Global Investors
Inception:	22-Mar–01

TOP 10 HOLDINGS

1) Petro-Cda	10.00%
2) Suncor Energy Inc	10.00%
3) Alberta Energy Ltd	10.00%
4) Talisman Energy Inc	10.00%
5) Canadian Nat Res Ltd	7.53%
6) Imperial Oil Ltd	6.80%
7) Nexen Inc	6.32%
8) Anderson Expl Ltd	4.81%
9) Shell Canada Ltd	3.46%
10) Precision Drilling Cor	3.20%

iUNITS S&P/TSE CANADIAN FINANCIALS INDEX FUND (XFN CN)

Expense Ratio:	0.55%
Total Net Assets:	N/A
Category:	Sector
Benchmark:	S&P/TSE Canadian Financials Index
Init Divisor:	36895
Exchange:	Toronto
Manager:	Barclays Global Investors
Inception:	29-Mar–01

TOP 10 HOLDINGS

1) Royal Bk Cda Montreal	10.00%
2) Toronto Dominion Bk On	10.00%
3) Bank of Nova Scotia	10.00%
4) Bank of Montreal	9.63%
5) Manulife Financial	9.61%
6) Canada Imperial Bk of Com	9.32%
7) Sun Life Financial	7.37%
8) Canada Life Finl Corp	3.37%
9) Clarica Life Insurance	2.96%
10) National Bk Cda	2.67%

IUNITS S&P/TSE CANADIAN GOLD INDEX FUND (XGD CN)

Expense Ratio:	0.55%
Total Net Assets:	N/A
Category:	Sector
Benchmark:	S&P/TSE Canadian Gold Index
Init Divisor:	36895
Exchange:	Toronto
Manager:	Barclays Global Investors
Inception:	29-Mar–01

TOP 10 HOLDINGS

1) Placer Dome Inc	10.00%
2) Franco Nev Mng Ltd	10.00%
3) Barrick Gold Corp	10.00%
4) Goldcorp Inc New A	10.00%
5) Meridian Gold Inc	6.66%
6) Agnico Eagle Mines Ltd	5.61%
7) Kinross Gold Corp	2.90%
8) N/A	0.00%
9) N/A	0.00%
10) N/A	0.00%

IUNITS S&P/TSE CANADIAN INFORM. TECH INDEX FUND (XIT CN)

Expense Ratio:	0.55%
Total Net Assets:	N/A
Category:	Sector
Benchmark:	S&P/TSE Canadian Inform. Tech Index
Init Divisor:	36895
Exchange:	Toronto
Manager:	Barclays Global Investors
Inception:	22-Mar–01

TOP 10 HOLDINGS

1) Celestica Inc	10.00%
2) Nortel Networks Corp	10.00%
3) ATI Technologies Inc	6.83%
4) C-Mac Inds Inc	6.11%
5) Onex Corp	5.85%
6) Cognos Inc	4.60%
7) Research In Motion Ltd	4.47%
8) Mitel Corp	3.71%
9) Groupe Cgi Inc A	2.61%
10) BCE Inc	2.49%

IUNITS S&P/TSE CANADIAN MIDCAP INDEX FUND (XMD CN)

Expense Ratio:	0.55%
Total Net Assets:	N/A
Category:	Mid Cap
Benchmark:	S&P/TSE Canadian MidCap Index
Init Divisor:	36901
Exchange:	Toronto
Manager:	Barclays Global Investors
Inception:	8-Mar–01

TOP 10 HOLDINGS

1) Canada Life Finl Corp	6.80%
2) Clarica Life Insurance	5.99%
3) Ballard Pwr Sys Inc	5.30%
4) Power Corp Cda	5.21%
5) Power Financial Corp	3.61%
6) Trizec Hahn Corp	2.81%
7) C-Mac Inds Inc	2.76%
8) Onex Corp	2.64%
9) Fairfax Finl Hldgs Ltd	2.52%
10) Shell Canada Ltd	2.39%

Source: AMEX and Morningstar data as of 6/30/2001.

ɪUɴɪᴛꜱ S&P/TSE Cᴀᴘᴘᴇᴅ 60 Iɴᴅᴇx Fᴜɴᴅ (XIC CN)

Expense Ratio:	0.17%	**Tᴏᴘ 10 Hᴏʟᴅɪɴɢꜱ**	
Total Net Assets:	N/A		
Category:	Country	1) Nortel Networks Corp	6.87%
Benchmark:	S&P/TSE Capped	2) Royal Bk Cda Montreal	6.58%
	60 Index	3) BCE Inc	6.13%
Init Divisor:	36901	4) Bombardier Inc B	4.64%
Exchange:	Toronto	5) Toronto Dominion Bk On	4.64%
Manager:	Barclays Global Investors	6) Bank of Nova Scotia	4.42%
Inception:	22-Feb–01	7) Bank of Montreal	3.92%
		8) Manulife Financial	3.91%
		9) Cdn Imperial Bk of Com	3.79%
		10) Alcan Inc	3.54%

Mᴀꜱᴛᴇʀ DJ Eᴜʀᴏ STOXX 50 (MSE FP)

Expense Ratio:	0.40%	**Tᴏᴘ 10 Hᴏʟᴅɪɴɢꜱ**	
Total Net Assets:	N/A		
Category:	Regional	1) Nokia Corp	8.02%
Benchmark:	DJ EuroSTOXX 50	2) Royal Dutch Petrol Co	7.67%
Init Divisor:	1/100	3) TotalFinaElf	6.35%
Exchange:	Euronext Paris	4) Vivendi Universal	3.77%
Manager:	Société Générale Group	5) Telefonica	3.54%
	(Lyxor Asset)	6) Siemens	3.52%
Inception:	19-Mar–01	7) ING Groep	3.16%
		8) Aventis	2.92%
		9) Deutsche Bank R	2.79%
		10) BCO Bilbao Vizcaya	
		Argentaria	2.57%

Mᴀꜱᴛᴇʀ Dᴏᴡ Jᴏɴᴇꜱ (DJE FP)

Expense Ratio:	0.50%	**Tᴏᴘ 10 Hᴏʟᴅɪɴɢꜱ**	
Total Net Assets:	N/A		
Category:	Country	1) Minnesota Mining	7.15%
Benchmark:	Dow Jones	2) IBM	6.84%
	Industrial Average	3) Johnson & Johnson	6.04%
Init Divisor:	1/100	4) ExxonMobil Corp	5.23%
Exchange:	Euronext Paris	5) United Tech Corp	4.84%
Manager:	Société Générale Group	6) Merck & Co Inc	4.39%
	(Lyxor Asset)	7) Microsoft Corp	4.33%
		8) Procter & Gamble	3.83%
Inception:	17-May–01	9) Boeing Co	3.79%
		10) General Motors	3.49%

Source: AMEX and Morningstar data as of 6/30/2001.

MASTER SHARE CAC 40 (CAC FP)

Expense Ratio:	0.30%
Total Net Assets:	N/A
Category:	Country
Benchmark:	CAC 40 Index
Init Divisor:	1/100
Exchange:	Euronext Paris
Manager:	Société Générale Group
	(Lyxor Asset)
Inception:	22-Jan–01

TOP 10 HOLDINGS

1) TotalFinaElf	10.00%
2) Vivendi Universal	6.82%
3) Aventis (Ex Rp)	6.82%
4) AXA Financial Inc	5.72%
5) L'Oreal	5.64%
6) France Telecom	5.59%
7) Carrefour	4.56%
8) BNP Paribas	4.41%
9) Suez Lyonnaise	3.79%
10) STMicroelectron	3.02%

MDAX Ex (MDAXEX GY)

Expense Ratio:	0.50%
Total Net Assets:	N/A
Category:	Country
Benchmark:	MDAX Index
Init Divisor:	—
Exchange:	Deutsche Börse
Manager:	IndexChange AG
Inception:	25-Apr–01

TOP 10 HOLDINGS

1) Ergo Vers.Gruppe AG O.N.	9.40%
2) Marsch. Laut. U.Pa. Vz O.St. O.N.	7.17%
3) Beiersdorf AG O.N.	7.12%
4) Amb Aachener U. Muench.Bet.-AG	4.80%
5) BHW Holding AG O.N.	4.32%
6) Altana AG O.N.	4.27%
7) Heidelberger Druckmaschinen AG O.N.	4.00%
8) Karstadt Quelle AG O.N.	3.37%
9) Wella AG Vz O.St. O.N.	2.89%
10) WCM Ltd Bet. - U.G. O.N.	2.88%

NEMAX 50 (NMKXEX GY)

Expense Ratio:	0.50%
Total Net Assets:	N/A
Category:	Country
Benchmark:	Nemax 50 Index
Init Divisor:	—
Exchange:	Deutsche Börse
Manager:	IndexChange AG
Inception:	11-Apr–01

TOP 10 HOLDINGS

1) T-Online Intern. AG NA O.N.	10.00%
2) Quiagen NV	9.67%
3) Aixtron AG O.N.	7.45%
4) Broadvision Inc	5.84%
5) Bb Biotech Sf 1(Euronotiz)	5.77%
6) Medion AG O.N.	5.75%
7) Comdirect Bank AG O.N.	4.64%
8) Direkt Anlage Bank AG O.N.	3.58%
9) Thiel Logistik AG O.N.	3.51%
10) Consors Disc.-Broker O.N.	3.03%

Source: AMEX and Morningstar data as of 6/30/2001.

SATRIX40 (STX40 SJ)

		TOP 10 HOLDINGS	
Expense Ratio:	0.30%		
Total Net Assets:	N/A	1) N/A	0.00%
Category:	Country	2) N/A	0.00%
Benchmark:	ALSI 40 Index	3) N/A	0.00%
Init Divisor:	—	4) N/A	0.00%
Exchange:	Deutsche Börse	5) N/A	0.00%
Manager:	INDEXCO Ltd	6) N/A	0.00%
Inception:	9-Nov–00	7) N/A	0.00%
		8) N/A	0.00%
		9) N/A	0.00%
		10) N/A	0.00%

SMI EX ANTEILE (SMIEX GY)

		TOP 10 HOLDINGS	
Expense Ratio:	0.50%		
Total Net Assets:	N/A	1) Novartis NA	10.00%
Category:	Country	2) Nestle SA NA	10.00%
Benchmark:	SMI Index	3) UBS NA	10.00%
Init Divisor:	—	4) Credit Suisse Grp. NA	10.00%
Exchange:	Deutsche Börse	5) Roche Holding Genußschein	9.82%
Manager:	IndexChange AG	6) Zürich Financial Services NA	5.23%
Inception:	22-Mar-01	7) Schweiz. Rückvers. NA	5.12%
		8) ABB Ltd NA	3.98%
		9) Cie Fin, Richem, A + Ps Inh	2.32%
		10) Adecco SA	1.95%

STOXX 50 EX ANTEILE (SX5PEX GY)

		TOP 10 HOLDINGS	
Expense Ratio:	0.50%		
Total Net Assets:	N/A	1) British Petroleum Plc	7.08%
Category:	Country	2) GlaxoSmithKline	5.94%
Benchmark:	DJ STOXX 50 Index	3) Vodafone Group Plc	5.80%
Init Divisor:	—	4) Nokia Corp	4.77%
Exchange:	Deutsche Börse	5) Royal Dutch Petrol Co	4.58%
Manager:	IndexChange AG	6) TotalElfFina SA Ser.B	3.83%
Inception:	27-Dec–00	7) HSBC Holdings Plc	3.80%
		8) Novartis NA	3.56%
		9) Shell Transport and Trading Co Plc	3.06%
		10) Nestle SA NA	2.81%

Source: AMEX and Morningstar data as of 6/30/2001.

STOXX 50 LDRs - AMSTERDAM

		TOP 10 HOLDINGS	
Expense Ratio:	0.50%		
Total Net Assets:	N/A	1) British Petroleum Plc	6.84%
Category:	Country	2) GlaxoSmithKline	6.65%
Benchmark:	DJ STOXX 50 Index	3) Vodafone Group	5.10%
Init Divisor:	1/100	4) Royal Dutch Petrol Co	4.57%
Exchange:	Euronext (Amsterdam)	5) HSBC Holdings Plc	3.87%
Manager:	Mercury Asset	6) TotalFinaElf	3.83%
	Management Ltd.	7) Novartis R	3.31%
Inception:	11-Apr–01	8) Nestle R	3.22%
		9) Nokia Corp	3.21%
		10) Shell Transport & Tradng	3.08%

STOXX 50 LDRs - PARIS (EUN1)

		TOP 10 HOLDINGS	
Expense Ratio:	0.50%		
Total Net Assets:	N/A	1) British Petroleum Plc	6.84%
Category:	Country	2) GlaxoSmithKline	6.65%
Benchmark:	DJ STOXX 50 Index	3) Vodafone Group	5.10%
Init Divisor:	1/100	4) Royal Dutch Petrol Co	4.57%
Exchange:	Euronext (Paris)	5) HSBC Holdings Plc	3.87%
Manager:	Mercury Asset	6) TotalFinaElf	3.83%
	Management Ltd.	7) Novartis R	3.31%
Inception:	11-Apr–01	8) Nestle R	3.22%
		9) Nokia Corp	3.21%
		10) Shell Transport & Tradng	3.08%

STREETTRACKS AEX INDEX FUND (AEXT)

		TOP 10 HOLDINGS	
Expense Ratio:	0.30%		
Total Net Assets:	N/A	1) Unilever	10.00%
Category:	Country	2) Royal Dutch Petrol Co	10.00%
Benchmark:	AEX Index	3) ING Groep 10.00%	
Init Divisor:	36901	4) Philips Elec(Kon)	9.22%
Exchange:	Euronext (Amsterdam)	5) AEGON	9.08%
Manager:	SSgA	6) Ahold(Kon) NV	8.90%
Inception:	30-May–01	7) Abn-Amro Hldgs	8.79%
		8) Akzo Nobel	3.81%
		9) Fortis Nl	3.62%
		10) Elsevier	3.03%

Source: AMEX and Morningstar data as of 6/30/2001.

TALI 25 (TALI IT)

Expense Ratio:	0.80%	
Total Net Assets:	N/A	
Category:	Country	
Benchmark:	TA25 Index	
	(aka MAOF Index)	
Init Divisor:	—	
Exchange:	TASE (Tel Aviv)	
Manager:	Ofek Leumi	
	Financial Instruments	
Inception:	28-May–00	

TOP 10 HOLDINGS

1) N/A	0.00%
2) N/A	0.00%
3) N/A	0.00%
4) N/A	0.00%
5) N/A	0.00%
6) N/A	0.00%
7) N/A	0.00%
8) N/A	0.00%
9) N/A	0.00%
10) N/A	0.00%

TRACKER FUND OF HONG KONG (TRaHK) (2800.HK)

Expense Ratio:	0.10%
Total Net Assets:	N/A
Category:	Country
Benchmark:	Hang Seng Index
Init Divisor:	—
Exchange:	Hong Kong
Manager:	State Street Global Advisors
Inception:	12 Nov 99

TOP 10 HOLDINGS

1) N/A	0.00%
2) N/A	0.00%
3) N/A	0.00%
4) N/A	0.00%
5) N/A	0.00%
6) N/A	0.00%
7) N/A	0.00%
8) N/A	0.00%
9) N/A	0.00%
10) N/A	0.00%

TSE 300 CAPPED INDEX FUND (TCF CN)

Expense Ratio:	0.25%
Total Net Assets:	N/A
Category:	Country
Benchmark:	TSE 300 Capped Index
Init Divisor:	—
Exchange:	Toronto
Manager:	TD Asset Management
Inception:	23-Feb–01

TOP 10 HOLDINGS

1) N/A	0.00%
2) N/A	0.00%
3) N/A	0.00%
4) N/A	0.00%
5) N/A	0.00%
6) N/A	0.00%
7) N/A	0.00%
8) N/A	0.00%
9) N/A	0.00%
10) N/A	0.00%

Source: AMEX and Morningstar data as of 6/30/2001.

TSE 300 INDEX FUND (TTF CN)

		TOP 10 HOLDINGS	
Expense Ratio:	0.25%	1) N/A	0.00%
Total Net Assets:	N/A	2) N/A	0.00%
Category:	Country	3) N/A	0.00%
Benchmark:	TSE 300 Index	4) N/A	0.00%
Init Divisor:	—	5) N/A	0.00%
Exchange:	Toronto	6) N/A	0.00%
Manager:	TD Asset Management	7) N/A	0.00%
Inception:	23-Feb–01	8) N/A	0.00%
		9) N/A	0.00%
		10) N/A	0.00%

XACTOMX (XACTOMX SS)

		TOP 10 HOLDINGS	
Expense Ratio:	0.30%	1) N/A	0.00%
Total Net Assets:	N/A	2) N/A	0.00%
Category:	Country	3) N/A	0.00%
Benchmark:	OMX Index	4) N/A	0.00%
Init Divisor:	—	5) N/A	0.00%
Exchange:	Stockholm	6) N/A	0.00%
Manager:	OM Group	7) N/A	0.00%
Inception:	27-Dec–00	8) N/A	0.00%
		9) N/A	0.00%
		10) N/A	0.00%

XMTCH (XMSMI SW)

		TOP 10 HOLDINGS	
Expense Ratio:	0.35%	1) N/A	0.00%
Total Net Assets:	N/A	2) N/A	0.00%
Category:	Country	3) N/A	0.00%
Benchmark:	SMI (Swiss Market Index)	4) N/A	0.00%
Init Divisor:	—	5) N/A	0.00%
Exchange:	SWX (Swiss Exchange)	6) N/A	0.00%
Manager:	Credit Suisse	7) N/A	0.00%
Inception:	15-Mar–01	8) N/A	0.00%
		9) N/A	0.00%
		10) N/A	0.00%

Source: AMEX and Morningstar data as of 6/30/2001.

streetTRACKS PAN-EURO (ERO)

		TOP 10 HOLDINGS	
Expense Ratio:	0.50%		
Total Net Assets:	N/A	1) British Petroleum Plc	4.09%
Category:	Regional	2) Vodafone Group	3.52%
Benchmark:	MSCI Pan_Euro	3) GlaxoSmithKline	3.44%
	Index Fund	4) Nokia Corp 2.	80%
Init Divisor:	1/10	5) Royal Dutch Petrol Co	2.66%
Exchange:	Euronext (Paris)	6) Novartis	2.35%
Manager:	State Street Global Advisors	7) HSBC Holdings Plc	2.35%
Inception:	19-Jun–01	8) TotalFinaElf	2.34%
		9) Astrazenica	1.69%
		10) Nestle	1.62%

Source: AMEX and Morningstar data as of 6/30/2001.

Index